AT HOME WITH THE ROUX BROTHERS

AT HOME WITH THE Roux BROTHERS

ALBERT AND MICHEL ROUX

BBC Books

Designed by Grub Street Design, London
Art Director: Roger Hammond
Photographer: Jan Baldwin
Stylist: Roisin Nield
Illustrators: Toula Antonakos (decorative illustrations); Azis Khan
(step by step illustrations)

We would like to thank the following for the loan of accessories for the photographs:
China, glassware and cutlery: The Conran Shop, Michelin House, 81 Fulham Rd,
London sw3;
Thomas Goode & Co, 19 South Audley St, London W1; Hutschenreuther, 57
Duke St, London w1.
Fabrics: Lizzie Cullen, 205, Lower Richmond Rd, London sw15; St Leger Fabrics,
68 Maltings Place, Bagleys Lane, London sw6.

First published in 1988 by BBC Books,
a division of BBC Enterprises Limited,
Woodlands, 80 Wood Lane, London w12 0TT
and Sidgwick & Jackson Ltd,
1 Tavistock Chambers,
Bloomsbury Way, London wc1A 2SG
© Taviscroft Ltd 1988
ISBN 0 563 21432 5 (paperback)
ISBN 0 563 21433 3 (hardback)

Printed and bound in Great Britain by
Butler & Tanner Ltd, Frome and London
Colour separations by Technik, Berkhamsted
Jacket printed by Belmont Press Ltd, Northampton
Cover printed by Fletchers, Norwich

CONTENTS

ACKNOWLEDGEMENTS

Albert and Michel Roux would like to thank:
Caroline Liddell, who collaborated closely and expertly on the preparation and testing of the recipes for the book, and gave the production team knowledgeable and practical support in the studio.

They would also like to thank all the following people for their invaluable help:
Chris Sellors, Sous Chef at the Waterside Inn, who tested and tasted most of the recipes, helped with the preparation of the food for the photographs, and provided infallible assistance throughout the recording of the television series; Samantha Ross, who typed the manuscript; Elizabeth David Ltd, 46 Bourne Street, London SW1W 8JD, who supplied equipment used in the BBC Television series and the photographs: Le Creuset, Cerafeu, Maxime Girard Sabatier, Lagostina Vega; Josiah Wedgwood and Sons Ltd; Robyn Roux; Dr Barry Lynch, Head of Features and Documentaries, BBC Wales Television; Jill Marshall; Frances Whitaker and Nigel Houghton.

INTRODUCTION

In the last twenty years, the Roux brothers have made a huge impact on the British food industry and on our eating habits. When they opened their first restaurant in England in 1967, they had £3,000 each and had to borrow the rest. They now control an extensive business empire employing hundreds of people, with an annual turnover of millions of pounds. Over the years, they have also won many awards that are a recognition of their culinary achievement in the UK and in Europe.

When they started that first restaurant, Le Gavroche, they made sure the ingredients for their small, selective menu were fresh by going to the market every day; and in their determination to obtain special ingredients of the highest quality, they became pioneers of cross-Channel shopping trips. Their requirements have now grown to the extent that they need their own import company to bring in products not obtainable in this country.

This venture is only one of the many that the Roux empire now controls. As well as Le Gavroche, and The Waterside Inn (opened in 1972), they have also established several of their proteges in joint venture restaurants in Britain, France and California.

MICHEL We both started cooking when we were small. Our father was a *charcutier*, and so was our grandfather, but neither of us felt drawn in that direction. We learnt a lot from our mother; we would both help her in the kitchen. She preferred me to help her, because I was tidier in the kitchen than Albert. She said she could never tell when I had been cooking, whereas with my brother it was a different matter. Albert is five years older, so he was the first one to leave home and become apprenticed to a *pâtissier*.

ALBERT I began my apprenticeship at the tender age of fourteen. My first boss was a man who believed in working his employees very hard, but he was a very fair man, and I learnt a great deal from him. A working day would regularly last twelve to fourteen hours, and at the weekend it would be nothing to work from Saturday morning, all through Saturday night, until eleven o'clock on Sunday morning, without a break. It was an apprenticeship that marked me for life. It was not just that I learnt how to make a beautiful cake; I learnt much, much more than that. I learnt about detail and organisation, order and discipline. In a way, I was lucky to start with the pastry-making side of my career, but I cannot emphasise too strongly how much I acquired from that man in other ways, such strong beliefs which have stayed with me for the rest of my life. He was such a good teacher – unlike a chef I worked under at the French Embassy in London. Another hard man, but so different. I was not allowed to do anything but watch. If I asked about a dish, I would be told 'It is none of your business!' Even so, I learnt an immense amount just by watching him, and that is still a good way for anyone to learn. But I still remember the chores: a big white table that had to be scrubbed with tar soap; a little piece of glass paper to clean the cookers – and it had to last you all week. He would not let you go home until he could see his face in the surface. Even worse, we started at six in the morning with a breakfast of porridge. It was not a time I shall easily forget, but it has certainly made me more sympathetic to the needs of the young people who come to study with me.

MICHEL After our apprenticeships we both worked in private houses. I went to work as *chef de cuisine* for Mlle Cécile de Rothschild, and Albert worked in various houses, including Fairlawne, in Kent, where he spent nine years with Major and Mrs Peter Cazalet. Although it sounds very luxurious to be the chef to a private household, it wasn't all grand cooking. It was a job that went from one extreme to the other, from cooking simple meals for the staff to preparing imposing banquets for the family and distinguished guests. Being required to travel with our employers meant having to adapt quickly to strange kitchens and conditions and to unscheduled meals and *ad hoc* ingredients. Time and money were not often a problem, though, it must be said.

The passing of the great house and its tradition is something that we both regret. There is no better place to learn to cook than a kitchen in a house where the old standards are still maintained. The taste and demands of such families evoke in those who are fortunate enough to work for them a constant striving for perfection. We in turn have carried the standards of those houses with us to our restaurants, and we try to pass them on to all the young people who come to work for us. We also feel that this experience has given us a domestic touch to complement the sophistication and knowledge that have come from our careers in our restaurants.

ALBERT I learnt so much from my time at Fairlawne. Not only the cooking, but from watching Mrs Cazalet run that house – how everything and everyone was looked after: the attention to detail, the flowers, the Malvern water by the bed. It was the same at Lady Astor's, where I worked when I first came to England when I was eighteen. It was not until I was twenty-five that I began to read all about her achievements, her family and its role in political history; at the time I joined her household I had no idea about any of that. But while I was there, I learnt so much about the sort of perfection that comes from attention to detail: things like messages being passed, not from hand to hand, but always on a silver tray. Although the cooking was what I was responsible for, I learnt so much about other things from being there, from observation.

MICHEL We had always wanted to open a restaurant together and in 1967 that opportunity came. With a little money of our own, and with the help of some good friends, we started in London in our first restaurant, Le Gavroche, which was then in Lower Sloane Street in Chelsea, where Gavvers now is, while Le Gavroche has moved to Upper Brook Street in Mayfair. It was just the two of us. To be truthful, I did not speak a word of English, so I had to be kept in the kitchen once the customers arrived. We worked eighteen hours a day, and it was hard work, really hard work. There was the marketing to do in the early morning and then dinner in the evening.

We made a certain innovation that the British were not used to: we had a short menu which changed with the seasons and what was available in the markets. Our customers in those early days were not always appreciative of what we were doing. But although we had our problems, and were both working so hard, it was good to be working in the kitchen with Albert – something I would still be happy to do.

Attitudes to eating, food and catering have changed in this country since we first opened that first restaurant. Travel has widened people's horizons and raised their expectations, and they have become much more adventurous and demanding about what they eat. People also read much more widely, so they are more knowledgeable about food. There was a time when Elizabeth David was the only cookery writer whose books you saw in people's homes. Now you go to someone's house, and they have a whole row of books by different writers, many of them master chefs. There is a greater interest in the subject than there was twenty or even ten years ago. Look at the way young chefs are emerging: English, Scottish, whatever – you would never have predicted that twenty years ago.

ALBERT It is not just eating habits that have changed – there has been a revolution. It really is the only word to describe what has happened. Once it was only people at a particular level of society who were able to enjoy a certain kind of food, not so much because they were the only ones who could afford it as because they were the only ones who understood about it. Now everyone talks about food, everyone cares about food. England is becoming more and more like France. An education about food has started, and you can see it in the shops. You can go to a chain store and buy a good deep-pan pizza, you can buy ready-prepared *sole au beurre blanc* and *caneton à l'orange* all over the place. This is all part of the process of educating people about food, and that has to be good news.

MICHEL You only have to look at any of the big shops to see what raw ingredients are available for the housewife. There is wider knowledge and more sophistication, more interest in food and eating than there was. People here are more aware of the quality of what they eat, and what they drink as well. Consumption of wine has increased fourfold in Britain in recent years, and people are more informed and knowledgeable about that too: they know about different wines and different grapes, they can discuss the Chardonnay and the Pinot Noir. They are more adventurous, as well, prepared to try wines from California, New Zealand and Australia, for instance.

Something else that has changed since we came here is the attitude of the suppliers. I realise that I am mostly talking about London and certain big cities, I cannot speak for those parts of the country that I do not know, but there is certainly a difference now. For instance, it was always hard to find supplies of the right type of vegetable. That is why we started our own company to bring in the vegetables that we wanted from France. It was the only way to make sure that we got the right type and size of carrots, turnips, peas, the fresh herbs, the flavours we needed. Everything here was too old and too big, and did not taste as good. Now all that is changing. Suppliers are more receptive to our needs, and to the needs of all the small restaurants that are being started up all over the country by young chefs who demand the same quality of fresh local ingredients.

Only the other day, a farmer wrote to ask what my requirements were. He sent me a very detailed questionnaire, and I answered the points in it, to help him. He and others like him are now realising that I and other restaurant-owners have certain needs, and he is prepared to change his methods and ideas to fulfil those needs. That is quite a dramatic change of attitude.

And we have to say that the change is due in part to what we have done. The Roux restaurants have been a flagship in the catering business, and others have followed us and our example.

I think our books have also had some influence. Our first book was *New Classic Cuisine – Nouvelle Cuisine Classique*. There is something I must say about that! It was just a coincidence that we happened to choose that title. The book was not about *nouvelle cuisine* as such, we were more interested in classic methods and techniques and how they could be adapted and changed to suit modern conditions. So-called *nouvelle cuisine* has certainly been one of the recent influences on food, but there is only one person who can really cook in that way, and that is Michel Guérard himself, who does it to perfection.

ALBERT Since the book was published, there have been changes in the big restaurants and hotels. Many of the medium-sized hotels have closed their restaurants, and transformed them into basic tea or coffee houses, cafés. The big hotels, what you might call the palaces, the Connaught, the Savoy, the Berkeley, will always have a restaurant, and a top restaurant at that, because that sells the rooms. If it does not sell them on the day, it works in the long run. Customers who go there for a meal and say 'What a beautiful hotel' might not otherwise have thought of actually staying there. But while the big restaurants are closing, at the other end there is so much happening. Obviously it is very nice to have a restaurant, but you have to have customers who are able to pay to come and eat at your restaurant. This is true at all levels. With the sort of economy we have at the moment, more people have money left in their pockets to spend on eating and entertaining, and that is going hand in hand with the invasion of all those youngsters who want to open their own little restaurants. Not only all those youngsters that we have trained, there have been other people training besides us, but it could be said that we started it. It is all good news. You might say that if it was a desert when we started, then now it is no longer a desert: it is at least an oasis.

I should point out that if it was left to me, there would not be any influence from books by the Roux Brothers at all. I do not have the sort of skill needed to put a book together, but luckily Michel is the writer of the family. I am delighted to say that I share the proceeds of his labours, just as he shares the proceeds of my labour on other things. We have been very fortunate in having such a happy partnership for so many years. It would be impossible to measure how much each one contributes because our contributions vary from day to day. And if we started to say that bit is mine and that bit is yours, we couldn't possibly work together so well. We have never done it like that.

MICHEL Now we have been working here for twenty years – it seems a long time since Albert had to persuade me to come to England. Instead of one restaurant, we now have an interest in several, and we run a big business, so there are different things now to think about than there were in those early days. There are only so many hours in the day, days in the week, and nowadays we have different priorities. But I still have to cook. Even if I am on holiday, or staying at a hotel, I cannot stop. After a little while, a few days, I have to ask if I can go into the kitchen and make something. I have to do it. Although I no longer spend 14 hours every day in the kitchen, I am still present and cooking each day with my brigade. I cannot live without cooking. For me it is a way of life: work, relaxation, everything.

ALBERT It is not the same for me. For one thing, I have Stephen Doherty who has been with me for years. I have to admit that now the pupil is better than the master.

I don't cook at home as often as Michel, but one time when I do is on New Year's Eve. It is a special date, a very important part of one's life, because one is, so to speak, a year older, like a racehorse. We get about twelve to fourteen people round the table, and the only reason they are there is because they are my dearest friends.

I must say one thing at this point about the difference between living here and in France. Here I can have a whole range of people round my table, with different political views, and we can sit and argue, discuss and learn. That simply is not possible in France. You only entertain people who come from the same sort of background as yourself. On New Year's Eve, I cook very cleverly. I cook for those friends, but I always manage to sit down with them. They never believe it, they are always amazed. I spend two or three minutes in the kitchen, and then I come in and sit down.

We eat in a very traditional way at home. For instance, take last weekend. I arrived home on Saturday morning, and lunch consisted of smoked fillet of haddock – which I had smoked myself. Stephen and I had bought a little smoker and we played with it on Friday, so I took my fillet of haddock home – and I had that with a few Jersey potatoes. Dinner? Well, it was a good meal; I remember banging my glass on the table and proposing a toast to the family. It all took place in the kitchen, which is a very, very big room, with a large pine table. We had all the children round the table, which is rather unusual – our daughter and her husband, and my son and his wife, and the four dogs sitting there too. The meal itself was a shepherd's pie, which I love, with a bottle of ketchup, which I also love. A great dollop of ketchup on shepherd's pie! The pie was made exactly the way I love it, slightly runny, from the leftovers from a leg of lamb which had been put in the freezer a couple of weeks ago, with the addition of a good little *jus d'agneau*. It was perfect … then with it I had some German sausage, which I bought at the Swiss Centre. I cannot pronounce the name of the sausage, but I certainly know where to find it.

I like brunch on Sundays. I like a good traditional English breakfast, about eleven o'clock in the morning. This might surprise you – though perhaps not, after the ketchup! – but I like my poached egg cooked the English way, and eaten with a piece of deep-fried bread, done in the fat we always keep from the roast pork, with back bacon, very crisply cooked like the Americans do it. And then some toast, with three or four pots of home-made jam on the table, and that is it.

MICHEL In our own lives, the greater the variety of demands on our time, the greater our productivity, and the greater our creativity. The main thing for me is to please myself. I cook things that I want to eat, and that I will want to eat again. It is no use if I am bored by something. It has to interest *me*. The best time for me is Ascot week. We have to arrange the dining room to seat more people than usual, and they start arriving at half past six. They have been racing all day, and often they are not happy. They might have lost some money on a bet; their horse might not have run well, or they have seen their wife with a boy-friend, anything like that. So they get here, and they are miserable. Then they sit in our beautiful dining room by the river, and have a lovely meal, and a little wine, and they begin to feel much better. And by the time I come out at ten o'clock to see them, to check that everything is all right, to greet my friends who have returned here – many of my clients have become my friends – they are happy. And that is what it is all about: to make people happy. If I ran a hotel, it would be the same. Not one with a lot of bedrooms, but small enough to look after the things that matter. There would always be fresh flowers in the rooms, the right kind of food sent up, the little extras that show you care and that make your establishment outstanding, one that people want to come back to again and again. Everything has to be exactly right.

ALBERT We have always wanted to give good value for money. If you take Le Poulbot as an example – we regarded it as the pub, but nevertheless we always felt that our customers were entitled to a proper grilled steak, with proper chips and a proper *béarnaise*. It has been the same with Le Gamin, which is a *prix fixe* brasserie. It has always been full, it has always given good value for money. The Rouxl Britannia operation, though it provides vacuum-packed meals not cooked on the premises, gives extremely good value for what it is. So in a way we like to think that we have helped with the revolution, helped to propagate the good word about food. We know it is not everybody who can afford to eat at Le Gavroche, but if you can educate people, then that is the right kind of progress. We have some customers who come to Le Gavroche only once a year, and they remember what they had for that particular meal, they are the kind of people we have educated. Some people come three times a week. Don't ask them what they have had for dinner, they will have forgotten it. They are just happy to be there.

Like Michel, when I cook, I cook for myself. The dishes on the menu at Le Gavroche are there for me. We both cook in the same way as we did when we opened our first restaurant twenty years ago – we have not changed our style of cooking at all. Of course, if there were a disaster in the kitchen and something were to be served up wrong, I should have to apologise. It would not happen, of course, disasters do not get through the door, but if it were to, then I would obviously offer my apologies. But if someone complains that they do not like the way a certain dish is cooked, and that is the way I cook it, then there is nothing I can do about it.

I personally get great pleasure from teaching, from passing on my skills and experience to others. We always have at least three youngsters training in the kitchen, and we have a two-year waiting list of applicants.

Anyone can teach how to cook if things are going right, what you need to be taught is how to rescue things when they go wrong. And to be taught why things go wrong, why the eggs go lumpy in a *hollandaise*, why something sinks when it should rise, that sort of thing. Once you know the reason why things go wrong, then you will not do it again. It is not as hard as it sounds, as nearly everything can be rescued or salvaged for another day. I love to teach. I love to find those young people who want to learn, and then to show them how to cook my way.

MICHEL It is especially rewarding to find someone who has come to you who develops real talent and skill, especially in the areas that you are fond of yourself. They learn by observation and practice.

THE ROUX REPERTOIRE

This chapter is a selection of recipes and bits of information which fall into no particular category. It includes some information basic to all cooking, as in the note about ovens (opposite); instructions in some techniques, such as clarifying butter (see page 16), which are essential to the Roux style of cooking; and recipes for some standard ingredients of the Roux repertoire, such as our chicken mousse (see page 23). This is an indispensable part of many of the dishes we offer at our restaurants, and we have included here a form of it which is specially adapted for the cook at home.

Some of the ingredients and techniques we call for in later chapters may sound a little daunting, but if you read this chapter first you will realise that most of them are not at all difficult to achieve. And you will find that the small amount of effort it takes to make your own stocks (see pages 18, 19) or bouquets garnis (see page 22), for instance, is amply repaid. Quite simply, using these ingredients in your dishes will help lift your cooking to another level.

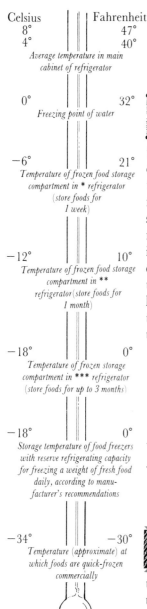

Celsius	Fahrenheit
8°	47°
4°	40°

*Average temperature in main
cabinet of refrigerator*

0°	32°

Freezing point of water

−6°	21°

*Temperature of frozen food storage
compartment in * refrigerator
(store foods for
1 week)*

−12°	10°

*Temperature of frozen food storage
compartment in **
refrigerator(store foods for
1 month)*

−18°	0°

*Temperature of frozen storage
compartment in *** refrigerator
(store foods for up to 3 months)*

−18°	0°

*Storage temperature of food freezers
with reserve refrigerating capacity
for freezing a weight of fresh food
daily, according to manu-
facturer's recommendations*

−34°	−30°

*Temperature (approximate) at
which foods are quick-frozen
commercially*

A NOTE ABOUT OVENS

Ovens vary, in the same way that every car coming off an assembly line is slightly different in performance from the next. You have to learn, and then work within, the virtues and shortcomings of your oven. However, an oven thermometer will remove some of the guesswork; and, of course, you should read all the manufacturer's instructions that come with the oven – it is surprising how many people do not! If you own one of the newer convection ovens this last point is particularly important. In this type of oven the fan-driven heat, circulating constantly in a sealed space, is constant and uniform throughout; and manufacturers may recommend lower temperatures and/or 10 to 20 per cent shorter cooking times. It is essential to make sure that you fully understand this different heat management.

•

A NOTE ABOUT REFRIGERATORS AND FREEZERS

Just as ovens cover a range of temperatures, so do refrigerators and freezers; and it is important not to be confused about the differences. The chart on the left gives a very simple illustration of the range of temperatures and their applications.

CLARIFYING BUTTER

 Clarifying butter is rather a laborious and messy process, but the result is well worth the trouble. Once the milk solids have been removed, you will be able to use the butter at a high temperature (for example, for frying steaks), and it will not burn, or lose its special flavour.

Note: about 20 per cent of the volume of butter is lost in clarifying. The exact proportion depends on the quality of the butter.

It is not worth clarifying butter in small quantities, so do about 2 packs of butter at a time. It is best to use unsalted butter. Cut the butter into pieces, put it in a pan and bring it to a good, bubbling boil. Remove from the heat and allow to settle. Meanwhile, wring out a double thickness of muslin in hot water, and use it to line a sieve. Set the sieve over a small bowl suitable for storing in the refrigerator. Carefully ladle the melted butter into the lined sieve, leaving the froth from the surface of the butter in the pan. The muslin will retain any remaining white milk solids; discard these and keep the cooled butter, covered, in the refrigerator. Use within 6 weeks.

·

FREEZING
EGG WHITES

 Many recipes leave you with surplus egg whites, but if you have a freezer, this presents no problem at all. The egg whites can be packed, just as they are, in small freezer containers. Label the containers with the contents, quantity and date, and they will keep for 6 months. When you are ready to use them, just put them in a bowl and allow to defrost: with the aid of an electric hand mixer you will be able to beat them stiff. There is even an added bonus – frozen egg whites give a better volume than fresh!

Note: if you are not very careful about labelling, it is easy to lose track of the number of egg whites frozen in a container. In this case, thaw them and measure the fluid whites on the basis of 1 egg white = 1 fl oz (30 ml).

PREPARING TRUFFLES

 Fresh truffles are a luxury available to very few, but should you have the amazing good fortune to obtain a truffle you will no doubt want to know how to treat it to get the best out of it.

Truffles are strange-looking things, black, lumpy and surprisingly hard. The fresher the truffle, the stronger will be the aroma; truffles of about a week old start to lose both flavour and aroma. The size varies considerably: a small truffle is about the size of a walnut, while very large specimens can be 4 in (10 cm) in diameter, or even more.

To prepare the truffle, the first step is to soak it in cold water in the refrigerator for a few hours. You should then scrub the truffle very thoroughly under cold running water – use something like a stiff nail brush to get out all the soil lodged in the crevices. Take care also to dig out any stones that might be embedded in the truffle.

If you want to keep the truffle some time before using it, freeze it, sealed in a heavy-duty plastic bag from which all air has been excluded. Do not freeze for longer than a month.

Put the truffle into a small saucepan and cover it with a mixture of two-thirds veal stock (see page 102) and one-third port. Bring to the boil and simmer gently until the truffle is cooked. Test with a thin metal skewer: when the truffle is done it should go in fairly easily, meeting only very slight resistance. An average-sized truffle will take 10–15 minutes.

The truffle can now be used as required. Should any be left over, this is best stored in a small jar with the reduced pan juices poured in to cover the truffle. They will set to a jelly forming a seal around the truffle. Packed like this and stored in the refrigerator, the truffle will keep perfectly well for up to a week.

QUICK CHICKEN STOCK

(Fonds de volaille rapide)

 A good stock will contribute subtle additional flavours to soups, stews, and other dishes. But remember that you will produce good stock only if you use good-quality ingredients. You cannot extract flavour and goodness from poor ingredients.

Chicken is specified in this recipe for a white stock, but you can substitute duck or other poultry, or lamb or veal.

Traditional methods of making stock can be time-consuming, but using a pressure cooker you can make stock very quickly. A note of warning: do not think you will improve your stock by steaming at pressure for longer than the 20 minutes specified. If pressure cooking is continued for longer than this too much is extracted from the meat bones, and some strange flavours can be brought out.

Makes about $2\frac{1}{4}$ pints (1.25 litres) unreduced

•

1 oz (25 g) butter	*1 medium onion, peeled and left whole*
2 medium carrots, peeled and diced	*1 clove*
1 leek (white part only), trimmed and diced	*A bouquet garni (see page 22)*
4 oz (100 g) button mushrooms, wiped, trimmed and coarsely chopped	*2 to $2\frac{1}{4}$ lb (1 kg) chicken (or boiling fowl) pieces, e.g. wings, neck, legs*

To cook

Melt the butter in the base pan of a pressure cooker and add the diced carrots, the white of leek, the chopped mushrooms, the onion stuck with the clove, and the bouquet garni, then stir. Add the chicken pieces, cover with cold water and bring to the boil. Skim thoroughly, then fit the pressure cooker lid in place. Bring up to pressure and steam for 20 minutes. Allow the pan to regain normal pressure before removing the lid, then pour the contents into a large sieve set over a large saucepan. Re-heat the strained stock and boil to reduce until the stock reaches the strength you require.

To store

The stock can be kept for several days in the refrigerator, and several weeks in the freezer. If freezing the stock, do so in the sort of quantities you are most likely to need, for example, packed in 5 or 10 fl oz (150 or 300 ml) separate containers.

AROMATIC STOCK

(Nage)

 This is a broth of vegetables, herbs, wine and wine vinegar, used mainly for poaching fish and shellfish. The quantity of salt can be increased if necessary (shellfish in particular benefit by being cooked in strongly salted liquid), but be careful not to add too much salt if you are intending to reduce the poaching liquor for a sauce, or you may find that your sauce tastes too salty.

Makes 2 pints (1.2 litres)

2 medium carrots, topped, tailed and peeled	2 tablespoons white wine vinegar
1 leek (white part only), trimmed and washed	A bouquet garni (see page 22)
½ celery stalk, scrubbed	1 clove of garlic, unpeeled
½ small fennel bulb, scrubbed	1 teaspoon coarse salt
1 medium onion	1 teaspoon black peppercorns, lightly crushed, tied in muslin
1 oz (25 g) butter	
10 fl oz (300 ml) dry white wine	

Preparation

If you have a food processor, fit it with the fine slicing disc and pass the carrots, leek, celery, fennel and onion through it; otherwise slice the vegetables thinly, using a cook's knife.

To cook

Melt the butter in a large saucepan and stir in the sliced vegetables. Cover and cook gently for 10 minutes. Take the lid off the pan and add the wine, vinegar, bouquet garni, garlic, salt and 1¾ pints (1 litre) of water. Bring to the boil, then lower the heat and simmer, uncovered, for 5 minutes. Add the crushed peppercorns tied in muslin and continue to simmer for a further 15 minutes. Strain the contents of the pan through a fine sieve. Use the stock as required.

NOTES ON SOME FLAVOURINGS

 In general, fresh herbs cannot be surpassed, for full flavour and aroma. If you have to substitute dried herbs, you should use much less, as they are more concentrated than the fresh. One teaspoon of the dried to 1 tablespoon of the fresh is a good rule to follow.

A word or two about the preparation and use of fresh herbs: we would emphasise very strongly that you must *never* chop them up. If you do that, you murder them. You do not take a chopper to a nice piece of meat: you use your best and sharpest knife to cut the meat neatly and finely. In the same way, you must treat herbs in the manner that is appropriate to them. 'Snip' them, or use a sharp knife to slice the herbs very finely.

You should also avoid overcooking herbs. It is always best to add delicate herbs such as tarragon and parsley to a sauce only 15 or 20 minutes before the sauce is finished, so that the colour and flavour of the herbs remains at its best when you serve the sauce.

Chervil is a favourite herb with both of us: it is delicately flavoured, it is never overpowering, and it looks beautiful, delicate and gentle.

Spices are also very important to us. We enjoy using them, especially with poultry. However, it is essential not to be excessive in your use of spices. As always, it is a case of looking for the right combination.

Only a few years ago, it was difficult to find another of our favourites, fresh ginger. Now it is everywhere. That is the result of influences from other parts of the world – although ginger was a common enough ingredient in France as long ago as the twelfth century. Rather more recently, Michel was using it in Paris twenty years ago, when he was at the Rothschilds'.

GREEN HERB ESSENCE

(Concentré de fines herbes)

 This essence of green herbs takes about $1\frac{1}{2}$ hours to prepare, and the result is some six tablespoons of green, gooey purée – and, yes, it *is* worth the effort! Make the concentrate during the summer months, when herbs are at their best and most plentiful. Store it either in a refrigerator, in a small screw-top jar covered with a fine film of oil, or in a freezer, in the form of ice cubes, and you will find that it quickly earns its place in a wide variety of dishes. Green herb essence will keep for about 2 weeks in the refrigerator. When you take a spoonful from the jar, add a little more oil to renew the seal. You can store it in the freezer for up to 2 weeks. After thawing a cube, transfer it to a plate. Using the flat of a knife blade, work the paste backwards and forwards to restore it to its former consistency.

Note: this recipe cannot be attempted without a food processor or blender; a blender produces a finer purée rather more efficiently. A standard processor needs time to cool between bouts of processing.

2 lb (1 kg) spinach	$1\frac{1}{2}$ oz (40 g) tarragon
5 oz (150 g) parsley	$1\frac{1}{2}$ oz (40 g) chervil
3 oz (75 g) onion or shallots, peeled	$\frac{1}{2}$ teaspoon salt
2 oz (50 g) chives	

Preparation and cooking

Thoroughly wash all the herbs and remove the thicker stalks.

Have ready $3\frac{1}{2}$ pints (2 litres) cold water measured in a jug, and a muslin-lined sieve or colander positioned over a large saucepan.

Process the herbs and onion or shallots a small batch at a time, adding sufficient water to give a thick 'soup'. Process each batch for 5 minutes, then pour it into the lined sieve. When all has been puréed, carefully gather up the ends of the cloth and twist it tightly, to extract the maximum liquid from the herb purée. Discard the pulp, rinse out the muslin in cold water and use it to line the sieve again. Now set the sieve over a large bowl.

Add the salt to the liquid in the pan and set the pan over medium heat. Stir with a wooden spoon until the liquid just begins to tremble. (At this stage a green layer will accumulate on the surface.) Immediately remove the pan from the heat before the liquid comes to the boil. Using a ladle, gently spoon the contents of the saucepan into the lined sieve. The muslin will retain the green purée; discard the brown water in the bowl. Using a rubber spatula or a palette knife, carefully scrape the green purée from the muslin, transfer it to a jar or ice cube tray and store as described above.

BOUQUETS GARNIS

One of the pleasures of cooking is to make up your own bouquet garni. In the mid-nineteenth century a famous chef defined a basic bouquet garni as one containing parsley, thyme and bay leaf. Taking this as a basis, you can add all manner of herbs and aromatics to suit your recipe. The collection of aromatics can be enclosed in a square of muslin, or packed between the curves of two short lengths of celery, or inserted into a slit in the white of a leek. Use a piece of string to tie the muslin into a bag or bind the celery or leek securely, leaving one long end of string free. When you lower the bouquet garni into the stock, soup, sauce, or whatever, you can use the length of string to secure it to the pan handle, so that the bouquet can easily be removed.

Note: do not leave any dangling ends of string that might catch fire!

The following very general categories may give you some idea of the combinations of herbs and aromatics suitable for different dishes. In general, think carefully about the dish for which the bouquet garni is intended and choose a few herbs that will complement and not dominate the flavour.

FOR FISH parsley, bay leaf, tarragon, chervil, white of leek, blade of mace, fennel

FOR MEAT parsley, thyme, bay leaf, clove-stuck onion, garlic clove (unpeeled)

FOR POULTRY celery, tarragon, bay leaf, parsley

FOR GAME rosemary, juniper, clove-stuck onion, strip of dried orange peel, thyme, parsley

POACHED CHICKEN MOUSSE WITH MUSHROOMS

(Mousselines de volaille aux champignons)

This chicken mousse provides a highly adaptable ingredient for many recipes. It is used, for example, in Veal chops with basil, in paper parcels (see page 106), and in Scrambled eggs Angélique (see page 70). It is worth preparing a larger quantity than you will need for your recipe, because the remaining mousse can be made into a simple and delicious supper dish: as described below, spoons of the mixture are gently poached in salted water to give the very light and tender dumplings known as mousselines. This recipe will make twelve mousselines; although they are light, they are rich and filling, so three per person is ample. Calculate that for every tablespoon of mousse taken out for use in another recipe, it will be one mousseline less here.

The mushrooms used can be of your choice; cultivated button mushrooms are good, but wild field mushrooms are delicious, and so are ceps, chanterelles and oyster mushrooms, if you can get them.

If you are mindful of calories, then a purée of fresh tomatoes could be served with the mousselines.

4 oz (100 g) chicken breast fillet	Per person:
1 small egg white	*½ oz (15 g) butter*
10 fl oz (300 ml) double cream, very cold	*1 teaspoon lemon juice*
Salt	*4 oz (100 g) mushrooms of your choice, trimmed, wiped and thinly sliced*
1 quantity Choron sauce (see page 32)	*2 tablespoons snipped chives*

Preparation and cooking

THE MOUSSE: Using a small, sharp knife, cut away any sinew from the breast fillet. Cut the meat into rough pieces and put them in a blender or food processor with the egg white. Process for about 2 minutes, until the mixture is reduced to a smooth purée.

Have ready a large bowl containing some cracked ice. Set a smaller bowl inside, on top of the ice, and rub the chicken purée through a fine sieve into the smaller bowl. Now beat in the cream a little at a time, beating well between additions. As the cream is added the mixture will slacken, but then as it is beaten it will resume its former thickness, and it will maintain this when all the cream has been added. Finally, beat in $\frac{1}{2}$ teaspoon salt. The mixture is now ready for use, or it can be covered and stored in the refrigerator for up to 3 days.

THE SAUCE: When ready to serve, first prepare the Choron sauce (or a sauce of your choice) and keep warm.

THE MUSHROOMS: Melt the butter in a sauté pan. When it is foaming, pour in the lemon juice and stir in the thinly sliced mushrooms. Cook over a fairly high heat until the moisture from the mushrooms has evaporated. Transfer them to a warmed shallow serving dish and keep them warm while you poach the mousselines.

THE MOUSSELINES: Briefly rinse out the pan, pour in water to a depth of about $1\frac{1}{2}$ in (4 cm), then return it to the heat. Add 1 tablespoon salt and heat until the surface of the water just trembles.

Stir the chives into the chicken mousse. Using 2 dessertspoons, scoop up a heaped spoonful of the mixture in one and use the bowl of the other to shape the mixture into a rounded oval. Now, carefully use one spoon to ease the mixture out of the other, keeping the oval shape, and slip it into the hot water. You will probably have room to poach 6 mousselines at a time. Working quickly, poach them for 4 minutes on each side, then use a draining spoon to remove them to the serving dish. When all are poached, quickly spoon a little sauce over each mousseline and serve immediately with the remaining sauce handed separately.

FRESH NOODLE DOUGH

(Pâte à nouilles)

Serves 6

•

9 oz (250 g) plain flour	1 teaspoon oil
2 eggs	1 teaspoon salt
3 egg yolks	1 tablespoon oil for boiling pasta

You will need a large work surface, because the dough will be rolled out to a circle 24 in (60 cm) in diameter.

Pour the flour into a mound on the work surface and make a well in the centre; put the remaining ingredients into the well. Start by beating the eggs lightly with your fingers, in a circular motion, gradually drawing in the surrounding flour. Use one hand for mixing and the other for rebuilding the flour wall and preventing the liquid egg from escaping. When the mixture ceases to be runny, push the flour over the dough and start using your palm and fingertips to combine the ingredients. It will come together in a non-sticky dough that will leave the work surface clean. Knead briefly. Leave the dough to rest, covered, for 30 minutes to 1 hour.

Dust the work surface with flour and roll out the dough, pushing it out and away from you, and turning it between rollings to keep it in either a square or a rectangular shape. You will need to roll it out to $\frac{1}{10}$ in (2 mm) thick and at least 24 in (60 cm) in diameter. Lightly dust the surface of the dough with flour, cover with a clean tea-towel and leave for 10 minutes. Now roll the dough up into a flat roll about 3 in (7.5 cm) wide. Using a sharp knife, cut the roll across in strips $\frac{1}{4}$ in (5 mm) wide. Unroll the individual strips and leave them to relax on the tea-towel for a few minutes. Meanwhile, bring a large pan of salted water to the boil and add to it 1 tablespoon of oil. Gather up the towel and tip the strips into the water; stir immediately with a wooden spoon. As soon as the water comes back to the boil, drain the pasta thoroughly, toss with melted butter and serve.

Note: the pasta can be dried and kept. The homely way of doing this is to unroll the freshly made pasta and drape it over a (clean) broom-handle. When dried, the pasta can then be stored in sealed plastic bags.

Green fresh noodles

Add 1 tablespoon of Green herb essence (see page 21) to the basic mixture, working it in with the eggs, oil and salt.

CHOUX PASTRY

(Pâte à choux)

People tend to assume that making choux pastry requires a considerable amount of expertise, but in fact it is quite a straightforward matter.

Makes 22 to 30 small buns or éclairs

•

$3\frac{1}{2}$ oz (90 g) butter, diced	$\frac{1}{2}$ teaspoon fine salt
$4\frac{1}{2}$ fl oz (135 ml) milk	5 oz (150 g) plain white flour, sifted
$4\frac{1}{2}$ fl oz (135 ml) water	4 eggs
$\frac{3}{4}$ teaspoon caster sugar	1 egg yolk beaten with 1 tablespoon milk, to glaze

Preparation and cooking

Put the butter, milk, water and sugar into a medium-sized saucepan. Add an extra $\frac{1}{2}$ teaspoon salt if you intend to make savoury choux pastries. Bring to the boil and boil for 1 minute, stirring with a wooden spoon. Take the pan from the heat and tip in the flour, all at once. Beat until the mixture forms a smooth, thick paste. Still beating, return the pan to the heat for 1 minute, to dry out the paste a little; but do not leave it on the heat any longer than this, or the pastry will not develop. Remove from the heat and transfer the paste to a bowl. Now beat in the eggs, one at a time.

When all the eggs have been incorporated, the choux paste is ready for use. If the paste is not required immediately, keep back 1 of the eggs and, instead of beating it in immediately, spread it over the surface of the paste. This will prevent a crust forming, and protected in this way and kept closely covered in a cool place, the paste will keep for up to 12 hours. When you are ready, beat in the surface egg and the paste will be ready to use.

Pre-heat the oven to gas mark 7, 425°F (220°C). Grease a baking tray, or line it with silicone paper. Choose an appropriate nozzle to pipe out the desired shapes. A $\frac{1}{2}$ in (1 cm) plain nozzle can be used for most buns, small and large, and is ideal for éclairs. Pipe the shapes on to the prepared tray. Now lightly brush the pastry shapes with the egg yolk and milk glaze.

Bake in the hot oven for 4 to 5 minutes, then open the oven door about $\frac{3}{4}$ in (2 cm) and continue to cook with the door ajar. From this point allow 10 to 20 minutes, according to the size of the buns. Cool on a wire rack.

To store

Choux buns can be stored in an airtight container for up to 3 days, or in the freezer for 1 week.

PANCAKES
(Crêpes)

 Pancakes are immensely versatile. To make a dessert, add a little sugar and a flavouring such as vanilla, orange flower water, lemon or orange zest, or a fruit-flavoured liqueur; fill or flame them or serve them with a sauce. For a main meal, a variety of herbs can be added to the batter. Pancakes also take well to storage in the refrigerator or freezer. Stack them on top of one another with a sheet of lightly oiled greaseproof paper in between each one. Enclose the stack in a plastic bag and the contents will keep in the refrigerator for a week. Wrapped in foil, then sealed in a plastic bag, they will keep for up to 4 weeks in a freezer (see page 15).

Makes 22 × 9 in (23 cm) pancakes.
You will need a large frying-pan with an 8½ to 9 in (22 to 23 cm) base. It should preferably be non-stick.

•

9 oz (250 g) plain flour, sifted	*1½ pints (900 ml) milk*
1 oz (25 g) caster sugar (dessert pancakes only)	*5 fl oz (150 ml) double cream*
Pinch of salt	*Flavouring of your choice*
4 eggs	*1 oz (25 g) clarified butter (see page 16)*

Preparation and cooking

Combine the flour, sugar (if used) and salt in a bowl. Make a well in the centre, break in the eggs and add a quarter of the milk. Using a wooden spoon, beat the eggs and milk together, gradually incorporating a little of the flour. Keep mixing until you have a smooth, thick batter, then gradually add the remaining milk and cream. Stir in the flavouring of your choice. Cover and leave in a cool place for 2 hours before using.

Set the frying-pan over moderate heat. Brush the base with clarified butter. Using a ladle, pour in some batter and immediately tilt the pan so that the batter covers the base. If you have put in too much, simply pour the excess batter back into the bowl; no harm is done, and the extra run of batter up the side of the pan can be neatly cut and lifted out with a spatula. If there is not enough batter to cover the base, quickly add small amounts to fill the gaps. By the second or third pancake you will be able to judge very accurately the amount of batter needed.

After about 30 seconds check the underside of the pancake; it should certainly need no more than 1 minute to become golden – if it does, turn the heat up a fraction. Turn the pancake with the aid of a palette knife. It will take less time to cook the other side – not more than 30 seconds. If they are to be eaten soon, the pancakes can be kept warm on a plate over a pan of simmering water with sheets of greaseproof paper between them but only for 5 minutes, or they will become rubbery.

SAUCES

A good sauce can make the difference between a dish which is ordinary and a dish which is great. A sauce should be delicate, complementing, and not overpowering, the dish with which it is served. In colour it should blend with the dish, but it should provide a contrast, though not too sharp a contrast, in texture and flavour.

When you have prepared a flour-based sauce in advance of your guests' arrival, it is usually better to let the sauce cool and then re-heat it, rather than try to keep it hot for a long time. Most sauces re-heat very well, though they will lose some flavour.

But however delicious your sauce, some people may dislike it – or they may think they will dislike it, but when they have tasted it, want more! So it is not a bad idea to serve just a little sauce on the plate, and have more in a separate sauce bowl. In some cases it may be best to serve the sauce quite separately, so that guests can help themselves.

MAYONNAISE

 A classic mayonnaise can be so quickly and easily made nowadays that there is no reason to buy the commercial product. And of course, if you make your own mayonnaise it can be tailored to your own taste. Firstly, you can choose the type of oil you use. For example, a groundnut oil will give a light, clear flavour, an ideal base when other flavours are to be added, as in *aïoli* (flavoured with garlic), *sauce tartare* (gherkins, capers, tarragon), or *sauce rémoulade* (similar, with the addition of anchovies). Olive oil will give a rich, robust flavour, something of an acquired taste, and mayonnaise made with olive oil is best served plain. As it is expensive to use olive oil in the quantities required for mayonnaise, try using half vegetable oil (for example, groundnut, sunflower or safflower oil – *not* corn oil) with half olive oil, for the best of both worlds.

Again, when you make your own mayonnaise, flavourings can be as varied and as strong as you choose.

To guard against mayonnaise separating, start with everything at room temperature (especially the eggs). If it is a cold day, rinse the bowl and the whisk in hot water just before using. If at all possible, avoid storing the made mayonnaise in the refrigerator; simply keep it, covered, in a cool place. But should refrigerator storage be absolutely necessary, remove the mayonnaise about three hours before you intend to use it and leave it without stirring until it comes up to room temperature; it will then usually survive.

Mayonnaise gets very thick in the final stage, and using a wire whisk can be hard work! You may need to resort to an electric hand mixer.

Note: to prevent discoloration, never allow mayonnaise to come into contact with any metal except stainless steel.

Makes 23 fl oz (650 ml)

•

3 egg yolks	*Freshly ground white pepper*
1 tablespoon Dijon mustard	*1 pint (600 ml) oil, of your choice*
1 teaspoon salt	*Juice of $\frac{1}{2}$ lemon or 2 teaspoons white wine vinegar*

Preparation

In a bowl, combine the egg yolks, mustard, salt and a little freshly ground white pepper. Position the bowl on a tea-towel to hold it steady as you work. Have the oil ready in a measuring jug. Start by whisking together the ingredients in the bowl. Then add the oil, a drop at a time, whisking it into the mixture. This is the critical stage: if the mayonnaise is to curdle it usually does it now, so take things very slowly until about 2 tablespoons have been added. The mayonnaise will now be getting thick, and the oil can be added about 1 tablespoon at a time. When about half the oil has been added, whisk in 1 teaspoon of the lemon juice or vinegar, then continue whisking in the oil in a steady stream. When all the oil has been added, stir in the remaining lemon juice or vinegar and any flavourings, if used. Taste and season with additional salt and freshly ground white pepper, if necessary. The finished mayonnaise will be a thick, wobbling mass. For a thinner sauce, stir in boiling water 1 tablespoon at a time until you reach the required consistency. Or you can stir in a tablespoon or two of double cream to soften the flavour.

If the mixture curdles during making or on standing, try beating in a tablespoon of boiling water. If this has no effect, simply put a fresh egg yolk in a separate bowl and gradually (just as slowly as before – or even more slowly) whisk in the curdled mix, a drop at a time.

Green sauce

(Sauce verte)

Add 1½ oz (40 g) Green herb essence (see page 21) to the made mayonnaise.

•

BUTTER SAUCES

 The following three sauces, White butter sauce, Béarnaise sauce and Hollandaise sauce, are all butter-based sauces, and they are very rich and very delicate. The most tender is the White butter sauce, which contains only butter, vinegar and flavourings. The other two also contain egg yolks.

Be sure to use stainless steel or tin-lined copper saucepans when making these sauces, as they are discoloured by, and discolour, most other metals. For the same reason, avoid serving them in silver sauce boats, or with silver spoons. You should not refrigerate any left-over sauce in a copper saucepan, either; if the tin lining is damaged, acids can erode the copper and create a dangerous reaction with the food. Of necessity, all these sauces are served lukewarm.

To rescue curdled butter sauces

A butter sauce that does not have an egg yolk base cannot be rescued, but you may be able to save a sauce that contains egg yolk. When a butter sauce curdles, it is usually because the mixture has been allowed to get too hot. If you suspect that this is the case, *instantly* remove the pan from the heat and sit it in a bowl of cold water.

Examine the sauce. If you can detect firmish flecks of cooked egg, abandon the mixture and start again: it is beyond help! If it has not reached the cooked-egg stage, try beating in a small ice cube, or put a tablespoon of cold water in a separate heatproof bowl and gradually beat in the sauce, as if making a mayonnaise.

On the other hand, if you have been very timorous it could be that the sauce has separated because it is too cold! In this case, with the pan over a low heat, beat in a tablespoon of *boiling* water, a drop or two at a time, until the sauce becomes emulsified and is thick and creamy throughout.

•

WHITE
BUTTER SAUCE
(Beurre blanc)

A sauce traditionally served with pike but one that is delicious with most grilled, poached or steamed fish. It should be made immediately before serving, because it easily becomes oily if any attempt is made to keep it warm. However, this is not quite as bad as it sounds as the sauce is very quickly made. When available, snipped fresh herbs such as chervil, chives, tarragon or flat-leaf parsley can be beaten into the sauce after all the butter has been added.

Makes 10 fl oz (300 ml)

•

3 fl oz (85 ml) white wine vinegar	*8 oz (225 g) butter, at room temperature*
2 shallots, very *finely chopped*	*Salt and freshly ground white pepper*

Preparation and cooking

Put the white wine vinegar and chopped shallots in a small saucepan. Boil to reduce the liquid to a tablespoon. Remove the pan from the heat and, using a wire whisk, beat in the butter, a small piece at a time, adding the pieces in quick succession. Taste, season and serve immediately.

BÉARNAISE SAUCE
(Sauce Béarnaise)

 This is a classic French sauce which is often used as a basis for other flavourings. It is usually passed through a sieve before serving, but we much prefer the coarser texture of the unstrained sauce: try our way and decide for yourself. Keeping the sauce warm before serving is difficult. The best advice is to keep it in a bain-marie over *warm* water for the minimum length of time. Any left-over sauce, kept at room temperature, is delicious served with vegetables or fish, grilled or poached.

Makes $\frac{3}{4}$ pint (450 ml)

8 oz (225 g) butter	1 teaspoon white peppercorns, coarsely crushed
2 shallots or 1 small onion, very finely chopped	4 egg yolks
5 tablespoons snipped fresh tarragon	3 tablespoons snipped fresh chervil or flat-leaf parsley
3 tablespoons red wine vinegar	Salt

Preparation and cooking

Melt the butter in a small saucepan and cool to tepid.

Put the shallots or onion, tarragon, vinegar and crushed peppercorns in another small saucepan. Bring to the boil and continue to boil until the free liquid is reduced to about 1 tablespoon. Remove the pan from the heat, add 1 tablespoon of water and leave to cool.

Beat the egg yolks into the cooled vinegar mixture. Place the pan over a base pan of hot water, or over very low direct heat, and whisk the mixture for about 8 to 10 minutes, until it is thick and creamy. Control the heat carefully: the temperature of the mixture should never exceed 150°F (65°C). Make sure too that you cover the whole of the base and sides of the pan with your whisk, so that none of the egg is allowed to overcook.

Take the pan off the heat and whisk in the melted butter, a little at a time. If the sauce becomes too thick, add 1 or 2 tablespoons of lukewarm water, then continue to beat in the butter. Do not add the milky sediment at the bottom of the pan. Just before serving, stir in the chervil or parsley, taste, and season if necessary.

Choron sauce

Peel and seed 2 tomatoes. Dice the flesh and cook in $\frac{1}{2}$ oz (15 g) butter to remove the excess liquid. Cool to tepid and stir into the Béarnaise sauce.

Opposite: Bouquets garnis (see page 22)

HOLLANDAISE SAUCE
(Sauce hollandaise)

 A very useful classic sauce to serve with vegetables, fish and poultry. If necessary the sauce can be kept warm, for a short time, in a bain-marie over *warm* water. On the whole, it is not worth trying to re-heat any left-over sauce as it will probably separate. But the sauce need not be discarded. Use it instead as an enrichment to beat into other sauces, just before serving.

Makes 15 fl oz (450 ml)

•

9 oz (250 g) butter	*3 egg yolks*
1 teaspoon white peppercorns, coarsely crushed	*Juice of $\frac{1}{2}$ lemon*
1 tablespoon white wine vinegar	*Salt*

Preparation and cooking

Melt the butter, skimming off any froth, and leave to cool to tepid.

In the top half of a double saucepan, or in a small saucepan, combine 2 tablespoons of water with the crushed peppercorns and white wine vinegar. Over direct heat, cook until only 1 tablespoon of free liquid remains. Remove the pan from the heat and add a further tablespoon of water.

When the reduction is cold, beat in the egg yolks, then place the pan over a base pan of hot water or over very low direct heat. Proceed exactly as for Béarnaise sauce (see page 32), *but* the temperature of the mixture should be kept a little lower, not exceeding 140°F (60°C).

When the mix is thick and creamy enough for the whisk to leave a trail on the surface, start whisking in the butter, a few drops at a time – if the additions of butter are too generous the sauce may curdle. Once the mix has begun to thicken, the liquid butter can be added a little faster. Do not add the milky sediment in the base of the pan. Just before serving, add a little lemon juice and salt to taste. Strain the sauce through a muslin if you would prefer a very smooth sauce of restaurant standard.

Mousseline sauce

Just before serving, fold 4 to 6 tablespoons of whipped double cream into the Hollandaise sauce.

Opposite: Cream of watercress soup (see page 40)

WHITE BORDELAISE SAUCE

(Sauce Bordelaise blanche)

This is a light, piquant sauce, particularly good served with poached or steamed fish, and a tasteful accompaniment to grilled white fish steaks.

Makes about 1 pint (600 ml)

•

15 fl oz (450 ml) dry white wine	*3 tablespoons finely chopped onion or shallot*
2 fl oz (50 ml) brandy	*A bouquet garni (see page 22)*
3 oz (75 g) butter	*1 tablespoon snipped fresh chives*
2 oz (50 g) flour	*1 tablespoon snipped fresh tarragon*
15 to 20 fl oz (450 to 600 ml) fish stock (see page 138)	*Salt and freshly ground black pepper*

Preparation and cooking

In a small saucepan, combine the wine and the brandy and boil briskly to reduce to about 5 fl oz (150 ml). Remove from the heat.

In a medium-sized pan, melt 2 oz (50 g) of the butter and stir in the flour. Cook for a minute or two before gradually stirring in 15 fl oz (450 ml) fish stock. Bring to the boil, stirring, then add the white wine and brandy reduction, the finely chopped onion or shallot and the bouquet garni. Reduce the heat and leave the sauce to simmer very gently for 45 minutes, skimming the surface from time to time.

Retrieve and discard the bouquet garni, stir in the snipped herbs and beat in the remaining butter. Adjust the consistency with a little additional fish stock if necessary, then taste and season with salt and freshly ground black pepper. Serve hot.

CHAMPAGNE SAUCE

(Sauce champagne)

For a touch of luxury on a special occasion, try this sauce of onions, mushrooms, champagne, fish stock and double cream – an ideal accompaniment to most poached or steamed fish.

Makes about 15 fl oz (450 ml)

•

$1\frac{1}{2}$ oz (40 g) butter	10 fl oz (300 ml) champagne
$1\frac{1}{2}$ oz (40 g) shallots or onions, thinly sliced	13 fl oz (375 ml) fish stock (see page 138)
$1\frac{1}{2}$ oz (40 g) mushrooms or mushroom trimmings	16 fl oz (475 ml) double cream
	Salt and freshly ground white pepper
About $1\frac{1}{2}$ oz (40 g) trimmings from white fish	

Preparation and cooking

Melt $\frac{1}{2}$ oz (15 g) of the butter in a medium-sized saucepan. Stir in the sliced shallots or onions, the mushrooms or mushroom trimmings, and the fish trimmings. Cook over a low heat for 2 to 3 minutes without allowing the fish bones or vegetables to colour. Pour in the champagne and the fish stock and boil until the sauce is reduced to a syrupy consistency. Add the cream and boil again to reduce to a consistency thick enough to coat the back of a spoon. Whisk in the rest of the butter, a little at a time, and season to taste with salt and freshly ground white pepper. Strain through a fine sieve into a clean pan. The sauce is now ready to use.

NANTUA SAUCE
(Sauce Nantua)

This sauce is the perfect complement to any seafood, especially prawns, scallops, mussels, and white fish. With the addition of a little snipped basil, it is delicious with tagliatelle.

Makes about 12 fl oz (350 ml)

3 oz (75 g) butter	*4 fl oz (120 ml) dry white wine*
3 oz (75 g) shallots, peeled and finely chopped	*4 oz (100 g) fish trimmings (optional)*
	10 fl oz (300 ml) fish stock (see page 138)
3 oz (75 g) mushrooms, peeled and finely sliced	*1 tablespoon snipped fresh tarragon*
8 crayfish heads (cooked or uncooked), chopped	*2 pinches of cayenne pepper*
	A pinch of salt
2 tablespoons cognac	*10 fl oz (300 ml) double cream*

Preparation and cooking

Melt half of the butter in a saucepan set over a low heat, add the shallots and the mushrooms and cook gently until the shallots are soft but not coloured. Add the crayfish heads, increase the heat, and cook for 2 minutes, stirring with a wooden spatula.

Add the cognac and, standing well back, ignite it. When the flames have died down, add the wine, and the fish trimmings if you are using them. Boil briskly to reduce by half.

Pour in the fish stock and boil to reduce by one-third. Add the tarragon, cayenne pepper and salt, then the double cream. Again reduce by one-third. At this point, the sauce should be just thick enough to form a film on the back of a spoon. Pour the contents of the saucepan into a blender and purée for 1 minute, to break up the crayfish heads further. Pass the sauce through a sieve into a smaller saucepan, pushing gently with the back of a ladle to extract the juices. Bring back to the boil, then remove the pan from the heat and whisk in the remaining butter. Taste and, if necessary, season with more salt.

SOUPS

Soups smell good, they look good, and they are good to eat. You don't even need to be hungry to enjoy a home-made soup; the smell is so appetising that alone will put you in the mood to eat it. And soup can be a meal in itself. After a rich or sophisticated lunch, a steaming bowl of a good vegetable soup may well be all you need for supper.

Soup is also easy to make, and you don't need to spend a lot of time making it. It keeps well in a covered bowl in the refrigerator, so in one soup-making session you can make enough for several meals.

Another nice thing about soup is that children love it. Or if they don't, that is their parents' fault, they just haven't brought them up in the right way! It is very important that children should enjoy soup, and respect it as a significant part of a meal.

There are different sorts of soup. The simplest soup is a broth composed of meat, fish or vegetables simmered in water or, for extra flavour, stock. This type of soup is often thickened with potato. For a purée, the ingredients are reduced to a uniformly smooth consistency by being passed through a sieve or (nowadays) worked in a blender or food processor. Cream soups, like the Cream of watercress soup and Cream of artichoke soup here (see pages 39, 40), are purées with cream added. Veloutés, such as our Frogs' legs velouté (see page 38), are purées enriched with egg yolks and cream. A consommé is a soup of great finesse and delicacy, full of flavour and perfectly clear. The ingredients are simmered for a long time, to extract all their flavour, then they are strained out; the soup is also carefully cleansed of every trace of fat. We have included here two of our favourite consommés, Autumn consommé and Cold consommé Francillonette (see pages 42, 43).

VELOUTÉ OF FROGS' LEGS

(Velouté aux grenouilles)

An unusual soup with a subtle aroma and delicate flavour. White wine and cream are often used when cooking frogs' legs, as they complement the delicate, chicken-like flavour of the meat.

Frogs' legs can rarely be bought fresh, but they can be obtained frozen, in pairs, from quality fishmongers.

Serves 6 to 7

•

2 lb (1 kg) frogs' legs	1 pint (600 ml) fish stock (see page 138)
Salt	A bouquet garni – thyme, bay leaf, parsley (see p 22)
1 leek (white part only), thinly sliced	10 fl oz (300 ml) double cream
1½ oz (40 g) butter	A good pinch of turmeric
1 medium onion, thinly sliced	2 egg yolks
12 fl oz (350 ml) dry white wine	8 sprigs of chervil

Preparation

Rinse the frogs' legs in cold water, pat them dry with absorbent paper and sprinkle them with salt. Rinse the sliced leek in cold water and drain thoroughly.

To cook

In a large saucepan, heat the butter and fry the frogs' legs until golden, about 1 minute on each side. Remove them to a plate. Add the sliced onion and leek to the pan, stir, then cover and cook gently for 2 to 3 minutes. Uncover, add the wine and cook for 5 minutes. Then add the fish stock and bouquet garni. Bring to the boil, add the cream and the turmeric and return the frogs' legs to the pan, reserving 6 for garnish. Adjust the heat to give a gentle simmer, and cook for 10 minutes.

Meanwhile, position a large sieve over a large bowl. Pour the contents of the pan into the sieve, discarding the bouquet garni. When cool enough to handle, remove the meat from the bones. Put the meat with the vegetables and the cooking liquid into a blender or food processor and process for several minutes. Rub the purée through a sieve into the rinsed-out pan and return the pan to the heat. Re-heat, taste and season with salt. While the soup is warming, put the egg yolks in a small bowl. Beating briskly with a wire whisk, add a ladleful of the hot soup. Stir this mixture into the pan of soup. Continue to heat, but do not allow to boil or the egg yolks will scramble.

To serve

Take the meat from the reserved frogs' legs, cut in small neat pieces and put into a tureen or individual soup bowls. Pour over the hot velouté and garnish with sprigs of chervil. Serve immediately.

•

CREAM OF ARTICHOKE SOUP
(Crème d'artichauts)

Globe artichokes of the Camus variety, grown in the north of France and especially in Brittany, are particularly good, and so we often specify them in our recipes. The large, very rounded head, made up of closely folded fleshy leaves, surrounds a substantial, succulent heart. Brittany artichokes are available in the shops from June to November.

Serves 6 to 7

•

4 large Brittany globe artichokes	*1½ pints (900 ml) milk*
Juice of 2 lemons	*Freshly ground black pepper*
Salt	*6 or 7 tablespoons double cream*
3 oz (75 g) butter	*6 or 7 sprigs of chervil*
1 medium onion, thinly sliced	

Preparation

Start by preparing the artichokes. Have ready a large bowl for the leaves, and a basin containing cold water and the juice of 1 lemon for the bottoms. First snap off the artichoke stems. Then, using a small, sharp knife or a pair of scissors, trim off and discard almost two-thirds of each leaf. Now, slipping a small knife under each leaf, cut it away at the base. Reserve the trimmed leaves in the large bowl. Continue until you reach the layers of thin, pale, papery leaves; discard these. Use a teaspoon to scrape away the hairy choke that covers the cup-like base. Then drop the artichoke bottom into the acidulated water, to prevent it discolouring.

To cook

Bring a medium-sized saucepan of water to the boil, add some salt and the juice of the second lemon and simmer the artichoke bottoms for 15 to 20 minutes, until they feel tender when pierced with a thin skewer. Drain and reserve.

Meanwhile, melt the butter in a large saucepan, stir in the sliced onion, cover, and cook gently for 3 or 4 minutes, making sure the onion does not colour. Stir in the trimmed artichoke leaves; cover, and cook for a further 5 minutes before adding the milk. Bring to the boil, then lower the heat and simmer gently for 10 minutes.

Pour the contents of the pan into a blender or food processor, and purée. Strain this purée through a sieve, pressing the pulp firmly.

Return the soup to the rinsed-out pan and re-heat. Skim if necessary, taste and season with salt and freshly ground black pepper.

To serve

Dice the artichoke bottoms and divide the dice equally between the soup bowls. Put a spoonful of cream in each bowl, ladle in the hot soup and garnish with sprigs of chervil. Serve immediately.

•

CREAM OF WATERCRESS SOUP

(Crème de cresson)

Sometimes the simplest recipes are the trickiest; a watercress soup is a good example of this. The freshness of flavour and appearance are hard to capture and impossible to hold, so delay as little as possible between preparation and serving. In fact, this soup is so quickly made you could start the recipe 30 minutes before the meal, and still have time to fry some diced bread in clarified butter until crisp and golden, to make croûtons to serve with it.

Serves 6
•

1¼ lb (500 g) watercress	1¼ to 1½ pints (750 ml to 900 ml) chicken stock (see page 18) or water
2 oz (50 g) butter	
2 oz (50 g) onion or shallots, thinly sliced	15 fl oz (450 ml) double cream
1 oz (25 g) leek (white part only), thinly sliced	4 oz (100 g) peeled potato, cubed
1 small carrot, peeled and finely diced	Salt and freshly ground black pepper

Preparation

Wash, drain and carefully pick over the watercress, discarding the thicker stalks and any damaged leaves.

THE GARNISH: Reserve 18 small, perfect leaves. Blanch them by dipping them in boiling water for 1 second, then immediately transfer them to a small bowl of iced water. Leave for a minute or two, then carefully remove and place on a sheet of absorbent paper and gently pat dry. Leave, covered with a damp cloth, until ready to serve.

To cook

In a large saucepan, melt the butter and stir in the remaining watercress, the thinly sliced onion or shallots and leek, and the diced carrot. Cover and cook for 2 minutes. Stir in $1\frac{1}{4}$ pints (750 ml) stock or water, followed by the cream and the cubed potato, and cook over a moderate heat for 15 minutes.

   Allow the contents of the pan to cool a little, then transfer to a blender or food processor and blend until smooth. Strain the soup through a fine sieve into the rinsed-out saucepan. Re-heat and adjust the consistency with a little additional stock if necessary, then season to taste with salt and freshly ground black pepper.

To serve

Pour the soup into warmed soup bowls or plates and carefully arrange 3 blanched watercress leaves on the soup in each bowl. Serve piping hot.

AUTUMN CONSOMMÉ
(Consommé automnale)

 This is a well-flavoured, crystal-clear soup. Served with the pistachio-coated croûtons arranged on a large oval plate, it makes a very elegant starter.

Serves 6
•

1 old partridge, plucked and drawn, or *half a pheasant*	2 tomatoes, chopped
	A sprig of thyme
4 oz (100 g) carrots, peeled and thinly sliced	2 egg whites
1 leek (white part only), trimmed, washed and thinly sliced	Salt and freshly ground black pepper
	2½ pints (1.5 litres) chicken stock (see page 18)
1 oz (25 g) celery stalk, scrubbed and thinly sliced	4 fl oz (120 ml) veal stock (see page 102)
1 oz (25 g) button mushrooms, wiped and thinly sliced	2 oz (50 g) shelled pistachio nuts
	12 very thin slices of French bread

Preparation and cooking

THE SOUP: Take a large cook's knife and chop the partridge (or half-pheasant) into rough pieces, leaving the breastbone and its meat intact. Place in a large saucepan. Add the thinly sliced carrots, leek, celery and mushrooms, the chopped tomatoes, the thyme and the egg whites. Season with salt and freshly ground black pepper and stir to mix thoroughly. Pour in the chicken stock, then bring to simmering point, stirring constantly. As soon as the liquid nears boiling point and begins to cloud, stop stirring and adjust the heat to maintain a very gentle simmer for 40 minutes. Leave the soup undisturbed during this time to allow the egg white to harden and clear the soup.

Meanwhile, rinse a clean cloth or a piece of butter muslin in cold water and use it to line a large sieve or colander. Position this over a large bowl and, when the consommé is ready, gently ladle the contents of the saucepan into the sieve, taking care to keep the cloth in place.

When it has thoroughly drained, return the clear consommé to the clean saucepan to re-heat. Retrieve the breastbone from the sieve and carefully remove the meat. Cut this in small strips and reserve, to garnish the soup.

THE CROÛTONS: To prepare the croûtons, boil the veal stock until reduced to a syrup.

Put the pistachio nuts in a small bowl and pour over boiling water; skin and finely chop.

Lightly grill the slices of bread on both sides, then brush them with the reduced stock. Sprinkle the surfaces with the chopped pistachios and arrange on a warmed plate.

To serve

Scatter the strips of breast meat into the soup and serve piping hot, with the croûtons.

•

COLD CONSOMMÉ FRANCILLONETTE

(Consommé froid Francillonette)

 A consommé the colour of a dark ruby, with a sublime flavour. The perfect complementary garnish is a duck breast fried quickly, so it remains pink, then cut into very small strips: arrange strips on top just before serving.

Serves 5 to 6

•

$2\frac{1}{2}$ pints (1.5 litres) chicken stock (see page 18)	2 egg whites
5 oz (150 g) lean beef, finely chopped	3 sheets fine leaf gelatine or
5 oz (150 g) lean duck, finely chopped	4 teaspoons granulated gelatine
8 oz (225 g) raw beetroot, peeled and grated	Salt and freshly ground black pepper
4 oz (100 g) raw celeriac, peeled and grated	

Preparation and cooking

Pour the stock into a saucepan and stir in the beef, duck, beetroot, celeriac and egg whites. Set the pan over high heat, stirring constantly. As soon as the liquid nears boiling point and begins to tremble, reduce the heat to very low and simmer, uncovered, for $1\frac{1}{4}$ hours, without stirring.

Have ready a large sieve or colander positioned over a large bowl. Rinse a clean cloth or piece of butter muslin in cold water and use it to line the sieve or colander.

Put the gelatine in a bowl and soak in 3 tablespoons of cold water for a few minutes. If you are using granulated gelatine transfer the bowl to sit over a saucepan of simmering water until the liquid is clear. The leaf gelatine requires only soaking: it will soften, not dissolve, and in this state is ready to be used. Gently stir either gelatine into the consommé and immediately remove from the heat.

Carefully ladle the consommé into the lined sieve, then taste and season with salt and freshly ground pepper. To remove any last vestige of fat, pass a sheet of absorbent kitchen paper across the surface of the consommé. (This should be done while the consommé is still liquid.) Leave to cool, then cover and refrigerate.

To serve

Allow 1 hour for the consommé to come up to room temperature before serving. Ladle into well-chilled soup bowls, garnish and serve.

•

CHEESE STRAWS
(Paillettes au fromage)

 Cheese straws are easily made, and they provide an interesting accompaniment to a soup. This recipe combines the flavours of mature Cheddar and Parmesan.

Makes about 4 dozen

•

8 oz (225 g) Quick or Classic puff pastry (see page 167 or page 164)	*A pinch of salt*
	2 oz (50 g) mature Cheddar, grated
1 egg yolk	*1 oz (25 g) Parmesan, grated*
1 tablespoon milk	*Sweet paprika or cayenne pepper*

Preparation

Pre-heat the oven to gas mark 7, 425°F (220°C).

THE PASTRY: On a lightly floured surface, roll out the pastry to an $8\frac{1}{2} \times 12$ in $(22 \times 30\,\text{cm})$ rectangle. In a small bowl, and using a fork, whisk together the egg yolk, the milk and a pinch of salt. Brush this over the surface of the pastry. Toss the cheeses together with some sweet paprika or a very little cayenne pepper to mix, and sprinkle evenly over the pastry. Press lightly on to the pastry using the flat of your hand. Using a long, sharp knife, cut the pastry in half lengthways, then across in strips to give pieces measuring about $4\frac{1}{4} \times \frac{1}{2}$ in $(11 \times 1\,\text{cm})$. Brush 2 baking trays with cold water, and use a palette knife to transfer the strips carefully to the baking trays.

Bake for about 10 minutes, until well risen and golden brown. Again, use the palette knife to transfer the cheese straws from the baking trays to a wire rack: leave to become cool and crisp. Cheese straws can be served cold, but are best eaten on the day of baking.

HORS-
D'OEUVRES
AND SUPPER
DISHES

The point of an hors-d'œuvre is to excite the appetite. An hors-d'œuvre should be fresh-tasting, and in colour, balance and texture it should anticipate what is next on the menu. Portions should be small, and you should never serve anything too rich or too heavy as an hors-d'œuvre. The intention is to leave your guests with clean palates, looking forward to the rest of the meal.

As, once your guests arrive, you will not want to spend all evening in the kitchen, we have selected for this chapter several starters, such as Eggs Albert (page 56) and Poulbot pasties (page 66), which can be prepared well in advance.

We have also included a range of dishes, from very simple ones, like Avocado Bering (page 46), which everyone can manage, to a sophisticated Fish terrine (page 62) which we often serve at our restaurants. This is really a dish for the more advanced cook, and it certainly takes a long time to prepare – but, equally certainly, it will be regarded as a masterpiece by your guests.

While the Fish terrine is definitely a starter for an impressive meal, most of the recipes in this chapter are suitable for either formal or informal occasions, and many can be adapted to make a main course for a family supper. The Poached egg soufflés (page 68), for example, served with a simple salad, would make an ideal meal in itself, as would Onion tarts with beef marrow (page 47) or Potato pie (page 71).

AVOCADO BERING

(Avocats à la Bering)

 If a fresh crab is available, boil it in heavily salted water, in a brine strong enough to float an egg; the crabmeat will then taste delicious. If you cannot find a fresh crab, buy a ready-boiled one from a reliable fishmonger.

Serves 4

•

Salt	Freshly ground black pepper
$1\frac{3}{4}$ lb (750 g) live crab	2 ripe avocados
$\frac{1}{2}$ quantity mayonnaise (see page 29)	Juice of $\frac{1}{2}$ lemon
1 tablespoon tomato ketchup	4 lettuce leaves (type of your choice)
1 tablespoon Worcestershire sauce	2 tomatoes
1 tablespoon cognac	2 black olives, halved and pitted
A few drops of Tabasco	

Preparation

THE CRAB: Bring a saucepan of salted water to the boil. Plunge in the crab and boil it for 20 minutes. If time allows, pull the pan aside from the heat and leave the crab to cool in the water; otherwise, drain and leave the crab to become cold, turned upside down, in a cool place for 2 hours. Have ready 2 bowls: one for the white meat and one for the brown.

Turn the cooled crab on its back, with the tail end towards you (see figs. 1 to 7, on page 153–4). Twist off the claws and legs, then, with your thumbs, push up the tail until it breaks free. Take out the central body section. Remove and discard the stomach sac and the gills (the pale-feathered 'dead men's fingers'); all that remains is edible. Using a teaspoon, scoop out all the soft yellow-brown meat from the shell and any brown meat still adhering to the central body section; put this in one bowl. Use a wooden mallet or something similar to crack the claw and leg shells. You will need a skewer to extract all the white meat from these, and from the crevices of the central body of the crab. As you work, put this white meat in the second bowl. Weigh the white meat; use the brown meat to make the weight up to 275 g (10 oz).

THE SAUCE: Put the mayonnaise in a separate bowl. Using a small wire whisk, stir in the tomato ketchup, Worcestershire sauce, cognac and Tabasco. Taste, and season with pepper if necessary. Cover and keep at room temperature.

THE AVOCADOS: Just before serving, cut the avocados in half and remove the stones. Brush the cut surfaces with lemon juice. Cut a thin slice from the base of each half so that they sit firmly on the serving plates.

To assemble

Mix two-thirds of the flavoured mayonnaise with the weighed crabmeat. Taste and season, then fill the avocado cavities, piling the mixture up high. Garnish the plates with the lettuce leaves and tomatoes. Finally, spoon some of the remaining mayonnaise over the crabmeat in each avocado half. Decorate each with half an olive, and serve.

·

ONION TARTS WITH BEEF MARROW

(Tartelettes aux oignons à la moelle de bœuf)

 These little tarts can be served as an hors-d'œuvre, or as a simple main course with a green salad. They make excellent outdoor food, or, if baked in little patty tins, an unusual accompaniment for roast pork or ribs of beef.
Note: for minimum tears and maximum speed, use a food processor to slice the onions.

Makes 6 individual tarts
You will need 6 individual tartlet tins, base measurement $3\frac{1}{4}$ in (8 cm), depth $1\frac{1}{4}$ in (3 cm).

·

2 oz (50 g) butter	*Salt*
$1\frac{1}{4}$ lb (500 g) onions, finely sliced	*2 eggs*
1 tablespoon black peppercorns, coarsely crushed	*8 oz (225 g) Quick or Classic puff pastry*
5 fl oz (150 ml) double cream	*(see page 167 or page 164)*
1 tablespoon currants	*4 × 4 in (10 cm) sections of beef marrow bones*

Preparation and cooking

THE ONION FILLING: In a large saucepan, melt the butter and stir in the finely sliced onions and crushed peppercorns. Cover and cook over a low heat for 30 minutes, stirring occasionally to check that the mixture is not cooking too fast and catching on the base of the pan. Uncover, and stir in cream, currants, and a little salt. Continue to cook gently, uncovered, for a further 15 minutes, stirring occasionally, then remove the pan from the heat and leave to cool. Break the eggs into a bowl and whisk them together until they are frothy; stir into the cooled onion mixture.

Pre-heat the oven to gas mark 7, 425°F (220°C).

THE PASTRY: Roll out the pastry thinly on a lightly floured surface. Using a small saucepan lid or saucer as a guide, cut out $6 \times 5\frac{1}{2}$ in (14 cm) rounds. Line the tartlet tins, gently pressing the pastry into the flutes with a floured finger. Divide the onion mixture equally between the pastry-lined tins, place them on a baking tray and transfer to the oven to bake for 20 to 25 minutes.

THE MARROW BONES: While the tartlets are baking, place the marrow bones in a saucepan, cover with cold water, add a little salt and bring to the boil over a high heat. When the water boils, lower the heat and simmer for 20 minutes. Remove the beef marrow to a plate and leave to cool for a few minutes. Run a small, thin-bladed knife around the marrow at both ends of each bone and it will slip out of the bone with little difficulty.

To serve

Cut the marrow into $\frac{1}{8}$ in (3 mm) slices and arrange them on top of the freshly baked tartlets. Serve piping hot.

LITTLE PIZZAS

(Petits feuilletés de tomate et basilic)

 These little pizzas would make tasty and attractive canapés for a drinks party. If you are unsure about the best way to peel tomatoes, see the recipe for Stuffed tomatoes with butter sauce (page 91).

Makes 40 canapés

•

1 oz (25 g) butter	*1 teaspoon snipped fresh basil*
3 oz (75 g) onion or shallot, thinly sliced	*Salt and freshly ground black pepper*
2 cloves of garlic, crushed	*8 oz (225 g) Quick puff pastry (see page 167) or puff pastry trimmings*
½ teaspoon sweet paprika	
1 lb (450 g) tomatoes, peeled, seeded and chopped	*12 pitted black olives*
A bouquet garni (see page 22)	*Anchovy fillets, to garnish*
¼ teaspoon dried oregano	

Preparation and cooking

Pre-heat the oven to gas mark 6, 400°F (200°C).

THE TOMATO TOPPING: Melt the butter in a medium-sized saucepan, and stir in the thinly sliced onion or shallot and crushed garlic. Cover and cook gently for 5 minutes. Sprinkle in the paprika and stir before adding the prepared tomatoes, bouquet garni, dried oregano and snipped basil. Cook over a low heat, uncovered, for 30 minutes, stirring 2 or 3 times during cooking. The sauce should now be thick enough to hold its shape on a pastry base; if not, continue cooking until this consistency is reached. Taste and season with salt and freshly ground black pepper. Cover and leave to cool.

THE CANAPÉ BASES: On a lightly floured surface, roll out the pastry to about ⅛ in (3 mm) thick. Using a plain cutter, stamp out 40 × 2–2½ in (5–6 cm) rounds. Brush a baking tray with cold water; use a palette knife to transfer the pastry rounds carefully to the tray. Use a fork to prick the pastry rounds, then put a heatproof wire rack on top of the pastry and weight it down (you can use the weights from a kitchen scales). Bake for about 5 minutes, until the pastries are crisp and golden. Again, use the palette knife to transfer the pastry rounds carefully to a wire rack to cool.

To serve

When ready to serve, chop or finely dice the olives. Drain the anchovy fillets and slice them into tiny strips. Spoon about $\frac{1}{2}$ teaspoon of tomato mixture on to each cooled pastry base and garnish each little pizza with a sprinkling of olives and a small strip of anchovy. Serve freshly made, warm or cold.

•

BLINIS

A classic Russian dish, these thick little wholemeal pancakes are ideal as a vehicle for smoked fish. Serve them straight from the pan, brushed with melted butter and topped with thinly sliced smoked salmon, or flaked trout or mackerel – or, most delicious of all, with salmon roe or caviare! Provide a bowl of soured cream as an accompaniment.

Makes about 36 × 1$\frac{1}{2}$ in (4 cm) blinis

•

$\frac{1}{2}$ oz (15 g) fresh yeast	2 eggs, separated
8 fl oz (250 ml) milk, warmed to blood-heat	A pinch of salt
1 oz (25 g) plain white flour	A little clarified butter (see page 16), for cooking
4 oz (100 g) wholemeal flour	

Preparation

In a mixing bowl, smoothly blend the fresh yeast and the tepid milk. Stir in the white flour, then cover and leave at room temperature for 2 hours.

Stir in the wholemeal flour and the egg yolks, then cover again and leave aside for a further hour, again at room temperature.

Have the egg whites ready in a clean bowl. Add a pinch of salt and whisk until stiff. Use a large metal spoon to fold them into the batter. The batter should now be used as soon as possible.

To cook

Heat a frying-pan or griddle and brush it with clarified butter. Either transfer the batter to a pouring jug, or use a ladle to pour it out on the heated pan, to form rounds about 1$\frac{1}{2}$ in (4 cm) in diameter. Leave space around each blini so they do not stick together and there is room to flip them over. They will need only about 30 seconds cooking on each side. Cook them in several batches, until no batter remains. Serve immediately.

GOUGÈRE

Burgundians claim the gougère as their own, and it certainly goes down well with a glass of Burgundy. The cheese-flavoured choux pastry, in the form either of individual small puffs or a large ring, makes an ideal hors-d'œuvre. The little buns can also be served as part of a selection of canapés, or, piped smaller, as a garnish for soup.

Makes 25 to 30 small puffs

•

1 quantity choux pastry (see page 26)	*3 oz (75 g) finely grated Gruyère and Parmesan cheese, mixed*
½ teaspoon salt	
Freshly ground black pepper	*Paprika or cayenne pepper, for dusting (optional)*

Preparation

Pre-heat the oven to gas mark 7, 425°F (220°C). Grease a baking tray, or line it with silicone paper.

Make the choux paste according to the recipe, adding an extra ½ teaspoon salt. Beat in the eggs, then the cheeses and some freshly ground black pepper. Fit a large piping bag with a plain ½ in (1 cm) nozzle and pipe little rounds on to the greased or lined baking tray. Dust with cayenne pepper or paprika, if used.

To cook

Bake for 4 to 5 minutes, then open the oven door about ¾ in (1–2 cm) and continue to bake for a further 5 to 8 minutes until the little puffs are golden-brown and crisp. Serve warm or cold.

LITTLE SWISS SOUFFLÉS WITH MUSHROOMS

(Petits soufflés suissesses aux champignons)

These little soufflés cause a sensation when they are brought to the table. Golden and fragrant, they make a deliciously light and unusual starter.

Serves 8
You will need 8 × 3 in (7.5 cm) tartlet tins.

•

3 oz (75 g) butter	*5 egg yolks*
1 small onion or 1 shallot, finely chopped	*Salt and freshly ground black pepper*
4 oz (100 g) mushrooms, trimmed, wiped and finely chopped	*1¾ pints (1 litre) double cream*
	6 egg whites
1 oz (25 g) flour	*7 oz (200 g) Gruyère cheese, finely grated*
10 fl oz (300 ml) milk	

Preparation and cooking

Pre-heat the oven to gas mark 6, 400°F (200°C). Brush the tartlet tins generously with 1 oz (25 g) of the butter. Arrange them on a baking sheet and put them in the refrigerator to chill.

THE MUSHROOMS: In a frying-pan, melt 1 oz (25 g) of the remaining butter. Stir in the chopped onion or shallot, cover, and cook very gently for 2 or 3 minutes, then take the lid off the pan, turn up the heat to medium, and add the chopped mushrooms. Cook, stirring frequently, for 5 to 7 minutes, until the moisture has evaporated from the mushrooms. Remove from the heat and leave to cool.

THE SOUFFLÉS: Melt the remaining 1 oz (25 g) butter. Stir in the flour and cook for 2 to 3 minutes, stirring, and then leave to cool a little. In a separate saucepan, bring the milk to the boil. Whisking briskly, pour the hot milk into the cooled roux. Bring to the boil, stirring; simmer gently for 3 minutes. Remove the pan from the heat and stir in the egg yolks. Season with salt and freshly ground black pepper. To prevent a skin forming, press a piece of buttered greaseproof paper on to the surface of the sauce.

Pour the cream into a fireproof baking dish, add a little salt and put the dish over direct heat; bring to the boil and continue to boil gently for 1 minute.

Pour the sauce into a large pan and warm it gently. In another bowl, whisk the egg whites until they are stiff but not dry. Remove the pan from the heat, then use the whisk to beat a third of the egg whites into the sauce. Stir in the cooked mushrooms. Now use a spatula to fold in the rest of the egg whites. Heap the mixture up high in the chilled tartlet tins, and shape quickly into rounded mounds. Immediately transfer the tins to the oven, and bake the soufflés for 3 to 5 minutes, until they are firmly holding their shape, and the tops are beginning to turn a light golden colour. Remove the soufflés from the oven and turn them out. Working as quickly as possible, flip them as gently as you can, into the warming cream. Sprinkle with the cheese and return to the oven to bake for a further 5 minutes.

Take the soufflés to the table as soon as they are baked, and serve them immediately, using a spoon and fork and of course taking care not to crush them as you do so.

.

SNAILS WITH HERB SAUCE

(Escargots aux herbes)

It has to be said, fresh snails *are* preferable to tinned, but the preparation of the fresh ones is quite a lengthy job, requiring considerable zeal and determination. The snails are first starved for a week; or some people do the exact opposite, and fatten them on things like fresh herbs, lettuce, milk, flour or bran. The next stage is to put them in a bowl and salt them (and it is a good idea to put some salt around the edge of the bowl to stop them escaping!). When they foam, rinse them and repeat the salting. Rinse once more and blanch in boiling water for about 3 minutes. Twist them free of their shells, using a fork, and discard the black spiral which is at the top of the shell. Rinse thoroughly, drain and simmer in chicken stock (see page 18) or Aromatic stock (see page 19; leave out the white wine if you use this stock) for 2 to 3 hours. The cooking time will depend on the size of the snail. Although snail farmers like to produce giants, small ones have a more delicate flavour, and will cook faster.

With tinned snails, of course, all this preparation has already been done. Snails can be served with or without their shells (tinned snails are often sold with a bag of shells attached), but, if you can, do serve them on snail plates.

Serves 6

•

6 oz (175 g) butter	Salt
2 oz (50 g) onion or shallot, finely chopped	2 teaspoons green peppercorns, drained
5 oz (150 g) sorrel, rinsed, drained and finely sliced	1 rounded tablespoon tarragon leaves
15 fl oz (450 ml) dry white wine	2 tablespoons chives
5 fl oz (150 ml) double cream	36 prepared snails

Preparation and cooking

Warm the serving plates for the snails, and have the snails drained and dried on absorbent paper.

THE SAUCE: Put 1 oz (25 g) of the butter in a medium-sized saucepan and melt over a gentle heat. Add the onion or shallot and cook for 2 or 3 minutes, without colouring, before adding the finely sliced sorrel, moistened with the white wine. When the volume of the sorrel has reduced by half, add the cream, a little salt, and the green peppercorns. Heat for a further minute, add the remaining herbs and continue to cook gently until the contents of the pan have again reduced by half. Transfer the mixture to a food processor or blender and process to a smooth sauce. Return to the rinsed-out pan and gently re-heat.

THE SNAILS: In a separate pan, heat the remaining butter until it is the colour of hazelnuts (no darker!), and throw in the snails. Swirl them in the hot butter, shaking the pan above the heat.

To serve

As soon as they are heated through, distribute the snails among the plates and spoon a little of the herb sauce over each. Serve piping hot.

ROLLED OMELETTE

(Roulade d'omelette)

This is a surprisingly adaptable recipe. Made as described below, it provides a good supper dish for four; it is especially delicious served on a bed of creamed spinach or accompanied by a mixed green salad dressed with a lemony vinaigrette. But it is simple to alter the recipe to produce attractive, and rather unusual, canapés. Just follow the recipe, but when you come to roll the omelette, roll it from one long side to the other. The roll can then be sliced into 25 small rounds. Use a plain biscuit cutter of a similar size to cut out rounds of bread, and fry these in clarified butter (see page 16) until they are golden brown. Place an omelette slice on each croûton, re-heat briefly in the oven, and serve straightaway.

Serves 4
You will need a small Swiss roll tin, base measurement 11 × 7 in (28 × 18 cm).

•

For the mushroom filling:	1 lb (450 g) tomatoes, peeled, de-seeded and diced
2 oz (50 g) butter	½ teaspoon sugar
2 shallots or 1 medium onion, finely chopped	Salt and freshly ground black pepper
10 oz (275 g) button mushrooms, wiped, trimmed and finely chopped	For the omelette:
	5 eggs
2 tablespoons finely snipped fresh flat-leaf parsley	7 tablespoons double cream
Salt and freshly ground black pepper	1 rounded tablespoon snipped fresh flat-leaf parsley
For the tomato filling:	1 rounded tablespoon snipped fresh chives
1 oz (25 g) butter	1 rounded tablespoon snipped fresh tarragon

Preparation and cooking

Line the Swiss roll tin with silicone paper and brush it with melted butter. Trim the paper fairly close to the rim of the tin.

THE MUSHROOM FILLING: Melt the butter in a frying-pan and add the finely chopped shallots or onion. Stir, then cover and cook over a low heat for about 5 minutes, until softened, but not coloured. Add the finely chopped mushrooms; turn up the heat and cook for 5 to 7 minutes, until the moisture has evaporated from the mushrooms. Stir in the finely snipped parsley, taste, and season. Keep warm.

THE TOMATO FILLING: Melt the butter in a medium-sized saucepan. Stir in the diced tomatoes and cook gently, uncovered, until reduced to a pulp. Add the sugar, then taste, and season.
Pre-heat the grill to a medium temperature.

TO COOK THE OMELETTE: Combine all the ingredients for the omelette together in a bowl and beat until well mixed. Pour the mixture into the prepared tin and transfer it to the grill, to a position about 4 in (10 cm) from the heat source. Cook gently until just firm, turning the tin so the cooking is even, and checking that the heat is not too high; it will take about 8 minutes.

TO FILL AND ROLL THE OMELETTE: Remove the omelette from under the grill and spread the surface first with the tomato pulp, then with the mushroom mixture.

Loosen the edges of the omelette from the paper with a palette knife, then lift up the paper at one short end and use it to guide the omelette into a firm roll: use the palette knife to ease the omelette from the paper. When the omelette is completely rolled up, leave the paper in position for a few minutes to allow it to set in the rolled-up shape, then remove the paper and cut the omelette into 8 slices. Serve immediately.

•

EGGS ALBERT

(Œufs froids Albert)

 A good well-behaved starter, that will keep happily in the refrigerator for up to 48 hours. However, do take care to use pure grated horseradish and *not* the sauce.

Serves 6

•

Juice of 1 lemon	*8 oz (225 g) smoked salmon slices*
6 Brittany globe artichokes	*10 fl oz (300 ml) double cream*
1 tablespoon flour	*1 teaspoon English mustard powder*
5 tablespoons white wine vinegar	*1 teaspoon grated horseradish*
Salt	*Freshly ground black pepper*
4 tablespoons fish stock (see page 138)	*6 size 4 eggs, very fresh*
$\frac{1}{4}$ teaspoon gelatine granules	*6 watercress or tarragon leaves, to garnish*

Preparation and cooking

THE ARTICHOKES: Have ready a large bowl of cold water to which the lemon juice has been added. Snap off the artichoke stems. Using a sharp stainless steel knife, pare the leaves from the base of each artichoke, much as you would pare the skin from

PREPARING THE ARTICHOKES

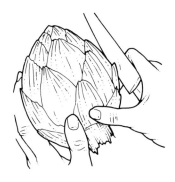

1 Using a sharp knife, pare the leaves from the base.

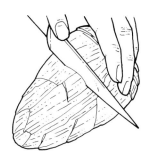

2 When the base is exposed, slice off the remaining cone of leaves.

3 Using a teaspoon, scoop out the hairy choke.

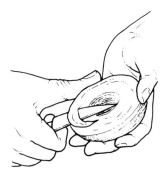

4 With a sharp knife, trim the base and bevel the top edge.

•

an apple (see figs. 1 to 4, above). Once the base is exposed, slice off the remaining cone of leaves. Finally, with the knife held at an oblique angle, trim the edge to round it off. As soon as each artichoke has been prepared, drop it into the acidulated water to prevent it discolouring.

In a large saucepan, combine the flour and 3 tablespoons of the vinegar, then fill the saucepan two-thirds full with water and bring to the boil. Add some salt and put in the artichokes. Simmer for about 20 minutes, until they are just tender when pierced with a thin skewer. Leave them to cool in the cooking water.

THE STOCK: In a small saucepan, heat the fish stock to boiling point, then remove it from the heat. Sprinkle in the gelatine, stir, and leave to become cold, but not set.

THE SALMON ROUNDS: Carefully lay the salmon slices on a work surface. Using a plain pastry cutter and firm pressure, cut out $6 \times 3\frac{1}{4}$ in (8 cm) rounds. Use a palette knife to transfer these to a lightly oiled sheet of greaseproof paper on a baking tray. Brush the salmon rounds with some of the fish stock. Transfer to the refrigerator to keep cool.

THE MOUSSE FILLING: Roughly chop the rest of the salmon pieces and place in a food processor or blender with half the cream. Process until smooth, then transfer to a bowl set in crushed ice and beat in 2 tablespoons of the cool, liquid fish stock, then the remaining cream, a little at a time. Stir the mustard to a smooth paste with a little water and add to the salmon mousse with the grated horseradish and salt and freshly ground black pepper to taste. Transfer the bowl to the refrigerator.

THE EGGS: Fill a shallow pan with water to a depth of about $1\frac{1}{2}$ in (4 cm). Add the remaining vinegar and heat until the surface of the water begins to tremble. Break the eggs into the water and poach for about 3 minutes, or until they are done to your taste. As soon as they are done, slip them into very cold water.

To assemble

When the artichokes are cold, drain them and scoop out the hairy chokes with a teaspoon. Pat them dry on absorbent paper. Divide the salmon mousse between the artichoke bases. Drain the eggs and place them on a clean cloth; trim the whites closely so that they sit nicely on top of the mousse. Place the smoked salmon rounds on top of the eggs, being careful to avoid breaking the yolks. Cover with cling film, and refrigerate until ready to serve. (*Note:* do not worry that the egg yolks may solidify during refrigeration – they do not.)

To serve

Arrange the artichokes on individual plates or a serving dish. Quickly blanch the watercress or tarragon leaves for 1 second in boiling water, then transfer them to a small bowl of very cold water. Remove, drain and gently pat dry on absorbent paper, then arrange one on top of each artichoke. Serve *very* cold.

SCOTCH POACHED EGGS

(Œufs pochés écossais)

 This is a quick supper dish for four, which adds interest to poached eggs by combining them with colourful strips of carrot, celery and leek, and crisp fried bread.

Serves 4

•

4 oz (100 g) carrots	*1 tablespoon white wine vinegar*
4 oz (100 g) celery stalks	*4 very fresh eggs*
2 oz (50 g) white of leek	*8 fl oz (250 ml) veal stock (see page 102), reduced by half*
3 oz (75 g) butter	
4 slices of white bread, each measuring about $4 \times 3 \times \frac{1}{2}$ in (10 × 7.5 × 1 cm)	*Salt and freshly ground black pepper*
	A little chopped parsley, to garnish
3 oz (75 g) clarified butter (see page 16)	

Preparation and cooking

THE VEGETABLES: Trim and wash the carrots, celery and leek, and cut them into matchstick strips. In a medium-sized saucepan, melt 1 oz (25 g) of the butter and stir in the carrot and celery strips. Cover and cook gently for 3 minutes. Take the lid off and stir in the leek strips. Cover again and continue cooking for a further 2 minutes. Take the pan off the heat and leave aside with the lid on.

THE CROÛTONS: Using a plain round cutter, about 2 in (5 cm) in diameter, cut a round from the centre of each bread slice. (These rounds are not needed in the recipe – use them to make breadcrumbs.) Heat the clarified butter in a sauté pan and fry the slices until golden on both sides. Remove and drain on absorbent paper, then arrange on individual plates; keep hot.

THE EGGS: Rinse out the sauté pan and fill with water to a depth of about $1\frac{1}{2}$ in (4 cm). Add the wine vinegar and heat until the surface of the water just trembles. Break the eggs into the water and poach for about 3 minutes, or to your taste.

Meanwhile, quickly add the reduced veal stock to the pan containing the vegetables. Re-heat, and stir in the remaining 2 oz (50 g) butter, a little at a time. Taste and season with salt and freshly ground black pepper.

To serve

Divide about two-thirds of the vegetables between the four pieces of bread, spooning a portion into the hole in the centre of each one. Using a draining spoon, take the eggs from the water and quickly place each one on top of one of the little piles of vegetables. Spoon over the remaining vegetables. Sprinkle with chopped parsley and serve at once.

·

EGGS ELYSABETH

(Œufs froids Elysabeth)

 A dish suitable as an hors-d'œuvre or as a supper dish, but it needs assembling at the last minute, as the pastry cases lose their crispness if they are left in contact with the filling for long. As the smoked salmon is incorporated, finely diced, in a cocktail sauce, it is not necessary to use top-quality salmon: off-cuts are quite adequate.

Serves 8
You will need 8 individual tartlet tins, base measurement 3¼ in (8 cm), depth 1¼ in (3 cm).

·

10 oz (275 g) shortcrust pastry (see page 162) or 9 oz (250 g) Quick puff pastry (see page 167)	1 tablespoon cognac
	Salt and freshly ground black pepper
1 tablespoon white wine vinegar	6 oz (175 g) smoked salmon, finely diced
8 very fresh eggs	2 tablespoons very finely diced celery
½ quantity mayonnaise (see page 29)	1 teaspoon snipped chives
1 tablespoon tomato ketchup	1 teaspoon truffle parings (optional)
1½ teaspoons Worcestershire sauce	4 black olives, halved
2 drops Tabasco	

Preparation and cooking

THE PASTRY CASES: Roll out the shortcrust or puff pastry on a lightly floured surface: shortcrust pastry should be rolled out to ⅒ in (2 mm) thick, puff pastry as thinly as possible.

Using a small saucepan lid or saucer as a guide, cut out 8 × 5 in (13 cm) rounds. Line the tartlet tins, gently pressing the pastry into the flutes with a floured finger. Prick the bases well with a fork and assemble the tins on a large baking tray; chill for 20 minutes.

Pre-heat the oven to gas mark 5, 375°F (190°C). Line the pastry cases with circles of silicone paper and fill them with baking beans.

Bake in the top half of the oven for 15 minutes. Carefully remove the paper and beans and return the pastry cases to the oven for a further 5 to 7 minutes, until crisp. Remove from the tins and cool on a wire rack.

THE EGGS: Fill a shallow pan with water to a depth of about $1\frac{1}{2}$ in (4 cm). Add the wine vinegar and heat until the surface of the water just trembles. Break the eggs into the water, no more than 4 at a time, and poach for about 3 minutes or until done to your taste. Use a draining spoon to remove them to a bowl of very cold water.

THE SAUCE: Put the mayonnaise in a bowl. Using a wire whisk, beat in the tomato ketchup, Worcestershire sauce, Tabasco and cognac. Taste and season; cover and keep at room temperature.

THE GARNISH: In a bowl, combine the diced smoked salmon, celery, snipped chives and truffle parings (if used), reserving a little truffle. Toss with a fork, then stir half into the cocktail sauce; reserve the rest.

To serve

Ten minutes before serving, sprinkle the remaining garnish into the pastry cases. Drain and thoroughly dry the poached eggs on a cloth, trimming the whites with a knife so the eggs fit the pastry cases. Put the eggs on top of the garnish and, using a large spoon, evenly coat them with just sufficient cocktail sauce to fill the pastry cases nicely. Put a halved olive (and a little reserved truffle, if any) on top of each egg, and serve.

FISH TERRINE LAYERED WITH SOLE AND ASPARAGUS

(Pâté de poisson aux asperges et fines herbes)

This delicate, subtle terrine is an ideal starter for a formal dinner party. It is a pleasing combination of flavours and textures; it looks very impressive; and it can be made well in advance.

Makes 12 to 14 slices

You will need a 3 pint (1.75 litre) loaf tin. Top measurement $9\frac{1}{4} \times 5\frac{1}{4}$ in (23.5×13.5 cm) and $2\frac{3}{4}$ in (7 cm) deep.

•

1 teaspoon melted butter	*1×15 oz (425 g) Dover sole, skinned and filleted*
1 lb (450 g) skinned, boned hake or whiting	*$1\frac{1}{2}$ tablespoons snipped fresh chervil*
3 small egg whites	*1 tablespoon snipped fresh chives*
15 fl oz (450 ml) double cream	*1 tablespoon snipped fresh tarragon*
Salt	*2 teaspoons snipped fresh basil*
8 asparagus spears, about the thickness of a little finger	*2 teaspoons snipped fresh flat-leaf parsley*
	1 teaspoon Pernod
5×9 in (23 cm) pancakes, flavoured with herbs (see page 27)	*1 egg yolk, lightly beaten*

Preparation

Brush the loaf tin with melted butter. Put the hake or whiting into the processor or blender with the egg whites. Process for about 2 minutes, until the fish is a smooth purée. (*Note:* in the restaurant the purée is then rubbed through a fine sieve into a bowl. Although this gives a smoother texture, it is a lengthy process, which can be omitted if time is short.)

THE MOUSSE: Put the bowl containing the fish purée inside a larger one containing cracked ice. Using a wooden spoon, gradually work the cream, a little at a time, into the purée. When it has all been added, the mousse will have a soft, dropping consistency, like that of a cake mixture. Season to taste with salt. Cover and leave on one side, sitting in the ice.

THE ASPARAGUS: Bend each spear and it will snap in half at the point where the tender stalk becomes tough and fibrous; discard the ends (or keep them to flavour soups, sauces, and so on), and rinse the spears in cold water. Bring a sauté pan of salted water to the boil and cook the asparagus spears for 5 minutes, until they are just tender. Drain in a colander, refresh with cold water and dry on absorbent paper.

Pre-heat the oven to gas mark 2, 300°F (150°C).

To assemble the pâté

Use 4 of the pancakes to line the base and sides of the buttered loaf tin, leaving a 2 in (5 cm) overhang. Halve the remaining pancake and use one half to line each end of the tin, leaving sufficient overhang to cover the pâté when the terrine is filled.

Spread a third of the fish mousse evenly in the tin. Flatten out the sole fillets a little by passing the flat of the blade of a cook's knife firmly over them. Lay 2 fillets on top of the fish mousse. Divide the remaining mousse into 2 portions of equal size. Stir the snipped herbs and the Pernod into 1 portion. Cover the 2 sole fillets evenly with the herb-flavoured mousse, then lay the asparagus spears at regular intervals on top of the mousse, pressing them in gently. Place the 2 remaining sole fillets on top. Cover with the remaining plain mousse, again spreading this final layer evenly. Fold the pancakes over the pâté to enclose it, and brush them lightly with the egg yolk.

To bake

Cover the loaf tin with foil and put it in a roasting tin. Pour boiling water into the roasting tin, to come about half-way up the sides of the loaf tin. Carefully slide this bain-marie into the oven and cook the pâté for about $1\frac{1}{4}$ hours, until a thin metal skewer inserted into it comes out clean. Transfer the pâté, in its tin and with the foil cover in place, to a wire rack, and leave it to cool for 3 to 4 hours. When it is completely cooled, put it in the refrigerator and chill for a minimum of 12 hours.

To serve

About 20 minutes before you intend to serve the pâté, pre-heat the oven to gas mark 2, 300°F (150°C). Take the foil cover off the tin and carefully slide a knife around the edge of the pâté. Turn it out on to a chopping board and use a sharp knife to cut it into slices $\frac{1}{2}$ in (1 cm) thick. Place each slice in a fold of buttered greaseproof paper, on a baking tray. Heat in the oven for 7 or 8 minutes, until they are warm, not hot. Serve on hot plates, accompanied by White butter sauce (see page 31).

SALMON TARTARE

(Tartare de saumon cru)

 The salmon in this recipe is eaten raw, rather like steak tartare. The cheaper salmon trout can be used instead of salmon, without detriment to the recipe.

Makes about 40 canapés

•

4 to 5 tablespoons dry white wine	*2 tablespoons finely chopped green pepper*
1 oz (25 g) onion or shallot, very finely diced	*2 tablespoons snipped flat-leaf parsley*
½ quantity mayonnaise (see page 29)	*Lemon juice, to taste*
8 oz (225 g) very fresh salmon or salmon trout fillet, skinned, boned, and cut into tiny dice	*Salt and freshly ground black pepper*
	2 dozen quails' eggs (optional)
2 rounded tablespoons finely chopped gherkins	*2 small French-style baguettes*
1 rounded tablespoon drained and finely chopped capers	*About 40 sprigs of curly parsley, or chervil, to garnish*
2 tablespooons finely chopped red pepper	

Preparation

THE SALMON MIXTURE: In a small saucepan, bring the white wine to the boil. Add the finely chopped onion or shallot and bring back to the boil; boil for 1 minute, then pour the contents of the pan into a small sieve and leave to drain and cool. (Do not waste the juices – keep them to add to a stew or broth.)

Have the mayonnaise ready in a bowl. Fold in the diced salmon, the finely chopped gherkins, capers and red and green peppers, and the snipped parsley. Press the cooled onion firmly to extract the moisture, then add this also. Taste, and flavour with lemon juice and season with salt and freshly ground black pepper, if necessary. Keep covered in a cool place for not more than 12 hours.

Opposite: Poulbot pasties (see page 66)

Overleaf, top, from the left: Courgette gratin (see page 83); Gratin of salsify (see page 81); Gratin of chicory (see page 84); below left: Eggs Albert (see page 56); below right: Fish terrine layered with sole and asparagus (see page 62)

THE QUAILS' EGGS: To cook the quails' eggs, bring a saucepan of water to a fast boil. Remove the pan from the heat and immediately add the quails' eggs, gently lowering them into the water. Leave for 5 minutes, then pour off the hot water and replace with cold. Leave covered for a further 5 minutes, then drain and peel under running water. (This is a time-consuming job, with some eggs trickier to peel than others: it doesn't demand any particular skill, but you will need a lot of patience – or someone willing to do the job for you!) Keep the peeled eggs in cold water until you are ready to serve.

THE CANAPÉ BASES: Cut the baguettes obliquely into thin slices. Either fry the slices in clarified butter (see page 16) until they are golden, then drain them on absorbent paper, or arrange them on a baking tray, put a heatproof rack on top of them (to keep them flat) and bake at gas mark 2, 300°F (150°C) for about 20 minutes, until they are crisp and golden.

To serve

Just before serving, pile a little of the mayonnaise mixture on each canapé and top with half a quail's egg and a sprig of parsley or chervil. Serve as soon as possible.

Opposite: Potato pie (see page 71)

Previous page: Little Swiss soufflés with mushrooms (see page 52)

POULBOT PASTIES

(Petits pâtés Poulbot)

 These little pies are a great favourite at Le Poulbot restaurant whenever they appear on the menu. If time is short, the recipe can be made up as one large pie. You can also leave out the final stage of pouring stock into the pie(s), but the addition of the stock does make the filling more moist. If you omit the stock, add the port to the meat mixture at the same time as the white wine.

Makes either *20 individual pies* or *1 large pie*
You will need either: 20 small brioche moulds, top measuring $3\frac{1}{4}$ in (8 cm); or 1 pie tin, top measuring $9\frac{1}{2}$ in (24 cm), base 7 in (18 cm), depth $1\frac{1}{4}$ in (3 cm).

•

7 oz (200 g) shoulder of pork, trimmed of fat	*1 teaspoon salt*
4 oz (100 g) veal rump	*Freshly ground black pepper*
7 oz (200 g) chicken livers, trimmed	*For 20 individual pies:*
7 oz (200 g) veal fat or fat from very fresh young lambs' kidneys	*$2\frac{1}{2}$ lb (1.25 kg) Quick puff pastry (see page 167)*
	For 1 large pie: 1 lb (450 g) Quick puff pastry
3 tablespoons snipped fresh flat-leaf parsley	*1 egg yolk beaten with 1 tablespoon milk, to glaze*
1 shallot, finely chopped	*About 15 fl oz (450 ml) gelatinous veal stock*
1 clove of garlic, finely chopped	*(see page 102)*
2 eggs, beaten	*1 tablespoon port*
8 fl oz (250 ml) dry white wine	

Preparation

Pre-heat the oven to gas mark 4, 350°F (180°C).

THE MEAT FILLING: Dice the pork, the veal, the chicken livers and the fat. Put all the diced meat into a mixing bowl, add the snipped parsley, chopped shallot and garlic, and stir to combine. Stir in the beaten eggs and the wine, and season with salt and freshly ground black pepper.

TO MAKE INDIVIDUAL PIES: Roll out the pastry to a thickness of $\frac{1}{10}$ in (2 mm). Take two plain round cutters, one $4\frac{1}{2}$ in (12 cm) in diameter, the other $3\frac{1}{4}$ in (8 cm). Cut out 20 circles with each cutter. Use the larger pastry rounds to line the brioche moulds, easing the pastry into the flutes and slightly above the rims of the moulds. Spoon in sufficient of the meat mixture to come three-quarters of the way up the moulds. Brush the edges of the pastry with the egg and milk glaze, lay the pastry lids on top, then pinch the edges between your thumb and forefinger to seal well. Roll out the pastry trimmings again and, using a small biscuit cutter or a knife, cut out leaf shapes to decorate the pies. Glaze the decorated tops of the pies and cut a good-sized hole in the centre of each one, to allow steam to escape. Transfer to baking sheets and chill for 1 hour.

TO MAKE 1 LARGE PIE: Divide the pastry into 2 equal-sized pieces. Roll out 1 piece to line the tin. Pour in the filling. Roll out the remaining pastry for the lid. Trim, then glaze the rim, then position the lid over the filling, and crimp the pastry edges together to seal well. Decorate and glaze the top of the pie and cut a central steam-hole, as for the individual pies. The only difference is that you should insert a small cylinder of stiff paper into the steam-hole. Place the pie, in its tin, on a baking sheet, and chill for 1 hour.

To bake

Transfer the pie or pies, on the baking sheets, to the oven, and bake for 1 hour. Remove from the oven and leave until almost cold.

To finish

If you wish to add stock, mix the cool but not liquid stock with the port. The easiest way to fill individual pies is to use a bulb baster. Fill the baster with the stock and port mixture. Holding the baster upright, insert the tip into the steam-hole of each pie and 'inject' the stock. You can pour the stock into the large pie through the paper cylinder. Leave the pie or pies in a cool place to allow the stock to set, but do not put them in the refrigerator, as refrigeration will impair the quality of the pastry. Serve on individual plates, or one large one, garnished with watercress leaves.

POACHED EGG SOUFFLÉS WITH FRESH HERBS

(Soufflés d'œufs pochés aux fines herbes)

These soufflés have a delightful flavour of fresh herbs. If necessary you can make the soufflés without Green herb essence, if you double the quantity of each fresh herb to compensate. But the flavour will not be as subtle.

Serves 6
You will need 6 soufflé dishes, 4 in (10 cm) in diameter and 2 in (6 cm) deep.

•

3 oz (75 g) butter	*1 tablespoon white wine vinegar*
1½ oz (40 g) flour	*2 tablespoons snipped fresh chervil*
1 pint (600 ml) milk	*2 tablespoons snipped fresh tarragon*
4 egg yolks	*2 tablespoons snipped fresh chives*
Salt and freshly ground black pepper	*1 tablespoon snipped fresh flat-leaf parsley*
	1 tablespoon Green herb essence (see page 21)
6 very fresh eggs	*12 egg whites*

Preparation and cooking

THE SAUCE: In a medium-sized saucepan, gently melt 2 oz (50 g) of the butter. Stir in the flour with a wire whisk and, stirring constantly, continue to cook gently for 2 to 3 minutes. Remove the pan from the heat and leave the roux to cool a little while you bring the milk to the boil in a separate pan. Whisking quickly, pour the hot milk into the roux in a steady stream. Bring the sauce to the boil, still stirring, and simmer for 3 minutes. Remove the pan from the heat and beat in the egg yolks and some salt and freshly ground black pepper. To prevent a skin forming, press a piece of buttered greaseproof paper on to the surface of the sauce. Keep at room temperature.

POACHING THE EGGS: Fill a shallow pan with water to a depth of 1½ in (4 cm). Add the wine vinegar and heat until the surface of the water just trembles. Break 3 of the eggs into the water and poach them very lightly, cooking for about 2 minutes. By this time the whites should be just set. Use a draining spoon to transfer the eggs to a bowl of very cold water. Poach the other 3 eggs in the same way.

All the preparation up to this stage can be done in advance.

THE SOUFFLÉS: Pre-heat the oven to gas mark 6, 400°F (200°C). Melt the remaining 1 oz (25 g) butter and use it to brush the insides of the soufflé dishes. Assemble them in a large roasting tin.

Whisk the herbs and the Green herb essence into the sauce and pour the mixture into a large bowl.

In another large bowl, whisk the egg whites with a pinch of salt until they form soft peaks. Using the whisk, quickly beat about a third of the egg white into the sauce, then, using a spatula, fold in the remainder. Half-fill the soufflé dishes with the mixture.

Place the roasting tin in the top half of the oven and quickly pour in sufficient boiling water to come half-way up the sides of the soufflé dishes. Bake for about 5 minutes, until the tops of the soufflés begin to cook.

Meanwhile, thoroughly drain the poached eggs on a cloth and trim to the size of the dishes (a large plain biscuit cutter is useful for this job).

Very quickly and delicately, arrange a poached egg on each soufflé and cover with the remaining soufflé mixture up to the level of the tops of the dishes. Bake for a further 10 minutes. Serve immediately.

SCRAMBLED EGGS ANGÉLIQUE

(Œufs brouillés Angélique)

 A very suitable dish for serving at brunch, this recipe combines eggs and cream with smoked fish, Chicken mousse, tomatoes, Drambuie, and crisp fried bread.

Serves 4

•

1 medium kipper	*Salt and freshly ground black pepper*
4 oz (100 g) smoked haddock	*2 slices of white bread, about 4½ in (12 cm) square,*
1 pint (600 ml) milk	*½ in (1 cm) thick*
3 tablespoons Chicken mousse (see page 23)	*3 oz (75 g) clarified butter (see page 16)*
½ tablespoon Drambuie	*12 eggs*
1½ oz (40 g) butter	*2 tablespoons double cream*
4 tomatoes, skinned, seeded and chopped	

Preparation and cooking

THE FISH MIXTURE: Put the kipper and haddock in a large, shallow pan and pour in the milk. Bring to the boil over a low heat. As soon as the mixture boils, remove the pan from the heat and leave to cool. Pour the contents of the pan into a sieve; return the strained poaching liquor to the pan and reserve. Flake the fish, discarding all the skin and bones. Gently fold in the Chicken mousse and the Drambuie into the flaked fish. Cover and keep on one side.

THE TOMATOES: Melt ½ oz (15 g) of the butter and gently heat the tomatoes with a little salt and black pepper. Reserve.

THE BREAD: Trim the crusts and cut each slice in half, then across twice to give 6 evenly sized rectangles. Then cut each rectangle diagonally in half to give 24 triangles. Heat the clarified butter in a frying-pan and fry the triangles of bread. Drain on absorbent paper; reserve. The recipe can be prepared ahead up to this point.

Just before serving, put the fried bread triangles to warm in the oven.

THE QUENELLES: Re-heat the poaching liquor. Take 2 coffee spoons: scoop up a little of the flaked fish mixture in one and use the other to shape the mixture into a rounded oval. Form 24 small quenelles. Poach the quenelles, about 8 at a time, in the barely simmering milk for 2 or 3 minutes, turning them carefully after a minute or so. Drain and reserve on a warmed plate. Discard the poaching liquor and rinse out the pan.

THE EGGS: Break the eggs into a large bowl and beat briefly with a balloon whisk. In the rinsed-out pan, melt the remaining 1 oz (25 g) butter and pour in the eggs. Cook over a low heat, stirring gently with a wooden spoon, until the eggs begin to set in creamy, soft curds. Remove the pan from the heat, stir in the cream, taste, and season.

To serve

Divide the eggs between 4 warmed plates. Quickly re-heat the tomatoes and put a spoonful in the centre of each one. Arrange 6 quenelles and 6 bread-triangles, alternately, around each plate. Serve immediately.

•

POTATO PIE

(Tourte aux pommes de terre)

 A pie of crisp puff pastry, enclosing a filling of sliced potatoes, onions and fresh herbs. Just before serving, pour in boiling cream. This is a dish that manages to be at the same time rustic and *haute cuisine* – and utterly delicious! It is traditionally baked on a *tourtière* (a round, flat baking tin, something like a pizza tin – a baking tray makes a good substitute). This means that there is a flat base of pastry, and the potato filling is heaped up on top, then covered with a pastry lid. When baked it looks a splendid, homely pie. If you prefer a more formal presentation, bake the pie in a more conventional manner, in a pie tin.

Serves 6 to 8
You will need either: a baking tray a minimum of 11 in (28 cm) wide, or a pie tin with sloping sides, base measurement 7 in (18 cm), top measurement 9½ in (24 cm), height 1½ in (4 cm).

•

4 oz (100 g) butter	*Freshly grated nutmeg*
3¼ to 3½ lb (1.5 kg) potatoes, peeled and cut into ⅛ in (3 mm) slices	*Salt and freshly ground black pepper*
	9 oz (250 g) Quick or Classic puff pastry (see page 167 or page 164)
8 oz (225 g) onions, very thinly sliced	
3 tablespoons snipped fresh flat-leaf parsley and tarragon, mixed	*1 egg yolk beaten with 1 tablespoon milk, to glaze*
	8 fl oz (250 ml) double cream

Preparation

Pre-heat the oven to gas mark 6, 400°F (200°C).

THE FILLING: In a large pan, melt the butter. Stir in the sliced potatoes and onions, the snipped parsley and tarragon, and some nutmeg, salt and freshly ground pepper. Cook over a moderate heat, stirring frequently, for 5 minutes. By this time the potatoes will only just have lost their crispness. Pour the contents of the pan into a large sieve or colander set over a bowl, and leave to drain and cool.

FOR THE BAKING TRAY: Divide the pastry into 5 oz (150 g) and 4 oz (100 g) pieces. On a lightly floured surface, roll out the smaller piece to a round about 10 in (25 cm) in diameter. Brush the baking tray with water and place the pastry on it. Pile the cooled potato and onion mixture on top of the pastry base, keeping it centred in a neat round. Glaze the pastry border. Roll out the remaining 5 oz (150 g) pastry to a round about 12 in (30 cm) in diameter and use this to cover the pie, lightly pressing the edges together. Leaving a border about $\frac{3}{4}$–1 in (2–2.5 cm) wide, trim off any excess pastry, then crimp the pastry edges together to seal. If you like, you can roll out the pastry trimmings again and, using a small biscuit cutter, cut leaf-shapes to decorate the top of the pie. Glaze the pie lid. To allow the steam to escape during baking, cut a good-sized hole in the middle of the lid and insert into it a small cylinder of stiff paper.

FOR THE PIE TIN: Divide the pastry into 2 equal-sized portions. Roll out 1 piece and use it to line the base of the tin; trim off the excess pastry around the edge of the tin. Fill the pastry-lined tin with the cooled potato and onion mixture. Roll out the remaining piece of pastry for the lid. Glaze the band of pastry covering the rim of the pie tin, position the lid over the filling, trim and crimp the edges together to seal well. If you wish, decorate the pie lid as described above. Glaze the lid, cut a steam-hole and insert a paper 'chimney'. Place the tin on a baking tray.

Baking the pie

Bake the pie in the centre of the oven for 1 hour. About 15 minutes before the end of the baking time, check to see that the pastry is not getting too brown; if it is, cover loosely with a sheet of foil. Continue cooking. After the full hour, remove and reserve the paper cylinder and insert a thin metal skewer through the steam-hole to check that the potatoes are tender. Remove the pie from the oven and replace the paper cylinder.

To serve

Bring the cream quickly to the boil and carefully pour it into the pie through the paper funnel. Leave for 5 minutes, then serve.

WHOLEMEAL BREAD TO SERVE WITH CHEESE

(Pain pour fromage)

A wholemeal bread made with baking powder and full of flavour: serve it with cheese and a salad or with a thick soup, for a simple, satisfying supper. Unfortunately, it does not keep its delicious fresh taste for long, so eat it the same day, if you can. Or, alternatively, you can freeze it for a few days, then thaw it, warm it, and eat the same day.

Makes 1 bread twist, 16 to 18 slices

•

6 oz (175 g) butter, at room temperature	*4 teaspoons baking powder*
1 teaspoon sugar	*1 teaspoon salt*
12 oz (350 g) wholemeal flour	*8 fl oz (250 ml) milk*
2 oz (50 g) plain white flour	*1 egg yolk beaten with 1 tablespoon milk, to glaze*
2 oz (50 g) fine oatmeal	*2 tablespoons sesame seeds*

Preparation and cooking

In a medium-sized bowl, beat the butter with a wooden spoon to soften it, then mix in the sugar. Put the wholemeal flour, the white flour, the oatmeal, the baking powder and the salt into a large mixing bowl, and pour in the milk. Add the softened butter and work the ingredients together for about 5 minutes, to form a smooth dough. Cover the bowl with a damp cloth to prevent the dough from drying out, transfer to the refrigerator, and leave for 2 hours, to rest the dough.

Pre-heat the oven to gas mark 7, 425°F (220°C). Grease a small baking tray.

Shape the dough into a roll about 9 in (23 cm) long. Starting about 1 in (2.5 cm) from the end of the roll, cut the dough into 3 strips along the rest of its length. Plait these to form an attractive-looking loaf, tucking the ends under, and form into a ring if you wish. Transfer to the baking tray. Chill and rest the dough for a further 30 minutes, then allow to come up to room temperature. Glaze with the beaten egg yolk and milk and sprinkle lightly with the sesame seeds.

Bake for about 25 to 30 minutes, until the loaf is well risen and looks nicely browned.

To serve

Cool the wholemeal bread on a wire rack, and eat the same day.

VEGETABLES
AND SALADS

Vegetables and salads can be used to add colour, flavour and texture to a meal; or they can themselves form the basis of a meal.

In recent years so many interesting vegetable varieties have become available, to the home cook as well as to the restaurateur. Many supermarkets carry a very wide and adventurous range of vegetables and salads, some produced at home, some flown in from other countries. Mange-tout, for instance, only a few years ago, were very difficult to obtain. Now you can get them easily all the year round. All the same, do not despise the more homely vegetables – the turnip, the carrot, the potato (but please do use them before they are monster size: flavour usually diminishes as size increases).

With all vegetables, the most important thing is to buy them as fresh as possible, and use them as soon as you can. The best vegetables are freshly picked, and cooked and served immediately; and often the best way of cooking them is the simplest. Cook them straightforwardly, put a knob of butter on them, and serve them just as they are. But the cooking of vegetables does require careful judgement. For many years, of course, it was the fashion to cook vegetables for far too long, and to serve them soaked with water. Now people seem to have gone to the other extreme: they just blanch vegetables and serve them practically raw – which is equally unsatisfactory.

When you are deciding on vegetable accompaniments, take into account the character of the main ingredient. Avoid duplicating colours, textures and flavours. For instance, we would never serve turbot with a champagne sauce accompanied by cauliflower: white, white, and more white. Instead, how about nice little mange-tout, lightly cooked, and a few French beans? Then add some steamed potatoes, just to enhance the flavour and bring a different texture to the dish, and you will have a perfect combination. A vegetable purée is often the ideal complement. For example, try serving a rib of beef accompanied by a little purée of spinach or carrot. The delicate flavour and texture of the vegetables will contrast beautifully with the full-bodied meat.

Do consider combinations of vegetables, as well. A plate of two or three little stuffed vegetables, for instance, makes a delicious starter.

Salads, also, deserve a lot more care, attention and thought than they get. Some people will produce the most incredible – and inedible – mish-mash and call it a salad: they seem to think that you can produce a salad by just opening the refrigerator door and mixing together whatever you find inside. In fact you can make a meal from a good soup and a good salad, or salad with a piece of cheese, or a salad with soft poached eggs, or mixed with diced fried bacon.

There are so many exciting salad ingredients available now, that there is really no excuse for a bad or boring salad. You only have to think of the seemingly endless variety of salad leaves: cos and oak leaf lettuces; lamb's lettuce; endive; the colourful Italian radicchio; and many more.

It is important to pay attention to the salad dressing too. Different salads need different seasonings, and you should consider the character of the salad when you are deciding on a dressing. Delicate ingredients must have a delicate dressing. For example, walnut oil is wonderful with curly endive; but if you serve it with a salad based on cos lettuce, its flavour will overpower the lettuce. The ideal oil for this lettuce is groundnut oil. Olive oil is fine for a mixed salad, and perfect with tomatoes or lamb's lettuce. And a watercress salad has a strong enough flavour to take a rich dressing with cream, lemon juice and freshly ground black pepper.

If you are not confident about what dressing to use, it is a good idea to set up a little trial of different dressings in separate cups. Then dip little leaves of whatever is in your salad into the dressings and taste them, until you find the dressing that you feel suits that particular salad best.

VEGETABLE PURÉES

Presentation as a purée gives a touch of luxury to even the most mundane vegetable. It is also a very convenient way of serving vegetables, particularly at a dinner party, when you don't want to spend too much time in the kitchen. Purées can be made in advance and thereafter need little attention. They can simply be re-heated in the top of a double saucepan, or in buttered ramekins in a bain-marie in the oven: the ramekins can go straight from oven to table.

A purée should have the consistency of softly beaten cream – it should not be at all sloppy. The texture is a matter of personal preference. Puréeing in a food processor will not give such a smooth result as using a blender. And if you want a purée with a really velvety texture, you will have to rub it through a fine sieve after either processing or blending.

·

ARTICHOKE PURÉE
(Purée d'artichauts)

Makes 15 fl oz (450 ml)
·

Juice of 1 lemon	*Salt*
About 3¼ lb (1.5 kg) globe artichokes	*2 oz (50 g) butter*
1 tablespoon flour	*2 tablespoons double cream*
3 tablespoons white wine vinegar	*Freshly ground black pepper*

Preparation and cooking

Add the juice of the lemon to a bowl of cold water.

Snap off the artichoke stems, then bend over the tops of the leaves so that they break off, leaving the fleshy section of the leaf still attached to the base. If the leaves do not readily snap off in this manner, use a small, sharp knife to trim off three-quarters of each leaf. Cut the artichoke into quarters. Use a teaspoon to scrape out the hairy choke and pale, papery leaves. Drop immediately into the acidulated water.

Combine the flour and the vinegar in a large saucepan, then pour in water to come two-thirds of the way up the pan, add a pinch of salt, and bring to the boil. Immerse the prepared artichokes, cover, and simmer for 15 minutes, or until the artichokes feel tender when tested with a thin skewer.

To purée

Drain the artichokes thoroughly, then transfer them to a food processor or blender, add the butter and cream, and blend until smooth. (If you want a very smooth purée, you can then rub it through a sieve.) Return the purée to the pan and re-heat, stirring. Taste, and season.

•

BRUSSELS SPROUTS PURÉE

(Purée de choux de Bruxelles)

Makes 1½ pints (900 ml)

•

2 lb (1 kg) Brussels sprouts	*2 tablespoons double cream*
Salt	*Freshly ground black pepper*
2 oz (50 g) butter	

Preparation and cooking

Trim the stems, removing any discoloured leaves, and put the sprouts in a bowl of well-salted cold water.

Bring a large saucepan of salted water to the boil. Drain the sprouts, put them in the saucepan, bring the water back to the boil and cook them for 2 minutes. Drain in a colander and refresh under cold running water. Now put the sprouts in a steamer over boiling water. Cover the steamer, and steam the sprouts for 10 minutes, or until they are quite tender.

To purée

Purée the sprouts in 2 batches, in a food processor or a blender, adding half the butter and cream to each batch. (For a smoother texture, rub the purée through a fine sieve.) Taste, season, then re-heat, stirring.

CARROT PURÉE
(Purée de carottes)

Makes 1¼ pints (750 ml)

•

2 lb (1 kg) carrots	2 tablespoons double cream
Salt	Freshly ground black pepper
2 oz (50 g) butter	

Preparation and cooking

Top and tail and scrape or thinly peel the carrots, then slice them into rounds ¼ in (5 mm) thick.

Put the carrots into a steamer over boiling water, sprinkle them with a little salt, cover, and steam for about 15 minutes, until they are quite tender.

To purée

Purée the carrots in 2 batches, in either a food processor or a blender, adding half the butter and cream to each batch. (If you want a very smooth purée, you can then rub it through a sieve.) Taste, season, then re-heat, stirring.

•

FENNEL PURÉE
(Purée de fenouil)

Makes scant 15 fl oz (450 ml)

•

2 lb (1 kg) bulb fennel	2 tablespoons double cream
2 oz (50 g) butter	Freshly ground black pepper
Salt	

Preparation and cooking

Pre-heat the oven to gas mark 5, 375°F (190°C).

Cut the fennel bulbs in half and wash them in cold water. Trim the green shoots from the tops of the bulbs, reserving any feathery leaves. Shave off the bases, then peel off the outer leaves if they appear coarse or damaged; slice thinly.

In a fireproof casserole, melt the butter, then stir in the fennel, and cover. Cook the fennel gently, without colouring, until it is just beginning to soften, then take the lid off and sprinkle the fennel with a little salt. Cover the casserole again, and transfer it to the oven to cook for about 20 minutes, until the fennel is completely tender.

To purée

Drain the fennel thoroughly, transfer it to a food processor or blender, and blend until smooth. (Then, if a smoother texture is preferred, rub it through a fine sieve.) Return the purée to the rinsed-out casserole. Cook over a high heat for about 2 minutes, stirring constantly, until the excess moisture has evaporated and the purée has the desired consistency.

Stir in the cream; taste, and season if necessary. Chop the reserved leaves finely, stir them into the purée, and serve.

.

LEEK PURÉE
(Purée de poireaux)

Makes scant 1¼ pints (750 ml)
.

2 lb (1 kg) leeks	2 tablespoons double cream
Salt	Salt and freshly ground black pepper
2 oz (50 g) butter	

Preparation and cooking

Trim and wash the leeks and slice them finely, discarding the greenest part.

Melt the butter in a large pan, and stir in the sliced leeks. Cover and cook gently, without colouring, for 5 minutes. Strain the leeks (keep the cooking liquid to use in stocks).

To purée

Purée the leeks in 2 batches in either a food processor or a blender, adding half the butter and cream to each batch. (For a very smooth purée, you can then rub it through a sieve.) Taste, season, then re-heat, stirring.

ONIONS WITH SULTANAS

(Oignons aux raisins de Smyrne)

 This recipe combines onions with the sweetness of sultanas and the sharpness of wine vinegar. Very simple and quick to make, it can be served as an hors-d'œuvre with some hot French bread.

Serves 4

•

2 lb (1 kg) button onions, peeled and left whole	*3 tablespoons olive oil*
4 oz (100 g) sultanas	*Salt*
3–4 tablespoons white wine vinegar	*Cayenne pepper*
3 tomatoes, peeled, de-seeded, and diced	*Juice of ½ lemon, strained*

To cook

Rinse the whole onions in cold water and put them in a large saucepan with 7 fl oz (200 ml) water, the sultanas, 3 tablespoons of white wine vinegar, the diced tomatoes, the olive oil and a little salt. Add a very little cayenne pepper, only sufficient to cover the tip of a pointed knife. Bring the liquid to simmering point, then insert a butter paper, or a double thickness of buttered greaseproof paper, into the pan, to sit on top of the onions. Cover with a lid and simmer very gently for 30 to 35 minutes, until the onions are tender, but by no means squashy. Remove the pan from the heat and leave to cool, covered.

To serve

When ready to serve, add the strained lemon juice, then taste and flavour with additional salt, cayenne pepper and white wine vinegar, if needed. Serve at room temperature.

GRATIN OF SALSIFY
(Gratin de salsifis)

 Although salsify and its 'twin' scorzonera have been around for centuries, they have never become commonplace in our diet. They are still rarely grown, and are obtainable from only a few specialist greengrocers. In an effort to bring a delicious vegetable to a wider public, we have included it here.

Serves 6 to 8

•

Juice of 2 lemons	1 tablespoon snipped flat-leaf parsley
2 to 2¼ lb (1 kg) salsify	15 fl oz (450 ml) double cream
2 oz (50 g) plain white flour	Freshly ground black pepper
Salt	2 tablespoons grated Gruyère
1 oz (25 g) butter	2 tablespoons dry white breadcrumbs
1 onion or 2 shallots, finely chopped	

Preparation

Have ready a bowl of cold water to which the juice of 1 lemon has been added. Wash the salsify, then peel it and cut it obliquely into lengths of approximately 1¼ to 1½ in (3 to 4 cm). Drop these immediately into the water and lemon juice.

In a medium-sized saucepan, blend the flour with a little water and the juice from the remaining lemon. Add a further 3½ pints (2 litres) cold water and some salt and bring it to the boil, whisking from time to time to prevent the flour from sinking to the bottom of the pan and possibly burning.

To cook

Drain the prepared salsify, transfer it to the saucepan, and boil gently for about 25 minutes, or until tender, but not soft. While the salsify is cooking, melt the butter in a separate medium-sized pan and stir in the chopped onion or shallots. Cover and cook gently for 2 or 3 minutes without allowing it to colour. Uncover and pour in the cream. Bring to the boil and simmer until reduced to about 10 fl oz (300 ml).

Meanwhile, pre-heat the oven to gas mark 6, 400°F (200°C).

As soon as the salsify is cooked, drain thoroughly in a colander, then transfer it to the saucepan containing the onion and cream. Re-heat to boiling point, add the snipped parsley, taste, and season with salt and freshly ground black pepper if necessary. Pour the contents of the pan into a heatproof serving dish. In a small bowl, combine the cheese and breadcrumbs; sprinkle this over the surface. Bake near the top of the oven for about 10 minutes, or until golden brown and bubbling. Serve hot.

POTATO GRATIN
(Gratin Savoyard)

 This is a classic potato gratin which can easily be prepared in advance. With its delicious blend of garlic and nutmeg and its moist creamy texture, this dish re-heats very well in a slow oven.

Serves 4

•

1½ lb (750 g) medium-sized potatoes	*4 tablespoons milk*
Salt	*Freshly ground white pepper*
½ clove of garlic	*Freshly grated nutmeg*
1 pint (600 ml) double cream	

Preparation and cooking

Slice the potatoes to a thickness of about $\frac{1}{10}$ in (2 mm), using a mandoline or a sharp knife. Put the slices on a flat surface and sprinkle them with salt. Mix them so that all their surfaces are covered with the salt, then pile into a mound, and leave them for 10 minutes.

Dip the $\frac{1}{2}$ clove of garlic in salt, to draw out the juices. Pre-heat the oven to gas mark $\frac{1}{2}$, 250°F (120°C). Prepare a gratin dish by rubbing the inside with the garlic.

Heat the cream and the milk together in a saucepan large enough to hold all the slices of potato. Add white pepper and nutmeg to taste. Bring to the boil and boil for several minutes over a high heat.

Shake the salt, and any additional water which the salt will have drawn out, off the potato slices.

Add the potatoes to the cream mixture, bring back to the boil, then immediately remove from the heat. Using a draining spoon, carefully lift out the potato slices. Arrange them in even layers in the gratin dish, and pour the cream mixture over. Bake for about 45 minutes, until the potatoes are tender and the cream has formed a golden-brown crust.

COURGETTE GRATIN

(Gratin de courgettes)

 This dish is easily made in advance and then re-heated in the oven and browned at the last minute under the grill. It is a very nice vegetable to serve at a dinner party or on its own as a light vegetarian dish.

Serves 6 to 8

•

9 oz (250 g) tomatoes	*1¼ lb (500 g) courgettes*
1½ oz (40 g) butter	*Salt and freshly ground black pepper*
1 onion, or 2 shallots, finely chopped	*4 fl oz (120 ml) double cream*
½ clove garlic, crushed	*2 tablespoons finely grated Gruyère*
A small bouquet garni (page 22)	

Preparation and cooking

THE TOMATOES: Peel the tomatoes by plunging them into boiling water for 10 seconds, then immediately transfer to very cold water. Remove the skins, cut each tomato in quarters and remove the pips. Melt half the butter in a pan and add the finely chopped onions or shallots. Cover and cook gently until lightly coloured, then add the crushed garlic, the quartered tomatoes and the bouquet garni. Cover again, and leave to cook over a low heat for 10 to 15 minutes.

THE COURGETTES: Meanwhile, wash the courgettes, then cut into slices ⅛ in (3 mm) thick. Heat the remaining butter in a frying-pan and fry the courgettes for a few minutes over a fairly high heat; season with salt and freshly ground black pepper. Tip the courgettes into a colander and leave to drain.

Boil the cream in a small saucepan until reduced by half. Now add the drained courgettes, then taste and season with salt and freshly ground black pepper if necessary.

To serve

Spread half the courgettes in the base of a gratin dish. Remove the bouquet garni from the tomatoes and pour the contents of the pan over the courgettes to form a layer. Cover with the remaining courgettes and sprinkle with the grated Gruyère. Place under the grill until brown and serve immediately.

GRATIN OF CHICORY

(Endive au gratin)

 Chicory is in common use as a salad vegetable, but, surprisingly, it is not often cooked. There is some confusion over just what is meant by the names 'endive' and 'chicory'. What the English call chicory, the French call an *endive*, and when the French refer to *chicorée* they mean what the English call endive. In fact it gets even more complicated – perhaps we'd better stop here!

Serves 4
•

4 heads of chicory, about 1¼ lb (500 g)	For the sauce:
	2 teaspoons butter
Juice of ½ lemon	2 teaspoons flour
A little butter	3 fl oz (85 ml) milk
A pinch of sugar	4 fl oz (120 ml) double cream
Salt and freshly ground black pepper	4 oz (100 g) Swiss cheese (e.g. Emmenthal or Gruyère), grated

Preparation and cooking

THE CHICORY: Trim off any withered outer leaves and, using a sharp knife, make a cross in each base to ensure even cooking. Wipe the chicory heads with a damp cloth, then put them in a saucepan with the lemon juice, a small nut of butter, a pinch of sugar, and some salt and black pepper. Add just enough water to half-cover the heads. Bring the contents of the pan to the boil. Place a piece of buttered greaseproof paper on top of the chicory, cover with a lid, and simmer gently for about 20 minutes. Test the chicory with the point of a sharp knife; it is cooked if the knife goes in easily, meeting a very slight resistance. (The chicory can be prepared to this stage in advance, and kept in the poaching liquid, in a covered container in the refrigerator, until just before the meal). Re-heat the chicory if necessary, drain thoroughly, and cut each head in half lengthways. Arrange, cut side down, in a buttered fireproof dish; keep hot while you make the sauce.

THE SAUCE: In a small saucepan, melt the butter and stir in the flour. Cook for 2 minutes before gradually adding the milk and the cream. Bring to the boil, stirring. Simmer for a further 5 minutes, then pull the pan off the heat. Stir in the grated cheese, return the pan to the heat and cook very gently until the sauce is smooth. Taste, and season.

THE GRATIN: Pour the sauce over the chicory and grill briefly. Serve hot.

POTATO CAKE WITH COURGETTES

(Pommes darphin avec courgettes)

 This can be made as 1 large potato cake (as in the recipe below), or 4 small ones. To make the small potato cakes you will need 4 buttered poaching rings, to enclose portions of the mixture in the frying-pan. Prepare the potatoes and the courgettes as described below, and sandwich a little of the shredded courgette between layers of potato in each ring. The cooking time is the same. A bonus in using the rings is that they are easier to turn half-way through cooking: just flip them over with the aid of a spatula.

Serves 4
•

4 large potatoes, about 2 to 2¼ lb (1 kg), peeled	*Salt and freshly ground black pepper*
2 small courgettes, about 7 oz (200 g), washed and topped and tailed	*About 4 oz (100 g) clarified butter (see page 16)*

Preparation

Using a mandoline, or the coarsest side of a box grater, shred or grate the potatoes into a bowl. Grate the courgettes in the same way, into a separate, smaller bowl. Season both with salt and freshly ground black pepper.

To cook

In a 10 in (25 cm) frying-pan, preferably non-stick, heat half the butter. Put half the potato into the pan, pushing it out to a firm, flat pancake. Sprinkle the grated courgettes over the surface, then top with the remaining potato, again pressing the mixture out evenly. Cook over a low to moderate heat, giving the potatoes time to both cook and brown. After about 15 minutes, use a spatula to lift the edge to check that the underside is golden-brown. If it is still pale, cook for a couple of minutes more, then check again. When it is well browned, invert the potato cake on to a plate. Heat the remaining butter in the pan, then slide the potato cake back into the pan to cook on the other side. After a further 20 minutes, check the degree of browning again, and make sure the potato is cooked. When the potato cake is done, turn it out on to a warmed plate. Serve piping hot, cut into generous wedges.

FILLED POTATO CASES

(Pommes de terre farcies)

An unusual but simple way of presenting vegetables. Once you have mastered the preparation and cooking of the potato cases you can experiment with your own combinations of vegetables to make different and attractive fillings. And seasonal herbs can be added to the fillings – but use them with discretion. These little potato cases look very impressive surrounding a joint of roast meat.

Makes 12

•

6 very large potatoes, each weighing about 1 lb (450 g), peeled	*2 medium leeks*
	2 medium carrots, topped and tailed and peeled
1 lb (450 g) butter	*Freshly ground white pepper*
Salt	

Preparation and cooking

THE POTATOES: Trim each potato to a rectangle and cut it in half horizontally. Use a large fluted cutter about 2 in (5 cm) in diameter to trim the potato pieces to rounds (see fig. 1). Now use a melon baller, or a teaspoon, to scoop out the centre, being careful to leave a minimum thickness of $\frac{1}{4}$ in (5 mm) in the bases and sides of each potato case. Reserve the cases in cold water.

Put 11 oz (300 g) butter in a large pan, or divide it between 2 smaller pans. Put in the potato cases and add sufficient water just to cover, plus 1 teaspoon of salt for each pan. Bring to the boil, and continue boiling until the water has evaporated and only the butter remains. From this stage on, watch the cooking carefully, turning the potato cases as soon as they have browned. Make sure both sides are evenly coloured and the potatoes cooked before removing to a plate.

When they have been prepared to this stage the potatoes can be kept warm in the oven (at gas mark 2, 300°F, 150°C) for up to 20 minutes. Or you can keep them in a cool place (but not the refrigerator), for up to 12 hours, and re-heat at the same temperature.

THE FILLING: Trim the leeks, retaining just a little of the green tops. Cut in half lengthways, then across into $1\frac{1}{2}$ in (4 cm) lengths and finally lengthways into matchstick strips. Rinse thoroughly in cold water and drain well.

Slice the carrots thinly lengthways, then across, to produce very small matchstick strips about 1 in (2.5 cm) long.

In each of 2 separate small saucepans, put 2 oz (50 g) butter, $3\frac{1}{2}$ fl oz (100 ml) water and $\frac{1}{2}$ teaspoon salt. Bring to the boil, and put the carrot strips in one pan, the leeks in the other. Boil until they are just tender, but still retain some bite; the leeks will take about 1 minute, the carrots 2 to 3 minutes. Drain both vegetables, mix, and season to taste.

To serve

Pile the vegetable strips into the potato cases and serve hot.

•

PREPARING POTATO CASES

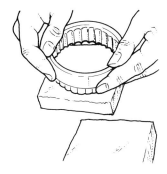

1 With a fluted cutter, trim potatoes to round shapes.

2 Scoop out the centres, leaving base and sides $\frac{1}{4}$ in (5 mm) thick.

COURGETTES STUFFED WITH RATATOUILLE

(Courgettes farcies à la ratatouille)

 If you fry the courgette, red and green pepper, aubergine and onion for the filling individually, each will retain its own colour, shape and taste.

Serves 12 (allowing 2 per person)

9 courgettes, each measuring about 6 × 1 in (15 × 2.5 cm)	*1 small onion, finely diced*
	1 oz (25 g) butter
2 red peppers	*Salt*
2 green peppers	*1 tomato, peeled, de-seeded, and finely diced*
1 small aubergine	*1 tablespoon Ricard*
About 3½ fl oz (100 ml) olive oil	*Freshly ground black pepper*
1 clove of garlic, peeled and left whole	

Preparation and cooking

Wash the courgettes, then trim each end. Use a zester to cut grooves the length of each courgette, then cut the courgettes into 2 in (5 cm) lengths; you should get 24 identical pieces. Now use a melon baller to hollow out each courgette piece down to about half-way. Keep the courgette shells on one side; dice the pieces removed from the courgettes and reserve separately.

Cook the peppers under a hot grill, turning them occasionally, until their skins are black. Remove them from the heat, cover them with a damp cloth and leave them to cool. Peel and de-seed them and dice them finely, keeping the colours separate. Chop off and discard the base and stalk from the aubergine; dice the flesh finely.

In a small frying-pan, heat 1 to 2 tablespoons of the oil with a clove of garlic. When the oil is hot, discard the garlic, then add the diced courgette flesh. Fry the courgette gently until it is tender, but do not allow it to colour. When it is cooked tip the contents of the pan into a large sieve; leave to drain. Wipe the pan clean with absorbent paper, and return it to the heat. Add a further 1 to 2 tablespoons of oil to the pan and, in exactly the same manner, fry the red pepper, then the green, then the aubergine, then the onion. As each is cooked, tip into the sieve to drain.

To cook the hollowed-out courgette pieces, stand them upright in a large, shallow pan and pour in 7 fl oz (200 ml) water. Add the butter and ½ teaspoon salt, bring to the boil, and cover with a lid. Continue cooking over a fairly high heat for 2 minutes. Be careful not to over-cook: use the point of a sharp knife to test if the courgette pieces are fairly tender. Remove them carefully from the pan and pour off most of the water, leaving just enough to cover the base of the pan. Return the courgette cases to the pan, with their hollowed sides uppermost.

Tip the vegetables for the filling into a bowl, add the diced tomato and the Ricard, taste, and season with salt and freshly ground black pepper.

Fill the courgette cases with the vegetable mixture, bring back to simmering point, cover the pan again, and cook for a further 2 minutes. Carefully transfer them to a warmed serving dish. Serve hot.

•

STUFFED MUSHROOMS
(Champignons farcis)

 In this recipe cultivated mushroom caps are stuffed with chopped wild mushrooms; and they are absolutely delicious. However, if it is difficult to find wild mushrooms in your area, don't despair, just use cultivated mushrooms instead. Wild mushrooms give out more liquid during cooking and therefore shrink more, so if you substitute cultivated mushrooms you won't need so many.

Serves 12 (allowing 2 per person)

•

24 cultivated mushrooms with caps about 1 to $1\frac{1}{2}$ in (2.5 to 4 cm) in diameter	*7 fl oz (200 ml) Madeira*
	4 oz (100 g) butter
7 fl oz (200 ml) dry white wine	*4 oz (100 g) onions or shallots, finely chopped*
Juice of 1 lemon	*5 fl oz (150 ml) double cream*
12 oz (350 g) wild mushrooms (e.g. girolles or ceps)	*Salt and freshly ground black pepper*

Preparation and cooking

THE MUSHROOM CAPS: Wipe the mushroom caps and remove the stems. Being careful not to break the caps, scoop out the brown gills and reserve with the stalks for inclusion in the stuffing. Pour the wine and juice of $\frac{1}{2}$ the lemon into a large, shallow pan. Put the mushroom caps, in a single layer, in the liquid in the pan – it will help keep them white while you prepare the stuffing.

THE STUFFING: Quickly rinse the wild mushrooms under cold running water. Trim off the earth attached to the bases of the stalks, and any blemished bits from the caps. Dry with absorbent paper.

Finely chop the wild mushrooms, and the mushroom trimmings. Pour the Madeira into a small saucepan and boil quite briskly to reduce to 2 fl oz (50 ml).

Melt the butter in a frying-pan, add the onions or shallots, and fry them gently for 1 or 2 minutes, until they are softened but not coloured. Add the finely chopped mushrooms and the remaining lemon juice. Cook briskly until all the liquid has evaporated. Add the reduced Madeira and the double cream, and cook for a further 3 minutes or so, until there is no free liquid and the mixture will hold its shape. Taste, and season with salt and freshly ground black pepper.

THE STUFFED MUSHROOMS: You can use a teaspoon or a piping bag (with or without a large plain nozzle) to fill the mushroom caps with the mixture. Bring the liquid in the pan to simmering point, then cover and cook for 5 minutes. Drain well and serve hot.

STUFFED TOMATOES WITH BUTTER SAUCE

(Tomates farcies au basilic)

 These tomatoes are a wonderful celebration of summer flavours. They make a vegetable dish that is a delightful starter or accompaniment, but is substantial enough to be served as a meal in its own right.

Serves 4 as a main meal, 6 as a starter or 12 as an accompaniment

•

12 medium tomatoes	3 oz (75 g) button mushrooms, trimmed, wiped, and finely chopped
1 large well-ripened tomato	
Salt	3 to 4 fl oz (85 to 120 ml) single cream
2 tablespoons olive oil	2 oz (50 g) soft, fresh goat's cheese
1 small onion, finely chopped	1 tablespoon snipped fresh basil leaves
1 small green pepper, de-seeded and finely diced	Freshly ground black pepper
1 small red pepper, de-seeded and finely diced	4 oz (100 g) butter
1 courgette, topped and tailed and finely diced	12 additional small basil leaves, to garnish

Preparation

Pre-heat the oven to gas mark 7, 425°F (220°C). Butter a baking dish that will hold the 12 medium tomatoes comfortably.

THE TOMATOES: To loosen the skin of the tomatoes, plunge them into boiling water for 10 seconds, then transfer them to very cold water. Depending on their ripeness they may need a little more time in the boiling water, but do not leave them there for too long or they will start to cook and become mushy. Peel all the tomatoes. De-seed the large tomato and cut it in very small dice; put on one side. With each of the 12 remaining tomatoes, slice the top off to form a little 'hat', and reserve. Carefully scoop the seeds from them, salt lightly and leave upside down on absorbent paper to drain.

THE FILLING: Heat the oil in a frying-pan and stir in the finely chopped onion. Cook gently without browning for 2 minutes, then add the diced peppers and courgette and the chopped mushrooms. Stir, cover, and cook for 5 minutes. Uncover and cook for a further 2 or 3 minutes until the vegetables are tender, but not soft; take off the heat and leave on one side for a few minutes.

In a small saucepan simmer the cream until it is reduced by half. Briefly mash the goat's cheese with a fork and add to the reduced cream with the tablespoon of snipped basil. Stir, and heat until smooth. Pour this on to the vegetable mixture, then stir in the reserved diced tomato. Mix, taste, and season with salt and freshly ground black pepper if necessary. Spoon 4 tablespoons of water into the buttered baking dish, then arrange the drained tomatoes in the dish. Fill them with the vegetable mixture, piling it up high. If you wish, prop the reserved lids on top.

To bake

Cover loosely with foil and bake in the oven for about 15 minutes until the tomatoes feel tender to the touch. Like the blanching time, the cooking time will depend on the ripeness of the tomatoes: the riper they are, the shorter the time they take to cook. Using a draining spoon, carefully transfer them to a warmed serving dish; keep warm.

To make the sauce

Meanwhile, transfer the juices from the baking dish to a small saucepan. Re-heat, reduce by half, and then beat in the butter, about a teaspoon at a time. Bring to boiling point, taste for seasoning, then spoon over the tomatoes. Garnish each tomato with a small basil leaf, and serve hot.

BRAISED GREEN CABBAGE

(Choux verts braisés)

 Any type of cabbage can be used in this recipe, but on the whole a cabbage of a firm, round, dark green variety is best.

Serves 4

•

1 green cabbage, about 1½ lb (750 g)	*1 clove of garlic, peeled and crushed*
7 oz (200 g) thick bacon slices, rind removed	*4 tablespoons dry white wine*
4 oz (100 g) clarified butter (see page 16)	*Salt and freshly ground black pepper*
7 oz (200 g) button onions, peeled and left whole	

Preparation

Pre-heat the oven to gas mark 6, 400°F (200°C).

Trim any coarse or damaged leaves from the cabbage, then cut it into quarters. Slice away the hard central stalk and finely shred the remaining cabbage. Rinse in cold water and drain thoroughly in a colander.

Cut the bacon into strips about ¼ × 1 in (5 mm × 1 cm). Put into a small saucepan of cold water and bring to the boil. Drain in a sieve and refresh under cold running water. Dry on absorbent paper.

To cook

In a fireproof casserole, heat the butter until a light haze forms. Add the blanched bacon strips and peeled onions and swirl in the hot fat until lightly browned. Stir in the garlic, then the drained, shredded cabbage, and cook for a minute or so, stirring. Spoon in the wine and season with a little salt and freshly ground black pepper. Cover with a lid and transfer to the oven to bake for about 30 minutes, until the onions and cabbage feel tender when tested with the point of a sharp knife. Serve hot.

BRAISED RED CABBAGE

(Émincé de choux rouges braisés)

 Red cabbage is a very accommodating vegetable when braised in this manner. It isn't easy to overcook it, and it re-heats very successfully. It makes an ideal partner to autumn and winter dishes such as rich roasts of game, or stews, and to pork, spicy sausage, and smoked meats.

Serves 4

•

1 small red cabbage, about 2 to 2¼lb (1 kg)	*2 tablespoons red wine vinegar*
4 oz (100 g) clarified butter (see page 16)	*4 tablespoons red wine*
½ medium onion, coarsely chopped	*Salt and freshly ground black pepper*
1 dessert apple (preferably a Cox's Orange Pippin), peeled, cored, and coarsely chopped	

Preparation

Pre-heat the oven to gas mark 4, 350°F (180°C).

Trim any withered or damaged leaves from the cabbage, then cut it into quarters and slice away the hard central stalk; shred the remaining cabbage very finely. Rinse in cold water and drain thoroughly in a colander.

To cook

In a fireproof casserole, heat the butter and stir in the sliced cabbage. Cook over a fairly high heat for 1 minute, stirring constantly, then add the onion and apple and continue to cook, stirring frequently, for a further 2 minutes. Add the red wine vinegar and the red wine and season with a little salt and freshly ground black pepper. Cover with a lid and transfer to the oven to bake for about 1½ hours, until quite soft. Stir once or twice during cooking and just before serving, taste for seasoning once more. Serve hot.

MARKET DAY SALAD

(La feuille de salade du marché)

 This is an ideal salad to serve as an hors-d'œuvre. Take care that the vegetables are blanched to just the right point: they should be tender but not soft; crisp, but not raw.

Serves 4
•

1 crisp lettuce with a firm heart	*2 tablespoons sherry vinegar*
¼ cauliflower head, cut into small florets	*Freshly ground black pepper*
4 oz (100 g) French beans,	*Pinch of sugar*
or 5 oz (150 g) shelled broad beans	*1 raw egg yolk*
Salt	*6 tablespoons olive oil*
2 tomatoes, peeled, de-seeded and quartered	*2 tablespoons snipped fresh chives*
2 oz (50 g) small button mushrooms, trimmed, wiped, and quartered	*4 spring onions, trimmed, washed and halved lengthways*
1 shallot, finely chopped	

Preparation

THE SALAD VEGETABLES: Remove any root and damaged, wilted leaves from the lettuce. Separate the leaves and rinse them briefly in very cold water. Drain them and gently shake them free of moisture, either in a salad basket or by gathering them up in a clean cloth and swinging the whole thing round (this manœuvre is best carried out in the garden!). Arrange the lettuce leaves on a dry tea-towel, roll it up loosely, and store at the bottom of the refrigerator.

Rinse the cauliflower florets and the French beans (if used) in cold water. Blanch the florets and the French or broad beans separately in boiling, salted water until they are just tender. Drain and refresh under cold running water; dry on absorbent paper. Cut French beans into 1 in (2.5 cm) lengths. Put these vegetables into a large bowl with the quartered tomatoes and button mushrooms and the finely chopped shallot.

THE DRESSING: In a separate small bowl, mix the vinegar with salt, the freshly ground black pepper and the sugar. Add the egg yolk and the oil, and whisk well with a fork to combine thoroughly. Alternatively, put all the ingredients in a food processor or blender and blend for a short time to combine.

To serve

When you are ready to serve, retrieve the lettuce from the refrigerator. Select 4 nice curved leaves, each one large enough to hold an individual serving of the salad, and put one on each serving plate. Tear half of the remaining lettuce leaves into pieces and add them to the vegetables in the bowl. (The rest of the lettuce should be sealed in a plastic bag and stored at the bottom of the refrigerator, ready to serve in the next day or two.) Lightly toss the vegetables in the dressing and serve them piled up on the individual lettuce leaves. Scatter each portion with some snipped chives. Finally, arrange a halved spring onion in the form of a cross on top of each salad, and serve.

•

JAPANESE SALAD
(Salade japonaise)

 Hearts of palm have an interesting texture, firm and delicious, that certainly adds something to this light little salad. Any hearts left over can be transferred, with the juice from the can, to a glass or plastic storage container. Covered, they will keep for about 10 days in the refrigerator.

Serves 4

•

14 oz (400 g) watercress	*1 teaspoon strong Dijon mustard*
2 heads of chicory	*2 oranges*
1 tablespoon white wine vinegar	*4 oz (100 g) tinned hearts of palm,*
Salt and freshly ground black pepper	*cut into matchstick strips*
4 tablespoons groundnut oil	*2 tablespoons chervil leaves or tiny sprigs of parsley*

Preparation

THE FRUIT AND VEGETABLES: Fill a bowl with very cold water. Plunge in the watercress and rinse very thoroughly, then transfer to a colander to drain. Dry on a tea-towel. Roll up loosely in a dry tea-towel and leave stored in the bottom of the refrigerator until ready to use.

Opposite: Japanese salad

Trim the base and discard the outer leaves of the chicory. Separate the rest of the leaves and rinse or wipe with a damp cloth. Put aside in a bowl.

With a very sharp knife, cut a slice from the top and bottom of the oranges, right down to the flesh. Sit the fruit on one cut end, or, if you prefer, hold it in your hand. Starting from the top and using a sawing movement, work your knife between the skin and the flesh of the oranges, cutting away all the white pith as well as the skin. Do this all around the oranges, then shave off any white pith that might have been missed.

Working with the fruit held over a bowl, cut each segment free of its membrane, folding back the layers of membrane like the leaves of a book, and letting the fruit drop into the bowl. Finally, squeeze the juice from the membranes into the bowl. You should be left with neat orange segments in a little juice.

THE DRESSING: In a separate small bowl, mix the vinegar and salt and freshly ground black pepper; add the oil and mustard and whisk well with a fork to combine thoroughly. Use a little of the dressing in which to separately toss the chicory and watercress.

To serve

Place some chicory leaves in the centre of each of 4 small plates or bowls and surround with a circle of watercress. Arrange the orange segments on the watercress and scatter the small strips of hearts of palm over everything. Sprinkle with the chervil leaves or sprigs of parsley, and serve.

•

SEGMENTING ORANGES

1 Cut slices from base and top. Then cut away pith and skin.

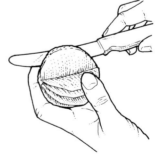

2 Cut segments free from membrane on each side.

Opposite: Leg of lamb with vegetables (see page 112)

MEAT

The way we buy meat for our restaurants is very different from the way most people buy it to eat at home. For the restaurants, we can buy the whole carcass. There are many advantages in this. First, we get the bones and trimmings, so we can make good stock; secondly, we get meat to feed our staff; and, thirdly, we get meat for our clients. Maybe we should put that in a different order: if we were talking to clients, we would put them first!

Whether you are buying meat for a restaurant or to eat at home, you should always buy the best-quality meat you can afford. By this we mean that you should buy meat from a good, reliable butcher, who buys and treats his meat properly: we do not mean that you should always buy prime cuts, such as fillet and sirloin. The cheaper second joints need different and slower cooking methods, but they can be turned into delicious meals. And do not overlook offal, which is nutritious, good value for money, and not used nearly as often as it should be. Usually, the only difficulty is that people simply do not know what to do with offal – no one has ever shown them. But some people are squeamish. When they hear the word liver, they think about their own liver. We do not know why: when they are eating ribs, they do not think about their own ribs. Any part of an animal is good to eat (though some, admittedly, are better than others).

One problem we all face when buying meat is that it is becoming more and more difficult to get meat which has been hung for long enough. The difficulty is mainly with beef. Veal, pork and lamb only need to be hung for four or five days, and any butcher who looks after his meat will hang it for that long. But beef can need as much as two to three weeks of hanging, and these days very few butchers are prepared to allow as long as that. So we have to do it ourselves.

Meat can be cooked to a whole range of points, from blue at one extreme, to well done at the other. In our opinion extremes are never very good (not only in food). We believe you should have beef from rare to medium, and lamb nicely pink. But in the restaurants, though we do not like to change the method of cooking, or the sauce or garnish, if people like their meat cooked to a certain point, we will cook it to that point. We may not approve, but we will respect their wishes!

FILLET OF BEEF WITH ANCHOVIES

(Tournedos de bœuf à l'anchoïade)

This very tender cut of meat *must* be sealed quickly, over a high heat, so fry the meat in two batches. If too many tournedos are crowded into the pan at once, the temperature quickly falls, and the meat is not sealed but starts cooking in its own juices, and toughens.

Serves 4
•

5 oz (150 g) butter	1½ oz (40 g) shallots, chopped
2 × 2 oz (50 g) tins anchovy fillets in oil	2 fl oz (50 ml) dry white wine
1 tablespoon goundnut oil	8 fl oz (250 ml) veal stock (see page 102)
Salt	Freshly ground black pepper
8 × 3½ oz (90 g) tournedos of beef, cut from the fillet	

Preparation and cooking

THE ANCHOVY BUTTER: Put 4 oz (100 g) butter in a food processor or blender. Drain and reserve the oil from the anchovies; also reserve 8 anchovy fillets, halved lengthways, for garnish. Process the remaining anchovies with the butter until smooth.

THE MEAT: In a large frying-pan, heat the groundnut oil and the rest of the butter over a very high heat. Lightly salt 4 of the tournedos and fry for about 1½ minutes, then turn them and continue cooking until they are done to your taste. (After a further 1½ minutes they will still be rare.) Fry the remaining meat, then transfer to a heatproof serving dish, and keep warm.

Pre-heat the grill.

THE SAUCE: Pour off all but 1 teaspoon of fat from the pan. Stir in the chopped shallots and cook over a low heat for 2 to 3 minutes. Turn up the heat and pour in the wine. Bring to the boil, briskly stirring and scraping the base and sides of the pan with a wooden spoon. Boil to reduce the wine by half; then add the veal stock and simmer gently for 5 minutes. Gradually stir in the anchovy butter, a little at a time, then taste, and season with salt and freshly ground black pepper if necessary. Strain the sauce through a sieve into a small saucepan; keep hot.

To serve

Quickly arrange the 2 halves of an anchovy fillet in a cross pattern on each tournedos, and brush with some of the reserved anchovy oil. Grill very briefly, just enough to warm through the garnish. Remove from the heat and quickly pour in sufficient sauce to cover the bottom of the dish. Serve the remainder in a warmed sauce boat, to accompany the tournedos.

·

SAUTÉ OF PORK WITH PAPRIKA AND PORT

(Sauté de porc au paprika et porto)

This is a rich and aromatic dish which can be served with grilled slices of fresh pineapple, and buttered spinach, or steamed potatoes.

Serves 4

·

$3\frac{1}{2}$ lb (1.5 kg) pork chump or shoulder (weighed on the bone)	1 teaspoon tomato purée
	A bouquet garni (see page 22)
5 oz (150 g) clarified butter (see page 16)	For the garnish:
1 medium carrot, peeled and cut into $\frac{1}{4}$ in (5 mm) slices	$1\frac{1}{2}$ oz (40 g) currants or sultanas
	9 oz (250 g) onions, very finely sliced
1 medium onion, peeled and cut into $\frac{1}{4}$ in (5 mm) slices	A pinch of sugar
2 cloves of garlic, crushed	1 tablespoon red wine vinegar
4 juniper berries, crushed	4 oz (100 g) salt belly of pork, trimmed and cut into strips $\frac{1}{4} \times 1$ in (5 mm × 2.5 cm)
2 tablespoons brown flour	
1 tablespoon mild paprika	2 oz (50 g) butter
$1\frac{3}{4}$ pints (1 litre) chicken stock (see page 18)	Salt and freshly ground black pepper
5 fl oz (150 ml) ruby port	

Preparation and cooking

Pre-heat the oven to gas mark 4, 350°F (180°C).

THE SAUTÉ: Have the butcher bone the meat, or do this yourself if you prefer. Trim and cut the meat into 1 in (2.5 cm) cubes. In a frying-pan, heat 2 oz (50 g) clarified butter until it is very hot. Add the meat to the pan, a small batch at a time, and fry over a high heat until it is evenly browned. Remove the meat to a colander and leave to drain. In a fireproof casserole, melt a further 1 oz (25 g) clarified butter and stir in the sliced carrot and onion. Cook over a gentle heat for 2 or 3 minutes. Stir in the crushed garlic and juniper berries and cook for a minute or two before sprinkling in the flour and the paprika. Stir and cook for a further minute before gradually adding the stock, the port and the tomato purée. Bring to the boil, stirring, then return the browned meat to the pan, and add the bouquet garni. Bring the contents of the pan to simmering point, cover with a lid, and transfer to the oven to bake for 1 to 1½ hours. Test for tenderness with the point of a sharp knife.

THE GARNISH: Bring a small saucepan of water to the boil. Add the currants or sultanas, boil for 1 minute, then drain and dry on absorbent paper; cover and keep on one side.

In the rinsed-out frying-pan, melt a further 1 oz (25 g) clarified butter and stir in the sliced onions and a good pinch of sugar. Cook gently until softened and golden. Add the red wine vinegar, and cook for 1 minute. Transfer the contents of the pan to a serving dish; keep warm.

Put the pork belly strips into a small saucepan of water, bring to the boil, and blanch for 1 minute. Drain and refresh under cold running water, then dry on absorbent paper. Heat the remaining clarified butter in the rinsed-out frying-pan and toss the pork strips in the hot fat until they are lightly coloured.

To serve

Use a draining spoon to remove the pork from the casserole and arrange it on top of the onions in the serving dish; keep warm. Quickly strain the contents of the casserole into a clean pan, pushing through just sufficient of the vegetables to give the sauce a good thick consistency.

Re-heat, whisk in the 2 oz (50 g) butter, taste, and season with salt and freshly ground black pepper. Add the currants or sultanas and pour the sauce over the pork and onions. Sprinkle with the pork belly strips and serve piping hot.

VEAL STOCK

(Fonds de veau)

 A well-made stock is a fundamental requirement of good cooking; and no stock that comes out of a packet or a tin can compare with the home-made product. Don't be put off by the amount of time it seems to take. If you are really in a hurry, use the recipe for Quick chicken stock (see page 18). But generally it takes very little effort to plan ahead to make a proper stock, like the one below. You can then refrigerate it or freeze it, ready for use as and when it is required. Stock will keep for about 10 days in the refrigerator or a month in the freezer.

It is particularly useful to have a supply of stock in the freezer, and it is worth giving a little thought to how you organise it. Consider the sort of amounts you are likely to use, and freeze the stock accordingly. We would recommend freezing stock in a range of quantities from ice-cube size, to provide a tablespoon to enrich a sauce, to $1\frac{3}{4}$ pints (1 litre) for a soup. If space in the freezer, or the refrigerator, is limited, you may prefer to reduce the stock to half its original quantity to obtain the syrupy sauce known as a demi-glace, or still further, to produce a concentrated meat glaze. Because reducing stock in this way considerably strengthens the flavour, correspondingly less of it is needed to bolster the flavour of sauces and stews.

Makes $1\frac{3}{4}$ pints (1 litre)

•

2 to $2\frac{1}{4}$ lb (1 kg) veal knuckle bones, coarsely chopped	*$\frac{1}{2}$ celery stalk, washed and thinly sliced*
1 calf's foot, split in half, or 2 pig's trotters, split in half	*1 clove of garlic, peeled and cut in half*
	7 fl oz (200 ml) dry white wine
4 oz (100 g) carrots, peeled and thinly sliced	*4 tomatoes*
4 oz (100 g) mushrooms, trimmed, wiped, and thinly sliced	*A bouquet garni (see page 22)*
	A sprig of tarragon
2 oz (50 g) onions, thinly sliced	

Preparation and cooking

Pre-heat the oven to gas mark 7, 425°F (220°C).

Arrange the veal bones and the calf's foot, or pig's trotters, in a single layer in a large fireproof roasting tin. Put the tin into the oven, near the top, and roast the bones for about 40 minutes, turning them occasionally so they brown lightly all over.

Transfer all the bones to a large saucepan. Add the carrots, mushrooms, onions, celery and garlic to the fat remaining in the roasting tin. Cook over a moderate heat for 3 or 4 minutes, stirring frequently, until the vegetables are softened, but not coloured. Pour in the white wine; cook, stirring briskly and scraping the base and sides of the pan with a wooden spoon, until most of the wine has evaporated. Add the vegetables to the veal bones and pour over enough cold water to cover – about $3\frac{1}{2}$ pints (2 litres). Bring the stock slowly to the boil, frequently skimming off the scum that rises to the surface. Adjust the heat to give a gentle simmer.

After 10 minutes add the tomatoes, bouquet garni and sprig of tarragon to the pan. Continue to simmer for a further 3 to 4 hours, skimming when necessary.

Strain the stock through a muslin-lined sieve into a bowl. If you do not intend to use it at once, cover it and leave it to cool before you refrigerate or freeze it.

•

SAUTÉ OF VEAL KIDNEYS WITH MUSTARD

(Rognons de veau sautés à la moutarde)

A quick supper dish that will be transformed into a gourmet feast if you serve the kidneys with some sautéed wild mushrooms and a saffron-flavoured pilaff.

Serves 4
•

2 veal kidneys, surrounding fat removed	3 fl oz (85 ml) veal stock (see page 102)
1 oz (25 g) clarified butter (see page 16)	1 tablespoon strong Dijon mustard
2 oz (50 g) butter	4 tablespoons double cream
4 oz (100 g) shallots or onions, finely chopped	1 tablespoon snipped fresh tarragon
3 fl oz (85 ml) dry white wine	Salt and freshly ground black pepper

Preparation and cooking

THE KIDNEYS: Slice the kidneys very thinly, removing the core where necessary.

In a frying-pan, heat the clarified butter until a light haze forms. Add the sliced kidneys to the pan and fry over a high heat for 1 minute. Immediately transfer them to a sieve and leave them to drain.

THE SAUCE: Pour off any fat left in the pan, wipe it clean with absorbent paper and melt the butter. Gently fry the finely chopped shallots or onions for 2 or 3 minutes. Then pour in the wine and boil briskly until reduced by half. Add the veal stock, mustard and cream, stir, then cook very gently for about 10 minutes, until the sauce is reduced to a syrupy consistency. Return the sliced kidneys to the hot sauce and cook for 1 minute to re-heat them. Finally, add the snipped tarragon, taste, season with salt and freshly ground black pepper, and serve on 4 deep serving plates.

•

ESCALOPES OF VEAL WITH WALNUTS AND ROQUEFORT

(Escalopes de veau aux noix et Roquefort)

This recipe calls for girolles (also known as chanterelles), mushrooms which grow in woods from spring to autumn, but they are difficult to get. Substitute tiny, cultivated button mushrooms if necessary.

Serves 4

•

$1\frac{1}{4}$ lb (500 g) girolles	1 bay leaf
4 oz (100 g) clarified butter (see page 16)	7 fl oz (200 ml) dry white wine
3 shallots, finely chopped	3 oz (75 g) Roquefort cheese
8 thin escalopes of veal, each weighing about $3\frac{1}{2}$ oz (90 g)	4 tablespoons double cream
	Freshly ground black pepper
Salt	9 oz (250 g) walnut halves
1 carrot, peeled and finely chopped	2 tablespoons snipped fresh flat-leaf parsley
1 sprig of fresh thyme	$\frac{1}{4}$ pint (150 ml) milk

Preparation and cooking

Pre-heat the oven to gas mark 3, 325°F (160°C).

THE GIROLLES: Rinse the girolles under cold running water if necessary. Trim away any discoloured areas and earth from the base of the stems. Dry on absorbent paper. In a frying-pan, heat 2 oz (50 g) clarified butter and fry the mushrooms over moderate heat for 3 or 4 minutes. Before the pan juices evaporate, add 1 finely chopped shallot; continue to cook until no free liquid remains.

Remove from the heat; keep hot.

THE VEAL: Lightly salt the veal escalopes. Put the remaining clarified butter in a frying-pan, set it over a high heat, and heat the butter until a light haze forms. Add the pieces of meat to the pan, and fry them for 30 seconds on each side. Remove to a plate and keep hot.

THE SAUCE: Turn down the heat under the pan and stir in the 2 remaining chopped shallots, the carrot, and the thyme and bay leaf. Cook for 2 or 3 minutes, then turn up the heat to moderate and pour in the wine. Mash the cheese with a fork and add to the pan with the cream. Cook the sauce until it is reduced to a syrupy consistency, then strain it into a clean pan. Re-heat, taste, season with salt and freshly ground black pepper if necessary, and leave to simmer.

Meanwhile put the walnuts in a small saucepan of boiling water; bring back to the boil, then drain and skin the nuts. Leave them to soak in the cold milk for 10 minutes.

To serve

Put 2 veal escalopes on each of 4 warmed plates, arrange the wild mushrooms around the veal; keep hot.

Drain the nuts and put them into the simmering sauce. Spoon this generously over the meat, scatter with the snipped parsley, and serve immediately.

VEAL CHOPS WITH BASIL, IN PAPER PARCELS

(Côtes de veau au basilic, en papillote)

This method of serving enclosed parcels of food is quite fun for a special occasion. The wrappings can be foil, greaseproof paper or baking parchment. Pierce a hole in the parcels when you take them from the oven, especially when using paper, and they will keep their puffed appearance. At the table, use a spoon and fork to open the parcels and serve the chops to your guests.

Serves 4
•

$3\frac{1}{2}oz$ (90 g) butter	Salt and freshly ground black pepper
2 oz (50 g) button mushrooms, trimmed, wiped, and finely chopped	4 trimmed veal chops, each weighing about 8 oz (225 g)
4 oz (100 g) onions, finely chopped	2 oz (50 g) clarified butter (see page 16)
4 tablespoons chicken mousse (page 23)	5 fl oz (150 ml) dry white wine
1 tablespoon double cream	10 fl oz (300 ml) veal stock (see page 102)
4 oz (100 g) unsmoked ham, finely chopped	2 tomatoes, peeled, seeded, and cut in thin strips
2 oz (50 g) snipped fresh basil	

Preparation and cooking

THE PARCELS: Cut 4 sections 12×18 in (30×46 cm) of foil, greaseproof paper or baking parchment. Fold each section in half to give 12×9 in (30×23 cm). Cut in a heart shape.

THE FILLING: In a frying-pan, melt $\frac{1}{2}$ oz (15 g) butter. Stir in the chopped mushrooms and cook over a moderate heat until the moisture has evaporated; transfer to a bowl.

In the same pan, melt a further 1 oz (25 g) butter and stir in the chopped onion. Cover and cook gently for 5 to 6 minutes, until the onion is softened but not coloured. Transfer to the bowl with the mushrooms. Mix in the chicken mousse, cream, chopped ham and two-thirds of the snipped basil. Season with a little salt and freshly ground black pepper.

THE CHOPS: Holding a filleting knife with the tip pointing towards the bone, cut a slit in the fat side of each chop. Fill the pockets with the stuffing mixture.

Heat the clarified butter in the frying-pan and fry the chops (probably 2 at a time is best) for 2 minutes on each side. Drain, reserving the pan juices. Lay each chop on one side of a cut-out foil or paper 'heart'. Fold over the other half and seal by turning the edges like a hem. (See illustration below.)

The chops can be wrapped in the parcels an hour before serving, and put in the oven to cook whilst the first course is eaten.

Pre-heat the oven to gas mark 6, 400°F (200°C). Put a baking tray to heat in the oven. Place the chops on the tray and bake for 15 minutes.

THE SAUCE: Meanwhile, heat the remaining buttery pan juices and pour in the wine. Boil briskly, stirring, until reduced by two-thirds. Pour in the veal stock and continue cooking for 5 minutes. Strain the sauce, return it to the heat, then add the remaining snipped basil and the tomato strips. Finally, stir in the rest of the butter, bit by bit. Taste and season with salt and freshly ground black pepper.

To serve

Take the parcels to the table on a large, heated dish, and serve the sauce separately in a warmed sauce boat.

•

WRAPPING VEAL CHOPS

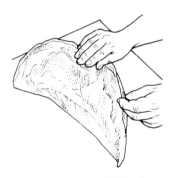

Wrap in foil or paper and fold edges together
firmly.

CALF'S LIVER WITH SWEETCORN

(Foie de veau aux grains de maïs)

Although tinned sweetcorn is used in this recipe, when fresh sweetcorn is available you might prefer to use that. Cook the cobs in boiling, salted water for about 8 minutes, then refresh in cold water. Drain well and slice off the kernels. One cob will give just under 4 oz (100 g) corn kernels. Buttered fresh noodles (see page 25) will complement this dish.

Serves 4

•

6 oz (175 g) clarified butter (see page 16)	10 fl oz (300 ml) veal stock (see page 102)
Salt	5 oz (150 g) tinned sweetcorn, rinsed and drained
4 thin slices calf's liver, each weighing about 5 oz (150 g)	4 tomatoes, peeled, seeded, and diced
	Freshly ground black pepper
4 shallots, finely chopped	4 tablespoons snipped fresh chives
10 fl oz (300 ml) sweet white wine (preferably Sauternes)	

To cook

THE LIVER: Set a large frying-pan over a high heat for about 45 seconds, then add 4 oz (100 g) clarified butter, swirling it around the pan. Lightly salt the liver slices, and fry them very briefly on both sides, so they are lightly browned, but still rosy inside (do not be afraid to err on the side of under-cooking, as the liver will continue to cook while you make the sauce). Drain and remove to a serving dish; keep warm (not hot!).

THE SAUCE: Pour off all but about 1 teaspoon of buttery juices from the pan. Add the chopped shallots to the remaining juices. Fry gently for 2 minutes, then cover and cook for a further 2 minutes. Uncover and pour in the white wine; boil briskly until the wine is reduced by half. Add the veal stock and continue to boil until the liquid is reduced to a slightly syrupy consistency. Stir in the sweetcorn and diced tomatoes, followed by the remaining butter. Taste, and season with salt and freshly ground black pepper if necessary. Quickly pour the sauce over the liver, scatter with the snipped chives, and serve.

LAMB CUTLETS WITH BASIL

(Côtes d'agneau au basilic)

 A delightfully quick and easy supper dish. Serve these cutlets with a pea purée and fresh buttered noodles or creamed spinach and steamed new potatoes tossed in parsley butter.

Serves 4

•

9 oz (250 g) tomatoes	7 oz (200 g) boiled ham, diced
2½ oz (65 g) butter	1 oz (25 g) clarified butter (see page 16)
1 small onion or shallot, finely chopped	
9 oz (250 g) button mushrooms, trimmed, wiped, and finely chopped	8 lamb cutlets, trimmed of fat
	3 fl oz (85 ml) dry white wine
4 tablespoons double cream	3 fl oz (85 ml) lamb or chicken stock (see page 18)
Salt and freshly ground black pepper	½ oz (15 g) snipped fresh basil

Preparation and cooking

Peel the tomatoes (see page 91), cut them in half, scoop out the seeds with the back of a spoon handle, then slice each half into 3 wedges. Trim each wedge into a lozenge or diamond shape.

In a frying-pan, melt 1 oz (25 g) of the butter and add the finely chopped onion or shallot. Cook gently for 2 or 3 minutes, then stir in the finely chopped mushrooms. Cook over a moderate heat until all the liquid from the mushrooms has evaporated. Stir in the double cream and season with salt and freshly ground black pepper to taste. Add the diced ham, then remove from the heat; keep warm.

In a separate frying-pan, heat the clarified butter until a light haze forms. Lightly salt the cutlets and fry them over a high heat for 2 minutes on each side, or more if you prefer them less pink. Transfer the cutlets to a plate, and keep them warm.

Pour off the excess fat and return the pan to the heat. Add the white wine and boil, stirring briskly and scraping the base and sides of the pan with a wooden spoon, until the wine is reduced by half. Stir in the lamb or chicken stock and continue to boil until the sauce is reduced to a syrupy consistency. Strain into a clean pan.

To serve

Put a quarter of the mushroom mixture in the centre of each of 4 warmed plates, arrange 2 cutlets on either side and keep warm while you finish the sauce.

Bring the sauce to the boil and throw in the tomatoes and the snipped basil. Gently whisk in the remaining butter, taste, and season with salt and freshly ground black pepper. Pour the sauce over the cutlets and serve immediately.

•

LEG OF LAMB VENISON-STYLE

(Gigot d'agneau en chevreuil)

 Venison is often marinated in red wine with vegetables and herbs to flavour. Here lamb is given the same treatment. Serve with a Potato gratin (see page 82), or some little stuffed vegetables (see pages 88, 89, 91).

Serves 6

•

A 7 lb (3 kg) leg of lamb	6 black peppercorns, crushed
2 necks of lamb, coarsely chopped, or 17 fl oz (485 ml) lamb stock (see Quick chicken stock, page 18), skimmed and cooled	1½ pints (850 ml) red wine (e.g. Gamay or Pinot Noir)
	2 tablespoons olive oil
1 onion, coarsely chopped	A bouquet garni (see page 22)
2 carrots, peeled and coarsely chopped	About 5 oz (150 g) clarified butter (see page 16)
1½ oz (40 g) mushrooms, trimmed, wiped, and coarsely chopped	1 to 2 tablespoons redcurrant jelly
	1 oz (25 g) butter
1 clove of garlic, peeled and sliced	Salt and freshly ground black pepper
6 juniper berries	

Preparation

Using a boning knife, remove the thigh bone only from the leg of lamb, then trim away the fat and sinew. Where the bone has been removed tie the joint around with string in 3 or 4 places. Reserve the bone and the meat trimmings and put them and the lamb into a large, deep bowl with the 2 chopped necks of lamb (if not using the lamb stock). Cover the meat with the coarsely chopped onion, carrots and mushrooms, the sliced garlic, the juniper berries and the crushed peppercorns. Pour in $1\frac{1}{4}$ pints (750 ml) red wine and the olive oil and push the bouquet garni in amongst the meat and trimmings. Cover tightly with greaseproof paper and refrigerate for 12 hours, turning the meat every 4 hours.

To cook

Pre-heat the oven to gas mark 8, 450°F (230°C). Remove the leg of lamb, the chopped necks of lamb (if used), the bone and the meat trimmings from the marinade; reserve the marinade. Put the clarified butter in a fireproof roasting tin and heat until a light haze forms. Over a high heat, brown the leg of lamb and all the chopped meat and trimmings. Remove the bone and all the meat trimmings and replace in the marinade. Transfer the leg of lamb to the oven to roast for 35 minutes; baste every 10 minutes with the juices in the roasting tin, and turn the joint over after 20 minutes.

Meanwhile, pour the rest of the marinade and meat trimmings into a saucepan, bring to the boil, and skim; simmer gently, uncovered, for 30 minutes. If using lamb stock, add this to the marinade. Pull the pan off the heat and reserve.

After 35 minutes, remove the leg of lamb from the oven and the roasting tin, wrap it in foil and leave it in a warm place for 20 minutes.

Set the roasting tin over a high heat and pour in the remaining red wine. Bring to the boil, stirring briskly and scraping the base and sides of the tin with a wooden spoon, then pour the contents of the tin into the saucepan containing the marinade and meat trimmings. Heat, stir in the redcurrant jelly, then strain the sauce into a clean pan. Boil until reduced to a syrupy consistency. Finally, whisk in the butter, taste, and season.

To serve

Carve the joint at the table, and serve the sauce separately in a sauce boat.

LEG OF LAMB WITH VEGETABLES

(Gigot d'agneau aux primeurs)

A very light, fresh alternative to the conventional stew. Timing is all-important for this dish: it is at its best, with the meat pink and each of the vegetables slightly crunchy.

Serves 8

•

Leg of lamb, weighing about 6 lb (2.75 kg)	*¼ teaspoon sugar*
1½ lb (750 g) carrots, trimmed and peeled	*1½ lb (750 g) turnips, trimmed and peeled*
4 oz (100 g) onions, diced	*1 lb (450 g) broccoli*
1 celery stalk, diced	*Juice of ½ lemon*
10 fl oz (300 ml) dry white wine	*6 Jerusalem artichokes*
A bouquet garni (see page 22)	*(preferably of a regular shape)*
A pinch of powdered saffron,	*2 tablespoons white wine vinegar*
or a few saffron strands	*2 oz (50 g) clarified butter (see page 16)*
1½ oz (40 g) butter	*Freshly ground black pepper*
Salt	*Parsley sprigs, to garnish*

Preparation and cooking

THE STOCK: If possible, prepare the stock the day before. Pre-heat the oven to gas mark 7, 425°F (220°C). Bone the leg of lamb (or have the butcher do this for you). Reserve the bones. Trim off the excess fat and sinews and cut the meat into 1¼ in (3 cm) cubes; refrigerate until ready to cook. Put all the bones and meat trimmings in a roasting tin and roast in the top of the oven for 25 minutes.

Meanwhile, dice 2 of the prepared carrots.

Remove the roasting tin from the oven and set it over a moderate heat. Add the diced carrots, onions and celery. Fry for about 5 minutes, until the vegetables are lightly browned. Using a draining spoon, transfer the bones, meat trimmings, and vegetables to a large saucepan. Pour the excess fat from the tin, re-heat, and add 5 fl oz (150 ml) of the white wine. Bring to the boil, stirring briskly and scraping the tin with a wooden spoon. As soon as the wine boils, pour it into the saucepan. The pour in sufficient water to cover the bones and the vegetables – about 2 pints (1.2 litres). Add the bouquet garni to the pan and set it over a low heat to simmer for 1 hour, skimming if necessary. Strain the contents of the pan through a sieve, then return the liquid to the rinsed-out pan. Boil to reduce to a well-flavoured stock – you will probably have about 15 fl oz (450 ml). Add the saffron, and stir. If leaving overnight, cool, then chill. The following day, skim the fat from the surface.

THE VEGETABLES:

Cut the remaining carrots in strips about $\frac{1}{4} \times 1\frac{3}{4}$ in (5 mm × 4.5 cm). Put them into a saucepan and pour in just enough boiling water to cover them. Add $\frac{1}{2}$ oz (15 g) of the butter, and $\frac{1}{4}$ teaspoon each of salt and sugar. Cook over a high heat for about 6 minutes, until the carrots are barely tender. Reserve.

Prepare the turnips in the same way as the carrots, but without the sugar. Cook for about 4 minutes; reserve.

Divide the broccoli into individual florets, rinse in cold water, drain and put in a saucepan. Pour in sufficient boiling water to cover; cook for about 4 minutes. Drain in a colander and rinse with cold water. Turn out on to a cloth and cover until ready to use.

Fill a bowl with cold water and add the lemon juice. Peel the artichokes, dropping each one into the acidulated water as soon as you have peeled it. When you have peeled them all, drain them and transfer them to a saucepan. Pour in sufficient boiling water to cover, and add the wine vinegar and some salt. Boil gently, covered, for 5 to 7 minutes, until the artichokes are just tender. Drain and dry on absorbent paper and cut into strips roughly the same size as the carrot and turnip strips.

THE MEAT:

Set a large pan over a high heat and add 2 oz (50 g) clarified butter. Fry the lamb cubes, a small batch at a time, until they are evenly browned, but still very pink inside; remove to a plate.

To finish

When all the meat has been fried, pour the fat from the pan. Return the pan to the heat, add the remaining wine, and bring it to the boil, stirring quickly and scraping the sides and base of the pan with a wooden spoon. Add the lamb stock and the rest of the butter, taste, and season with salt and freshly ground black pepper. Bring back to the boil, then gently stir in all the vegetables and meat. Continue to heat only long enough to bring the contents of the pan up to serving temperature; pour quickly into a large, warmed serving dish, garnish with parsley sprigs and serve immediately.

POULTRY AND GAME

Practically everyone likes poultry, especially, of course, chicken. If you do not know your guests very well, a chicken dish is generally a safe choice. All we would suggest is that if you are not entirely about the provenance and quality of your chicken, you should not serve it as a plain roast, because it may lack flavour.

Try to find a butcher who can supply a good-quality chicken; or select from the fresh – not frozen – poultry range at one of the major supermarkets. We used to find that British free-range chickens were not much better than French battery chickens, and ducks were so fatty that they were only acceptable cooked for 2 hours longer than we would have expected, and then served with an apple sauce. But the quality and range of poultry available in Britain is improving all the time.

We have always been fortunate with game: British game is of excellent quality, and it is good value for money. But people do not eat enough of it, and so a lot is exported.

Game is most readily available during the winter, and it is an ideal choice for a winter meal: the fairly heavy meat, served with a delicious sauce, will make a warming and satisfying dish to keep out the cold.

A trademark of the Roux restaurants is the combination of fresh fruit with poultry and game, in dishes such as Duck breasts with blackcurrants (see page 125), Medallions of venison with cherries (see page 135), and Quail with grapes (see page 126). In recent years it has been regarded as rather eccentric to serve fruit with meat (except in some traditional dishes, such as lamb with redcurrant jelly or gammon with pineapple), but it is in fact a classic combination. The fruit provides a contrast to the meat, and brings out its flavour. When a rich meat, such as duck, is served with sharp-tasting fruit, such as blackcurrants, the sharpness of the fruit balances the richness of the meat, and cleanses the palate. Quail with grapes is a different sort of combination. Quail can be a bit bland: grapes complement the mild flavour, without overwhelming it – an example of the basic Roux philosophy.

CLASSIC CHICKEN STOCK

(Fonds de volaille)

 It is well worth including all the ingredients we specify, when you make this classic chicken stock. The vegetables and the bouquet garni will give extra flavour, and the veal bone, or tongue, will add flavour and gelatine.

Makes 1¾ pints (1 litre)

¾ oz (20 g) butter	4 oz (100 g) mushrooms, washed and finely sliced
4 oz (100 g) carrots, washed and finely sliced	2 to 2¼ lb (1 kg) chicken carcasses (necks, wings and feet), or 1 boiling fowl
1 leek (white part only), trimmed, washed, and finely sliced	1 veal knuckle bone or 1 calf's tongue
	1 onion, stuck with a clove
½ celery stalk, washed and finely sliced	A bouquet garni (see page 22)

To cook

Heat the butter in a saucepan and cook the vegetables until they are lightly coloured. Add the chicken carcasses and other pieces, or the boiling fowl, and the veal knuckle bone, or tongue. Pour over enough cold water to cover, and bring to the boil. Lower the heat and simmer gently, frequently skimming the surface. After 10 minutes, add the onion with the clove, and the bouquet garni.

Cook for a further 2 hours 20 minutes, then strain the stock through a muslin-lined sieve into a bowl. Set aside in a cool place. As with all stocks, do not refrigerate until absolutely cold.

To store

This stock will keep in the refrigerator for one week, or for several weeks in the freezer.

BONING, STUFFING AND TYING A POUSSIN

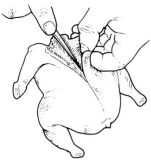

1 Turn chicken breast-side down. Cut along spine and separate flesh from rib cage down to breast bone, severing wing and leg joints.

2 Carefully free the top of the breast bone. Remove the thigh bones but leave the drumstick bones.

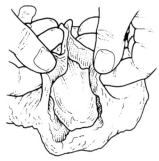

3 Place stuffing in the centre of the boned chicken, then bring up the flesh on each side to reconstruct shape.

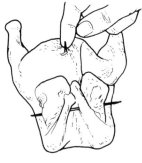

4 Use a cocktail stick to close its length and another one to close the neck end and hold the wings together.

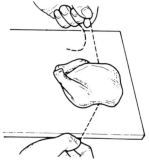

5 Turn the chicken breast-side up, and position the string underneath so it will hold the wings in place.

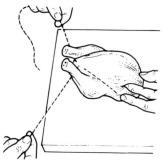

6 Bring the string up and over the drumsticks, then cross and loop under the ends of the drumstick bones. Tie on top.

CHICKEN COOKED IN CIDER

(Poulet au cidre)

 This recipe is an attractive, autumnal dish of golden-sauced chicken, which is perfectly complemented by the rich amber of sautéed apples.

Serves 4
•

$4\frac{1}{2}$ lb (2 kg) oven-ready chicken	8 oz (225 g) carrots, trimmed, peeled, and diced
Juice of $\frac{1}{2}$ lemon	5 oz (150 g) onion, diced
6 medium-sized crisp eating apples (e.g. Cox's Orange Pippins), washed	1 celery stalk, diced
	1 pint (600 ml) medium-sweet cider
4 oz (100 g) clarified butter (see page 16)	A bouquet garni (see page 22)
1 teaspoon sugar	10 fl oz (300 ml) double cream
Salt	Freshly ground white pepper

Preparation and cooking

TO PREPARE THE CHICKEN: Joint the chicken, and shape the joints, following the instructions given in the recipe for Baked chicken heart's delight including tying them with string (see page 122). Chop the chicken carcass. Refrigerate the 4 chicken joints, and the other carcass pieces.

THE GARNISH: Cut each apple into 6 wedges. Remove the core, peel, and round off the cut edges, so that each wedge becomes an oval. As you work, transfer the apple to a bowl containing the lemon juice, and toss. Reserve the apple peel and trimmings. Heat 2 oz (50 g) of the butter in a frying-pan. Add the apples and cook over a medium heat. Half-way through, sprinkle with sugar. Cook until brown but still crisp to the bite; keep them warm.

TO COOK THE CHICKEN: Pre-heat the oven to gas mark 7, 425°F (220°C). In a fireproof casserole, heat the rest of the butter. Lightly salt the chicken joints and fry over a moderate heat for about 6 minutes on each side, until just coloured. Using a draining spoon, transfer to a plate. Stir in the carcass pieces and brown them lightly before adding the vegetables, the reserved apple peel and trimmings. Cook for 5 minutes to colour slightly, then lay the chicken joints on top. Pour in the cider and tuck in the bouquet garni under the chicken. Bring to the boil, cover, and transfer to the oven to bake. After 8 to 10 minutes transfer the chicken breasts to a warmed serving dish; keep hot. Return the casserole to the oven for a further 10 minutes, then transfer the chicken legs to the serving dish; keep hot. Discard the pieces of carcass.

THE SAUCE: Process the remaining contents of the pan in a food processor (probably in 2 batches). Process for 2 minutes, then rub the resulting purée through a sieve. Return the purée to the rinsed-out casserole and reduce for about 10 minutes, stirring frequently. Stir in the cream and bring to the boil. Taste, and season.

To serve

Discard the string from the chicken joints and arrange the apple segments in rosettes around the dish. Pour over the sauce and serve immediately.

•

POUSSINS WITH CALVADOS AND APPLES

(Poussins Sarthoises)

This recipe blends traditional Norman ingredients – poussins, veal, mushrooms, apples, calvados, sweet cider and double cream to produce a delicious dish for a special occasion.

Serves 4

•

4 × 14 oz (400 g) oven-ready poussins	*1 egg*
4 oz (100 g) clarified butter (see page 16)	*1 pint (600 ml) double cream*
1 shallot or small onion, finely chopped	*Salt and freshly ground black pepper*
4 oz (100 g) cup mushrooms, trimmed, wiped, and finely chopped	*Juice of ½ lemon*
3 oz (75 g) veal fillet, cut in pieces	*4 small, crisp eating apples (e.g. Cox's Orange Pippins or Reinettes)*
3 oz (75 g) chicken breast, skin removed, cut in pieces	*4 fl oz (120 ml) calvados*
	15 fl oz (450 ml) sweet cider

Preparation and cooking

TO PREPARE THE POUSSINS: To bone the poussins, follow the step-by-step illustrations (see figs. 1 and 2, on page 116). (The bones removed from the poussins will make excellent stock for another recipe, so do not throw them away.) Cover and refrigerate the boned poussins while you prepare the stuffing and the apple garnish.

THE STUFFING: In a frying-pan, melt 1 oz (25 g) of the clarified butter. Add the finely chopped shallot or onion and mushrooms. Stir, cover, and cook over a low heat for 5 minutes. Then take the lid off the pan and turn up the heat for a minute, so that most of the juices evaporate. Transfer the mushrooms and shallot to a sieve set over a bowl and leave to drain and cool.

Pass the veal and chicken pieces through the fine blade of a mincer. Transfer to a bowl set in a larger bowl of crushed ice. Using a wooden spoon, beat in the egg. Now add 5 fl oz (150 ml) of the double cream, a little at a time, beating well after each addition. When all this cream has been added the mixture should readily hold its shape. Finally, fold in the cold, finely chopped mushrooms and shallot, taste, and season. Cover and leave in the refrigerator for about an hour.

THE GARNISH: Squeeze the lemon juice into a bowl. Wash the apples, then cut each one into 6 wedges. Remove the core, peel, and round off the cut edges, to turn each wedge into an oval shape; as you work, transfer the apple pieces to the bowl and toss them in the lemon juice. Reserve all the apple trimmings.

In a frying-pan, melt a further 1 oz (25 g) of the clarified butter. Add the apple pieces, cover, and cook very gently, without allowing them to colour. When they are almost tender but still retain some bite, remove them from the heat and keep warm.

TO STUFF THE POUSSINS: Lay the poussins, opened out, skin side down, on a wooden board or work surface. Lightly salt, then place an equal quantity of stuffing in the centre of each bird. Pull up the skin on both sides to reconstruct the original shape, and secure with cocktail sticks and string (see figs. 3 to 6, on page 116).

TO COOK THE POUSSINS: Pre-heat the oven to gas mark 7, 425°F (220°C). In a large fireproof casserole, heat the rest of the clarified butter. When a light haze forms, put in the poussins, 2 at a time, and cook until they are a light golden colour all over. Add the apple parings. Allow to heat through, then cover and bake the poussins in the oven for 15 to 20 minutes.

Remove the poussins from the casserole; to check that they are cooked, insert the point of a small knife, or a skewer, into the thickest part of the drumstick – the juices should run clear. Lift the poussins on to a warmed heatproof serving dish, making sure no apple parings go with them. Cover the birds loosely with foil and return them to the switched-off oven to keep warm while you prepare the sauce.

THE SAUCE: Re-heat the contents of the casserole on top of the stove. Heat the calvados in a large soup ladle or small saucepan. *Take great care with the next stage*; protect your hands with a cloth and stand well back as you ignite the calvados and pour it over the contents of the casserole, shaking the casserole as you do so. When the flames subside, pour in the cider and boil briskly until reduced by half. Now pour in the remaining cream and continue boiling for a further 5 minutes. Strain the sauce through a fine sieve into a clean pan, pressing the apple pieces to extract all the juices. Re-heat the sauce. It should lightly coat the back of a spoon. If it is still a little thin, boil until it reaches the required consistency. Taste, and season.

To serve

Remove the strings and cocktail sticks from the poussins and, using scissors, trim off the wing tips and ends of the leg bones, to neaten them. Arrange the apple segments around the edge of the dish. Put the poussins on the dish and pour some sauce around them. Serve immediately, accompanied by the rest of the sauce in a sauce boat.

•

BAKED CHICKEN HEART'S DELIGHT

(Poulet poêle mon cœur)

 This is a novel way to prepare chicken, the shape of the chicken joints being formed to suggest the 'heart' shape of the title. This is not nearly so difficult as it sounds! Serve with leaf spinach and a pilaff or plain steamed rice.

Serves 4

•

2 × 2¼ lb (1 kg) oven-ready chickens	9 oz (250 g) carrots, trimmed, peeled and diced
1¼ lb (500 g) cucumber	4 tablespoons mild paprika
Salt	12 fl oz (350 ml) dry vermouth
24 large white grapes, about 9 oz (250 g)	15 fl oz (450 ml) chicken stock (see page 18)
4 large slices white bread, about ½ in (1 cm) thick	
5 oz (150 g) clarified butter (see page 16)	10 fl oz (300 ml) double cream
6 oz (175 g) onion, diced	Freshly ground black pepper

Preparation and cooking

TO PREPARE THE CHICKENS: Pick up a chicken by one leg. This will enable you to see clearly where to cut through the skin between the leg and the body. Break open the leg joint at the junction with the body and cut through with a knife. Cut off the other legs of both chickens in the same manner. With the point of a knife, work the meat free from the thigh bones. Sever the thigh bones at the 'knee' joint, and discard them. Fold the boned flesh of the thighs down alongside the drumsticks, wrapping it round the lower leg bone; tie it in place with string, but not too tightly or the string will mark the meat, and detract from the finished appearance.

Next, remove the breast meat and wing as one piece, on both sides of each bird. Fold the breast over on top of the wing joint; tie with string. You should now have 8 joints (see figs. 1 to 3 overleaf).

Chop the remaining chicken carcasses (they are to be used to add flavour to the stock) and refrigerate with the prepared chicken joints.

THE GARNISH: Cut the tapering ends from the cucumber; peel the remainder. Cut in quarters lengthways, then across to give 6 equal-sized sections – 24 pieces in all. Using a small knife, trim each section into the shape of a large grape, keeping them all evenly shaped and of comparable size. Reserve all the cucumber trimmings and peel for the stock. Cook the cucumber shapes for 1 minute in boiling salted water, then drain and refresh with cold water. Dry on absorbent paper and reserve.

Peel, halve and de-seed the grapes. Reserve in a heatproof bowl.

Pre-heat the oven to gas mark 7, 425°F (220°C).

Using a sharp, pointed knife, cut each slice of bread into a heart shape, about the same size as the chicken joints. Heat 2 oz (50 g) of the clarified butter in a frying-pan and gently fry the croûtons until they are golden on both sides. Drain on absorbent paper and reserve.

TO COOK THE CHICKENS: Melt the remaining clarified butter in a large fireproof casserole set over a low heat. Lightly salt the chicken joints and place them in the pan. Cook very gently, so they do not colour, turning them after 5 minutes. Cook for a further 2 minutes, then add the diced onion and carrot and the reserved cucumber trimmings. Cook until heated through, then cover the casserole and put it in the oven. Cook for 10 minutes, then, using a draining spoon, transfer the breasts to a plate; cover the plate and keep the joints warm. Cook for a further 10 minutes, then remove the casserole from the oven. Transfer the leg joints to the plate; cover again and keep warm.

THE SAUCE: Set the casserole over a high heat, and add the chopped carcasses. Stir, and cook for 5 minutes. Sprinkle in the paprika, stirring, and cook for a further 2 minutes before pouring in the vermouth. Boil briskly to reduce by half. Pour in the chicken stock and continue boiling until the liquid is reduced by two-thirds. Strain the sauce through a sieve into a clean saucepan. Add the cream and reduce the liquid further, until it has a syrupy, coating consistency. Turn the heat down low, so the sauce is barely simmering. Taste, and season with salt and freshly ground black pepper, if necessary.

To serve

Remove the string from the chicken joints and put them in the sauce for 2 minutes. Then add the cucumber shapes for just long enough to heat through.

Put the grapes over a pan of simmering water to warm.

Arrange the chicken joints on a warmed large, shallow serving dish. Pour the sauce with the cucumber over and scatter with the warmed grapes. Finally, arrange the heart-shaped croûtons on the chicken breasts; serve immediately.

•

PREPARING CHICKEN JOINTS

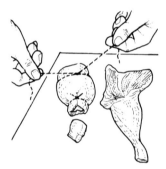
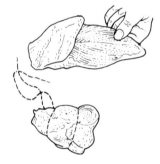

1 Remove legs and cut out thigh bones, severing 'knee' joints. Fold boned flesh down alongside drumsticks; secure with string.

2 Remove breast fillet and wing in one piece; bring tip of fillet up to cover wing bone. Secure with string.

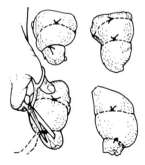

3 The joints should be heart-shaped: wing and breast joints (above), leg joints (below).

DUCK WITH HONEY AND CLOVES

(Canard au miel et aux clous de girofle)

 This recipe is best prepared over 2 days. If the duck is partially cooked and the stock made on the first day, then the recipe is quickly and easily finished on the second day. At The Waterside Inn this dish is served garnished with candied red pepper and 2 puff pastry containers in the shape of ducks, filled with celeriac purée. If you would like to try this presentation, you can prepare candied pepper as follows. Cut the skin, and a little flesh, from the red pepper. Shred into very thin hair-like strips. Blanch these briefly in boiling, salted water, refresh, and put into a small saucepan with sufficient water to well cover, and 1 oz (25 g) sugar. Simmer for about 10 minutes, until almost all the syrup has evaporated. Drain in a sieve, separating the strands, and leave to cool. Use Classic puff pastry (see page 164) to form pastry containers, and fill them with one of the vegetable purées given on pages 76–79.

Try to get hold of a duck that is not too fat, and use a honey with a flowery flavour for the glaze.

Serves 2
•

4 lb (1.75 kg) duck	*2 teaspoons lemon juice*
Salt	*3 tablespoons olive oil*
5 shallots, unpeeled	*Salt and freshly ground white pepper*
4 oz (100 g) honey	*14 cloves*
1 quantity chicken stock (see page 18)	*2 oz (50 g) butter*

Preparation and cooking

THE DUCK AND THE STOCK: Trim the duck, cutting off the neck, wings and wishbone (or ask the butcher to do this for you). Put these pieces in a roasting tin; cover and keep on one side. Pre-heat the oven to gas mark 7, 425°F (220°C). Wrap the duck in a clean cloth or tea-towel, tying it with string at the head and tail ends. Bring a large saucepan of salted water to the boil, lower in the duck and simmer for 10 minutes, then lift it out and leave it to cool before you unwrap it. Carve off the legs and cut them through at the 'knee' joint to give separate drumsticks and thighs. Put the thighs and what remains of the main body of the duck on a plate, cover it, and place it in the refrigerator. Chop the drumsticks into small pieces and put them into the roasting tin with the neck, wings and wishbone. Bake for about 30 minutes, until nicely browned.

Meanwhile, slice the unpeeled shallots finely. Put 3 oz (75 g) of the honey in a large saucepan and when it is runny add the sliced shallots. Mix well, and cook until the honey has browned and caramelised the shallots. Add the roasted bones, pour in chicken stock to cover, then leave the stock to simmer away very quietly for 4 hours. Pour the contents of the pan through a fine sieve into a clean pan and return to the heat. Boil until the stock has reduced to a sauce consistency so that it coats the back of a spoon.

The recipe can be prepared ahead to this stage.

The following day, remove the duck from the refrigerator and allow it to come up to room temperature. Pre-heat the oven to gas mark 7, 425°F (220°C).

THE GLAZE: Put the remaining honey, the lemon juice and the olive oil into a blender or food processor, season with salt and freshly ground white pepper, and blend for 30 seconds.

TO COMPLETE THE COOKING: Stud the duck breast on each side of the carcass with 7 evenly spaced cloves. Coat the breast and thighs with the honey glaze. Place the carcass and thighs in a roasting tin and bake in the hottest part of the oven for 10 to 12 minutes, until the meat is golden brown.

Remove the carcass and keep warm, breast side down. Leave the thighs in the oven for a further 6 minutes.

Bring the duck stock to the boil and whisk in the butter, a little at a time. Pour the sauce through a fine sieve into a clean pan. Taste, and season with salt and freshly ground white pepper.

To serve

Using a sharp carving knife, remove the duck breasts from the carcass. Carve each breast diagonally into 6 even slices. Leave the cloves in the meat but warn your guests not to eat them. Arrange these breast pieces and the thighs on a serving plate and pour the sauce round them. If you wish, garnish with candied red pepper and pastry cases filled with a vegetable purée, as suggested in the recipe introduction.

DUCK BREASTS WITH BLACKCURRANTS

(Magret de canard aux baies de cassis)

 This is an autumnal dish with particularly rich, strong flavours. It is delicious served with fried wild mushrooms or Potato gratin (see page 82) as an accompaniment.

Serves 4

•

1¼ lb (500 g) duck trimmings (wings, neck, carcass)	2 tablespoons crème de cassis
2 carrots, peeled and coarsely diced	1 oz (25 g) butter
2 shallots or 1 small onion, coarsely diced	Salt and freshly ground black pepper
1 clove of garlic, cut in 3	¾ oz (20 g) clarified butter (see page 16)
A sprig of thyme	4 duck breasts (or magret), each weighing about 12 oz (350 g)
1 bay leaf	
9 oz (250 g) blackcurrants, fresh or frozen	A pinch of sugar
7 fl oz (200 ml) Burgundy	

Preparation and cooking

TO PREPARE THE SAUCE: Pre-heat the oven to gas mark 7, 425°F (220°C). Coarsely chop the duck trimmings and place them in a fireproof roasting dish. Roast in the oven for about 20 minutes, until lightly browned. Then remove the dish from the oven and set it over a moderate heat. Add the coarsely diced vegetables, garlic cut in 3, thyme and bay leaf. Select 4 oz (100 g) of the best blackcurrants and reserve; add the rest to the roasting dish. Cook for 2 minutes, then add the red wine. Turn up the heat and bring to the boil, stirring briskly and scraping the base and sides of the roasting dish with a wooden spoon. Then, if you prefer, tip the contents of the pan into a large saucepan, and pour in just sufficient cold water to cover the bones, or continue cooking in the roasting dish. Bring to the boil, adjust the heat to a gentle simmer, and cook for 30 minutes. Pour the stock into a large sieve set over another pan. Return the strained stock to the heat, and boil until reduced to a syrupy consistency. Add the *crème de cassis* and whisk in the butter, a little at a time. Taste, season, and keep warm.

TO COOK THE DUCK: Heat the clarified butter in a frying-pan over a high heat. Fry the duck breasts, skin side down, for 3 minutes, then on the other side for 5 minutes. They will be very pink. Wrap in foil.

TO COMPLETE THE SAUCE: Pour off the fat from the pan, and return the pan to the heat. Add the reserved 4 oz (100 g) blackcurrants and a pinch of sugar. Heat for a minute, then sprinkle on to the surface of the warm sauce; continue to keep the sauce warm.

To serve

Slice the duck breasts very thinly, lengthways, trimming away any fatty skin. Arrange the slices from each breast in a fanned-out rosette on 4 warmed serving plates. Spoon some blackcurrants into the centre of the rosette, or around the sliced duck. Coat the meat with the sauce and serve immediately.

•

QUAIL WITH GRAPES
(Cailles vigneronnes)

 Farm-bred quails are readily available in supermarkets, fully prepared and ready to cook. Don't go looking to buy wild quails; they are a protected species in Britain. Courgettes, briefly steamed then quickly fried in butter, would make a good accompaniment.

Serves 4
•

2 oz (50 g) clarified butter (see page 16)	2 strips of lemon zest
6 × 6 oz (175 g) prepared quails	3 tablespoons red port
20 whole green grapes	7 fl oz (200 ml) chicken stock (see page 18)
Salt and freshly ground black pepper	2 oz (50 g) butter
1 carrot, trimmed, peeled, and diced	2 medium-sized heads of chicory
2 shallots, diced	32 green grapes, peeled and pipped, for garnish
A bouquet garni (see page 22), including a sprig of tarragon	

Preparation and cooking

Pre-heat the oven to gas mark 3, 325°F (160°C)

THE QUAILS: In a medium-sized casserole, heat the clarified butter. Lightly brown the quails all over, then add the 20 whole grapes and a little salt and freshly ground black pepper; cover and leave to cook gently for 7 to 8 minutes. Pull the casserole aside from the heat and remove the quails to a chopping board. Use a small sharp knife to lift off the breast and thighs, in one piece, from each bird. Wrap these in foil, and reserve.

THE SAUCE: Chop the remaining carcasses and return them to the casserole with the diced carrot, shallots, bouquet garni and lemon zest. Re-heat and continue to cook gently for a few minutes before stirring in the port and the chicken stock. Bring to the boil and continue to cook until reduced by two-thirds. Whisk in 1 oz (25 g) of the butter, a little at a time, then pour the contents of the casserole into a large sieve set over a clean pan. Season the sauce to taste with salt and freshly ground black pepper; keep warm.

THE CHICORY: To prepare the chicory, first trim off any withered or marked outer leaves. Wipe the heads with a cloth, then cut them lengthways into matchstick strips. Heat the rest of the butter in a frying-pan, add the chicory-strips and cook them briefly over a high heat, so they remain a little crisp; keep warm.

To serve

Arrange the chicory in the centre of a warmed heatproof serving plate. Place 3 pieces of quail on either side of the chicory and arrange the peeled and pipped grapes in a border around the dish. Put the dish to heat in the oven for 2 minutes, then spoon the sauce over the meat. Serve immediately.

RICH STEW OF HARE WITH SULTANAS

(Les culs de capucins en civet aux raisins de Smyrne)

This dish needs 2 days of preparation. Ask your butcher to give you leverets – young hares, about a year old; the French call them *capucins*. Saddle of hare, the most tender cut of the animal, is spoiled by being cooked in a stew, so the saddle is not used here. A more appropriate method of cooking this joint is given in the recipe for Saddle of hare with cream (see page 131).

This stew is a rich, highly flavoured dish, copiously sauced, and the ideal accompaniment is the traditional one of riced potatoes. These are steamed potatoes passed through a potato ricer, which gives a fine, light, fluffy texture (like rice grains – hence the name). A less usual accompaniment, but one which we would also recommend, is a purée of Jerusalem artichokes.

Serves 4
•

2 × young hares, skinned, with blood and livers reserved	4 oz (100 g) sultanas
	7 oz (200 g) smoked bacon, in one piece
1 large carrot, trimmed, peeled, and sliced	6 oz (175 g) clarified butter (see page 16)
1 large onion, sliced	5 oz (150 g) button mushrooms, trimmed and wiped
3 cloves of garlic	A pinch of caster sugar
A bouquet garni made with celery stalks (see page 22)	5 oz (150 g) button onions
3 tablespoons olive oil	8 × ¼ in (5 mm) thick slices of white bread, cut into heart-shaped croûtons
5 tablespoons red wine vinegar	10 fl oz (300 ml) veal stock (see page 102)
4 tablespoons armagnac	2 tablespoons double cream
1¾ pints (1 litre) red wine (e.g. Burgundy)	Salt and freshly ground pepper
1 teaspoon black peppercorns, crushed	2 sprigs curly-leaf parsley, finely chopped

Opposite, top: Medallions of venison with cherries (see page 135); below left: Baked chicken heart's delight (see page 120); below right: Duck with honey and cloves (see page 123)

Preparation and cooking

JOINTING THE HARES: Have the butcher joint the hares, cutting them into hind-legs, saddles, ribs and forelegs, or do this yourself following the illustrations in figs. 1 to 3 overleaf. Reserve (or freeze) the saddles and ribs for another dish.

THE MARINADE: Put the front and back legs of the hare into a large bowl. Sprinkle in the sliced carrot and onion, add 1 unpeeled, crushed garlic clove and the bouquet garni, spoon over the olive oil, the vinegar and 2 tablespoons of the armagnac, and pour in the red wine. Add the crushed peppercorns. Cover the bowl closely with cling film and refrigerate for 24 hours.

THE GARNISH: The following day, start by putting the sultanas to soak in lukewarm water for a minimum of 2 hours.

Remove the rind from the bacon and cut it into small dice. Put in a small pan of water and bring to the boil; drain and refresh with cold water. Dry on absorbent paper. Heat $\frac{1}{2}$oz (15 g) of the clarified butter in a frying-pan and lightly brown the bacon. Use a draining spoon to remove the bacon bits to a plate.

In the same pan melt a further $\frac{1}{2}$oz (15 g) of the clarified butter and fry the mushrooms for 5 minutes; remove to the same plate as the bacon.

In a small saucepan melt a further $\frac{1}{2}$oz (15 g) of the clarified butter and add a pinch of sugar. Add the onions and swirl in the butter until lightly browned. Now add sufficient water to half-cover them. Place a piece of greaseproof paper on top of the onions, and put the lid on the pan. Cook for about 8 minutes, or until the onions are just tender when tested with a thin skewer. Remove the paper and boil briskly to reduce the liquid in the pan and glaze the onions to a golden brown. Put them with the bacon and mushrooms; cover and reserve.

In a clean frying-pan, heat 2 oz (50 g) of the clarified butter and fry the croûtons until they are crisp and golden on both sides. Drain on absorbent paper.

TO COOK THE HARES: Pre-heat the oven to gas mark 3, 325°F (160°C).

Position a large sieve over a saucepan and pour in the marinade, vegetables and meat. Bring the strained marinade to the boil and keep hot. Pat the hare joints dry with absorbent paper. Heat the remaining butter in a fireproof casserole and brown the meat. Add the well-drained vegetables from the marinade and cook until browned, about 8 to 10 minutes. Now heat the remaining 2 tablespoons of armagnac in a soup ladle or small saucepan. Standing well back, ignite the alcohol and pour it into the casserole. When the flames subside, pour in the marinade and stock, bring to the boil, then cover and cook in the oven for 1 hour 20 minutes.

Opposite: Duck breasts with blackcurrants (see page 125)

THE SAUCE: Meanwhile, put the reserved blood and livers, the 2 remaining garlic cloves (peeled), and the double cream into a food processor or blender. Blend until smooth, then pass through a fine sieve into a bowl; cover and reserve.

To serve

Lift the cooked back legs of the hare from the casserole and arrange them on a warmed serving dish. Take out the front legs, transfer them to a chopping board, and remove the meat from the bones. Shred the meat finely and sprinkle it around the back legs. Put the bacon, mushrooms and button onions on top. Cover and return to the oven.

Strain the cooking liquid into a clean saucepan, rubbing the vegetables through the sieve with the back of a spoon. Boil briskly to reduce the liquid by half, skimming if necessary. Return the pan to the heat, bring to the boil again, then pull aside from the heat. Add a ladle of hot sauce to the blended blood and liver in the bowl; stir, and pour into the rest of the sauce. Add the sultanas and re-heat gently, but do not let the sauce boil, because if the blood and liver are allowed to boil their consistency will be unpalatable. Taste, season with salt and freshly ground black pepper

JOINTING A HARE OR RABBIT

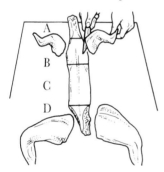

1 Cut forelegs and hind legs off the body. Trim rib cage (B) level with saddle (C).

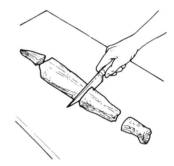

2 Cut off neck (A) and tail end (D). Divide rib cage (B) from saddle (C).

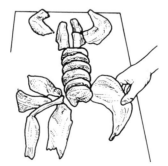

3 Depending on size, the rib cage, saddle and hind legs can be further divided.

if necessary, and coat the hare and garnish generously with the sauce. Arrange the warmed croûtons around the edge of the dish, sprinkle with parsley and serve.

•

SADDLE OF HARE WITH CREAM

(Civet de lièvre au crème)

 Richly flavoured, simple to prepare and inexpensive, this is the companion recipe to the Rich stew of hare with sultanas (see page 128). Note that there are delicious little nuggets of meat to be found *under* the saddle, when you come to carve it. Detach these with a small knife and serve with the rest of the sliced meat. Spinach or mange-tout would make a good vegetable accompaniment.

Serves 2

•

2 saddles cut from young hares, plus *2 livers, and the rib trimmings*	*3 tablespoons brandy*
	3½ fl oz (100 ml) red wine (e.g. Côte du Rhône)
3 oz (75 g) clarified butter (see page 16)	*10 fl oz (300 ml) double cream*
1 carrot, trimmed, peeled and diced	*1 oz (25 g) butter*
2 shallots or 1 medium onion, diced	*Salt and freshly ground black pepper*
A sprig of thyme	*16 spring onions, trimmed and washed*
4 juniper berries	*A small bunch of watercress, washed, trimmed, and dried*
1 bay leaf	

Preparation and cooking

Pre-heat the oven to gas mark 7, 425°F (220°C).

THE MEAT: Wipe the saddles of hare with absorbent paper. Set a heavy frying-pan with a heatproof handle over a high heat. Leave it to heat for 1 minute, then add 2 oz (50 g) of the clarified butter. Let this get very hot before putting the meat into the pan to brown. When it is evenly browned all over, transfer it to the top half of the oven to continue cooking for 6 minutes. Remove the meat, wrap it in foil, and keep it warm. Reduce the oven temperature to gas mark 3, 325°F (160°C).

THE SAUCE: Pour off the excess fat from the pan, then return it to the heat. Add the coarsely chopped ribs of the hares, cook for 1 minute, then add the diced carrot and shallots or onion, and the thyme, juniper berries and bay leaf. Stir, and leave to cook over a moderate heat for a further 2 minutes. Pour the brandy over the contents of the pan, stand well back and ignite, shaking the pan as you do so. When the flames subside add the wine and boil briskly until reduced by half. Now add the cream and reduce by half again. Put the butter in a small bowl with the 2 livers and crush together with a fork until well mixed. Pull the pan off the heat and briskly stir in the butter and liver, a little at a time. Strain the mixture through a fine sieve into a clean pan, taste and season. Keep the sauce warm, but from now on it should not boil.

THE GARNISH: Heat the remaining clarified butter in a frying-pan and fry the spring onions until cooked but still crisp; keep warm.

To serve

Use a sharp knife to free the meat and lift the fillets from the saddles. Carve the fillets lengthways in thin slices, then re-form and replace them on the saddles. Place on a warmed serving dish and heat in the oven for 2 minutes. When you remove the saddles coat them generously with the sauce and arrange the spring onions and watercress around them. Serve immediately.

•

GAME STOCK

(Fonds de gibier)

 You can make this rich, full-flavoured stock using the carcasses and trimmings (necks, wings, knuckles, etc.) from any type of game, bird or animal.

Makes $1\frac{3}{4}$ pints (1 litre)

•

2 tablespoons peanut oil	*1 pint (600 ml) veal stock (see page 102)*
2 to $2\frac{1}{4}$ lb (1 kg) game carcasses and trimmings, chopped in small pieces	*A sprig of sage*
	6 juniper berries
1 carrot, washed and coarsely diced	*6 coriander seeds*
2 oz (50 g) onion, coarsely diced	*A bouquet garni (see page 22)*
1 pint (600 ml) full-bodied red wine	

To cook

Heat the oil in a saucepan and brown the game pieces all over. Add the carrot and onion to the pan, lower the heat, and sweat the vegetables for a few minutes. Pour off any excess oil before adding the red wine. Boil to reduce by one-third. Add $1\frac{3}{4}$ pints (1 litre) water and the veal stock, and bring to the boil. Lower the heat and simmer gently, frequently skimming the surface. After 10 minutes, add the sage, juniper berries, coriander seeds and bouquet garni, and cook for a further $2\frac{1}{2}$ hours. Strain the stock through a muslin-lined sieve, skim off the fat from the surface and set aside in a cool place. As with all stocks, do not refrigerate until absolutely cold.

To store

Game stock will keep for 1 week in the refrigerator, or several weeks in the freezer. If you simmer the stock until it is reduced to half its original quantity, you will obtain a game *demi-glace*.

•

RABBIT WITH TARRAGON SAUCE

(Fricassée de lapereau sauce l'estragon)

 The French consider rabbit a delicacy and consequently treat the meat with care and attention in the kitchen, emerging with some delicious dishes as a result. In this recipe young rabbit is pan-fried and served with a sauce made with stock from the rabbit trimmings. Serve the dish garnished with seasonal baby vegetables, such as carrots, onions, turnips, fennel or salsify.

Serves 8

•

2 × 3 lb (1.5 kg) young rabbits, skinned	1¾ pints (1 litre) chicken stock (see page 18)
4 medium carrots, trimmed, peeled, and coarsely chopped	¾ oz (20 g) sprigs of fresh tarragon
	A bouquet garni (see page 22)
4 medium onions, peeled and coarsely chopped	Salt and freshly ground black pepper
2 garlic cloves, peeled and crushed	1½ oz (40 g) clarified butter (see page 16)
8 fl oz (250 ml) dry white wine	1 oz (25 g) butter

Preparation and cooking

Pre-heat the oven to gas mark 8, 450°F (230°C).

Cut the rabbits into joints according to the instructions on page 130, or ask the butcher to do this for you. Cover and keep in a cool place.

Put the bones from the back legs, the rib cage, the front legs and any other trimmings into a fireproof roasting dish and cook in the hottest part of the oven for 25 minutes. At this stage sprinkle the chopped carrot and onion and the crushed garlic into the roasting dish and return it to the oven to cook for a further 10 minutes. Now transfer the roasting dish to direct heat. Pour in 4 fl oz (120 ml) of the white wine and stir briskly with a wooden spoon, scraping the base and sides of the dish. Boil for a minute or two, then tip everything into a large saucepan and add the remaining wine and the chicken stock. Strip the tarragon leaves from the stalks, reserve the leaves and add the stalks to the pan, with the bouquet garni. Bring to the boil, then adjust the heat to give a gentle simmer; cook, uncovered, for $1\frac{1}{2}$ hours, skimming occasionally. Strain through a large sieve set over a clean saucepan. Return the pan to the heat and boil to reduce to the consistency of a thin sauce, skimming occasionally if necessary. Cover and keep on one side.

Lightly season the rabbit joints with salt and freshly ground black pepper. In a large frying-pan, heat the clarified butter. Fry the rabbit joints, several pieces at a time, being careful not to overcrowd the pan. After 5 to 8 minutes, when they are evenly browned and cooked, remove the rabbit joints to a plate and keep warm. When all the meat has been cooked, tip any excess fat from the pan, then return the pan to the heat. Add the reserved stock made from the rabbit trimmings and boil to reduce to a good sauce consistency. Whisk in the butter a little at a time and finally add the snipped tarragon leaves. Taste, and season with salt and freshly ground black pepper if necessary.

To serve

Transfer the rabbit pieces to 8 warmed plates and spoon a little sauce over each portion. Serve hot.

MEDALLIONS OF VENISON WITH CHERRIES

(Médaillons de chevreuil aux cerises)

 In this recipe the sourness of the cherries helps to cut through the richness of the venison, which is also complemented by the subtle flavour of asparagus.

Serves 2
•

2 oz (50 g) sugar	1 shallot, diced
4 oz (100 g) sour red cherries	A sprig of thyme
Lemon juice	1 bay leaf
12 asparagus spears	3 fl oz (85 ml) red port
Salt	4 oz (100 g) butter
1 oz (25 g) clarified butter (see page 16)	Freshly ground black pepper
6 × 2 oz (50 g) medallions of venison	4 oz (100 g) tagliatelle
1 carrot, trimmed, peeled and diced	20 pink peppercorns, crushed

Preparation and cooking

THE CHERRIES: Put the sugar in a saucepan, pour in 7 fl oz (200 ml) water, and stir over a fairly low heat until the sugar dissolves. Add the cherries and a good squeeze of lemon juice and simmer for about 5 minutes until they are softened.

THE ASPARAGUS: Peel the asparagus, then bend each spear and it will snap in half at the point where the tender stalk becomes tough and fibrous. Discard the ends or keep them to flavour soups and sauces. Rinse the spears in cold water. Cook in boiling salted water for about 5 minutes, or until just tender, then drain and refresh under cold running water. Cut the spears into short lengths, leaving the tips with about 2 in (5 cm) of stalk attached, and reserve.

THE MEDALLIONS: In a frying-pan, melt the clarified butter over a high heat. Cook the medallions for 1 minute on each side, or to your taste; remove to a plate and keep warm.

THE SAUCE: Pour the excess fat from the pan, then return the pan to the heat, stir in the diced carrot and shallot and the thyme and bay leaf and cook gently for 2 minutes before turning up the heat and adding the port. Stir briskly with a wooden spoon, scraping the base and sides of the pan. Now add 2 tablespoons of the syrup the cherries were poached in and reduce the liquid in the pan by half. Whisk in 2 oz (50 g) of the butter, a little at a time, then pour the contents of the pan through a fine sieve into a clean saucepan. Taste, season with salt and freshly ground black pepper, and keep warm.

To serve

Cook the tagliatelle in boiling salted water until it is *al dente* (just cooked, but still firm to the bite). Drain thoroughly and return to the dry pan with the rest of the butter and the chopped asparagus stalks (but not the tips). Heat sufficiently to melt the butter and warm the asparagus, then divide between 2 warmed plates. Arrange the medallions of venison on top, with the reserved asparagus tips in between.

Bring the sauce back to the boil; add the drained cherries, and when these are heated through pour the sauce over the meat. Sprinkle the tagliatelle with the crushed pink peppercorns, and serve.

FISH

We have both noticed a trend in our restaurants towards eating fish – which is, of course, low in fat, high in protein, high in vitamins and minerals, in fact one of the healthiest foods you can eat. Fresh fish, lightly cooked, is also among the most delicious of foods. And there is such a range of cooking methods for fish, from steaming, which we like especially for the way it retains the texture and flavour of the fish, to baking in the oven. What they have in common is that they all require precise judgement of the exact point at which the fish is cooked to perfection.

When you are buying fish, check for freshness. The eyes and the gills should be bright and should not look stale or dull; there should be a smell of the sea; there should be a sheen on the skin. A large fish, such as a salmon, should be firm when you pick it up, it should hold its shape and not flop about.

Shellfish are among our favourite ingredients: just look at the versatility and range of them. From the winkle to the oyster, the lobster to the mussel, there is almost no end to the sort of dishes you can prepare with shellfish. We are always surprised when people resist eating shellfish because they think they are difficult to eat. We have noticed a great reluctance in the British to risk looking foolish. Many people will not tackle a crab, for example, because they are afraid they might look clumsy or ignorant. This is very different from the confidence of the French – who think they know everything, when in fact this is often far from being the case!

FISH STOCK
(Fonds de poisson)

 Now, don't just look at the list of ingredients and think that you would never be able to assemble fish trimmings in such quantity. Whenever you are trimming or filleting fish, put the bits you cut away into the freezer. You will find that you soon have sufficient to make a stock. And when you have made your stock, it can go into the refrigerator, where it will keep for 1 week, or, packed in whatever amounts you find most useful, back into the freezer, where you can keep it for several weeks. In this way stock, or the ingredients to make it, will always be available. If space is limited you can reduce the stock by gently simmering until you have half or one-third of the original amount, and freeze it in this concentrated form. It can then be used in smaller quantities, to enrich and add body to fish sauces, such as White Bordelaise sauce (see page 34).

Makes 3 pints (1.75 litres)

•

2 to 2¼ lb (1 kg) fish heads and bones, taken from white-fleshed fish (e.g. sole, turbot or whiting)	*1 leek (white part only), trimmed, washed, and chopped*
2 oz (50 g) butter	*3½ fl oz (100 ml) dry white wine*
2 oz (50 g) onions, chopped	*A bouquet garni (see page 22)*
2 oz (50 g) mushrooms, trimmed, wiped, and chopped	

Preparation and cooking

Remove the gills from the fish heads (their bitter flavour would impair the stock). Soak the bones and heads in cold water for 3 to 4 hours. Drain them, and chop them roughly.

Melt the butter in a large saucepan. Stir in the vegetables and cook them over a low heat for 2 or 3 minutes, until they are softened but not coloured. Add the bones and cook for a further 2 or 3 minutes before you pour in the wine. Increase the heat and cook to reduce the wine by half. Add 3½ pints (2 litres) water and bring it slowly to the boil, skimming frequently. Adjust the heat to give a gentle simmer. After 5 minutes add the bouquet garni and continue to simmer, uncovered, for 20 minutes, skimming when necessary. Strain through a muslin-lined sieve and leave to cool before refrigerating.

SOLE HEART'S DESIRE

(Sole mon désir)

If you have the time, it is always worthwhile putting the mussels in cold, sea-salted water with a handful of fine oatmeal or flour. Left for an hour or two they gorge on the flour, while ridding themselves of grit, to emerge clean and plump for cooking.

Serves 4
•

4 × 14 oz (400 g) Dover soles, whole, skinned on both sides	4 fl oz (120 ml) fish stock (see page 138)
1 pint (600 ml) mussels	Salt
15 fl oz (450 ml) dry white wine	10 fl oz (300 ml) double cream
12 large oysters in the shell	¾ oz (20 g) truffle, cut in small strips (optional)
4 scallops	Freshly ground white pepper
Butter	Snipped chervil or flat-leaf parsley, to garnish
2 medium shallots, thinly sliced	A few puff pastry fleurons (see page 164 and page 167), to garnish

Preparation

THE SOLES: Using a pair of scissors, cut off the bony edges of the Dover soles; then remove the heads. With a sharp filleting knife make an incision down the length of the backbone to ensure even cooking. Then, using the scissors, snip twice through the exposed backbone, once towards the head, then at the tail end of the fish. This makes the fish remain flat during cooking.

THE MUSSELS: Put the mussels in a bowl of cold water and scrub well with a stiff brush. Pull out the stringy 'beard' and rinse again, discarding any mussels that remain open. Put into a saucepan with 5 fl oz (150 ml) of the dry white wine, cover the pan and set over a high heat for 5 minutes. Holding the lid firmly in place, shake the pan vigorously once or twice during cooking to ensure the mussels cook evenly. Discard any mussels that are still closed. Scoop the mussels from their shells into a bowl; strain the cooking liquor from the pan through a muslin-lined sieve, and reserve.

THE OYSTERS: When opening the oysters, work over a bowl to catch all the juices. Insert a strong, rigid knife between the two shells, next to the hinge. Push in and twist the knife to break the hinge and open the shell; scrape free the oyster and put it into a sieve. Sluice with plenty of cold water, strain the juice through a muslin-lined sieve, and reserve.

THE SCALLOPS: Using the same knife as for the oysters, lever the scallop shells apart. Sever the scallops from the rounded half of the shell, then rinse them in cold water, discarding the membrane and retaining only the round white muscle (known in France as the *noix*) and the orange tongue. Separate these and cut the *noix* in small strips.

Pre-heat the oven to gas mark 5, 375°F (190°C).

To cook

Butter a fireproof dish or roasting tin large enough to take the soles in a single layer. Strew the base with the sliced shallots and lay the soles on top. Pour in the rest of the wine, the strained juices from the mussels and oysters, and the fish stock. Season with a little salt. Set the dish over a high heat and bring to the boil. Cover with a double thickness of buttered greaseproof paper and transfer to the oven for about 8 minutes, until the fish are just cooked. Drain and carefully arrange the soles on a large, warmed serving dish; cover again with the buttered paper and keep warm.

Strain the cooking liquor through a fine sieve into a large saucepan and boil briskly until reduced by about two-thirds. Add the cream and boil for a further 3 minutes. Turn the heat down low and stir in the mussels, oysters, scallops, and truffle (if used).

To serve

Taste, and season if necessary. As soon as the sauce mixture begins to bubble, pour it over the soles. Serve immediately, sprinkled with snipped chervil or parsley and garnished with a few puff pastry *fleurons*.

BAKED WHITING WITH TOMATO BUTTER SAUCE

(Merlan gratiné au beurre de tomate)

 For this recipe it is best if the whiting are boned and cleaned through the back. This is a slightly tricky operation, so you may prefer to ask your fishmonger to do it for you.

Serves 4

•

4 × 12 to 14 oz (350 to 400 g) whiting, with the gills removed	*2 oz (50 g) fresh white breadcrumbs*
	3 oz (75 g) Parmesan cheese, grated
7 oz (200 g) butter	*4 large tomatoes*
Salt and freshly ground black pepper	*1 tablespoon double cream*

Preparation and cooking

Pre-heat the oven to gas mark 5, 375°F (190°C).

THE FISH: Using a pair of scissors, remove the fins from the top, bottom and sides of each whiting, then trim the tails. The fish now need to be boned through the back; don't worry, this is easier than it sounds. Place each fish on its side and use a sharp filleting knife to cut along the backbone. Holding the knife horizontally, cut the flesh away from the rib bones on either side of the fish, stopping just before you reach the underside. Take a pair of scissors and snip the backbone as near to the tail as possible, and again as near to the head as you can. Carefully withdraw the backbone and the guts; use tweezers to remove any bones that remain in the fish. Rinse the fish with cold water and pat dry with absorbent paper.

Melt 1 oz (25 g) of the butter in a small saucepan. Select a baking dish just large enough to contain the fish comfortably, and brush it with some of the melted butter. Arrange the fish in the dish, belly side down, and brush them with the rest of the melted butter. Season with salt and freshly ground black pepper. In a small bowl, toss together the breadcrumbs and cheese; sprinkle the mixture over the boned whiting. Bake in the top half of the oven for about 10 minutes. Test the fish with the point of a sharp knife to make sure it is cooked; the flesh should be ivory-white.

THE SAUCE: Meanwhile, prepare the sauce. Purée the quartered tomatoes in a food processor or blender. Pour into a small saucepan and cook to reduce by two-thirds. Add the cream and bring back to the boil. Whisk in the rest of the butter, a little at a time, but do not boil once the butter has been added, or the sauce will curdle. Taste, and season with salt and freshly ground black pepper. Strain through a sieve.

To serve

Arrange the fish on a warmed oval plate; pour the sauce into the base of the plate around the fish. Serve hot.

•

HALIBUT WITH MINT AND PEPPERCORN BUTTER

(Tronçonettes de flétan grillés)

The French title may have you slightly perplexed! The halibut is cut in half lengthways, then across into thick slices – the 'tronçonettes' of the title. This is rather an unusual way of portioning fish, but the slices look attractive when presented on a plate, and they are very easy to serve.

Serves 8

•

7 oz (200 g) butter	8 medium courgettes, cut into matchstick strips
2 rounded teaspoons finely chopped mint	1 × 3¼ to 3½ lb (1.5 kg) halibut
1 tablespoon crushed white peppercorns	Olive oil
1 red pepper	Salt and freshly ground white pepper
1 green pepper	

Preparation and cooking

Pre-heat the grill to a high heat; pre-heat the oven to gas mark 6, 400°F (200°C).

THE BUTTER: In a small bowl, thoroughly mix 4 oz (100 g) of the butter, the chopped mint and the crushed peppercorns. Place the butter on greaseproof paper or cling film and roll it into a cylinder 4 in (10 cm) long. Refrigerate until very firm.

THE GARNISH: Put the peppers in a grill pan or baking tray, and cook them under the hot grill, turning them occasionally, until they are black. Remove them from the heat, but leave the grill on a high heat, and put a grill rack directly underneath the heat. Peel the peppers under cold running water, then de-seed them, and cut them first into broad strips, then into diamond shapes. Melt 1 oz (25 g) of the remaining butter in a frying-pan and fry the peppers gently until they are tender. Turn them out on to a plate, and keep warm. Wipe the pan with a piece of absorbent paper, then melt the rest of the butter in it. Quickly fry the strips of courgette – they should remain quite firm. Transfer them to the plate with the peppers, and keep warm.

THE FISH: Cut off the head of the halibut and, using scissors, trim off the fins. Now cut the fish in half down the backbone. You will need a very sharp serrated knife for the next step. Cut each half across in slices about $\frac{3}{4}$ in (2 cm) thick; you should get about 8 slices from each half, giving 16 slices in all. Brush these with the olive oil and season lightly with a little salt. Quickly arrange the fish slices on the red-hot grill rack and grill them for 2 minutes. Without turning the fish pieces, transfer the rack of fish to the oven to finish cooking. This will probably take about 3 minutes: the fish is cooked when the bones in the middle can be moved, with perhaps a little resistance. Remove the black skin – the white skin can be left on the pieces – and grind a little white pepper over the halibut.

To serve

Arrange the fish, with the crisscross pattern from the very hot grill rack uppermost, on a warmed oval serving dish. Sprinkle the vegetable garnish around the fish. Immediately before serving, slice the flavoured butter into 16 pieces and put a slice on top of each piece of fish. Serve immediately.

STEAMED SALMON WRAPPED IN SPINACH

(Saumon en habit vert à la nage de coquillages)

 This fresh-flavoured salmon dish goes well with young steamed broad beans. We suggest a garnish of mussels but you can substitute prawns, or any other small shellfish.

Serves 6
•

6 × 4 to 5 oz (100 to 150 g) pieces of salmon, cut from the tail end of the fillet and skinned	*2 oz (50 g) mushrooms or mushroom trimmings, coarsely chopped*
Salt and freshly ground black pepper	*1 small onion or shallot, coarsely chopped*
About 4 oz (100 g) large spinach leaves, rinsed well	*1 tablespoon double cream*
	8 oz (225 g) butter
About 36 mussels	*Clarified butter (see page 16)*
½ quantity Aromatic stock (see page 19)	

Preparation and cooking

TO PREPARE THE SALMON: Season the fish lightly with salt and freshly ground black pepper. Have ready a pan of boiling water and a bowl of very cold water. Remove the stalks from the spinach leaves and plunge the leaves, a few at a time, into the boiling water. Leave for a second or two, then remove and transfer immediately to the bowl of cold water. Remove and dry carefully on absorbent paper. Wrap the salmon pieces neatly in the blanched spinach leaves.

TO PREPARE AND COOK THE MUSSELS: Prepare the mussels according to the directions given in the recipe for Sole heart's desire (see page 139). Pour the Aromatic stock into a large saucepan. Add the prepared mussels and cook over a high heat for 3 to 5 minutes, shaking the pan vigorously once or twice to ensure the mussels cook evenly. Discard any mussels that remain closed. Empty the contents of the saucepan into a colander set over a saucepan. Drain well, then remove the colander and transfer the pan to direct heat. Add the chopped mushrooms and onion or shallot and boil briskly to reduce to a syrupy consistency. Strain through a fine sieve and return to the heat; re-heat and add the cream, then whisk in the butter a little at a time; keep hot but do not reboil.

TO STEAM THE FISH: Bring about 2 in (5 cm) of salted water to the boil in the base pan of a steamer. Arrange the leaf-wrapped fish in the steamer and position it over the boiling water. Cover and steam for between 3 minutes (for thinner fillets) and 5 minutes (for thicker pieces).

To serve

Place each piece of fish on a warmed serving plate. Remove the mussels from their shells and reheat gently in the sauce. Spoon a little of the sauce and mussels around the fish. To give this dish a professional-looking finish, brush a little melted clarified butter on to the spinach to give an attractive gloss. Serve immediately.

•

BACK OF SALMON ON CRISP SLICES OF FENNEL

(Dos de saumon sur croquants de fenouil)

 A most wonderful summer dish with a delightful fennel flavour. Simple and easy to prepare, this could make an elegant lunch or dinner for friends.

Serves 4

•

For the salmon:	The fennel trimmings, roughly chopped
1½ lb (600 g) salmon fillet, skinned and boned	A sprig of thyme
1 large bulb fennel, leaves still attached	A few leaves of basil
½ cucumber	8 fl oz (250 ml) fish stock (see page 138)
1 tablespoon olive oil	1 tablespoon Pernod or Ricard
For the sauce:	7 fl oz (200 ml) double cream
1 tablespoon olive oil	2 oz (50 g) butter
1½ oz (40 g) shallots or onions, sliced	Salt and freshly ground black pepper

Preparation

The thick end of the salmon fillet is best, so try to use that if you can. Cut the salmon into 4 pieces across the fillet and then cut each piece into 3 lengthways, making 12 portions of equal length. Reserve in the refrigerator.

Wash the fennel and cut off the top leaves, keeping the most attractive leaves to use as a garnish. Remove the core and the outer layers of the fennel, and keep the trimmings for the sauce. Thinly slice the fennel lengthways. Fry for 30 seconds in very hot oil so the fennel remains crisp. Keep in a warm place.

Peel the cucumber and cut in half lengthways. Use a teaspoon to remove the seeds from the centre, then cut the two halves into very thin, hairlike strips, using a sharp knife or mandolin. Reserve in the refrigerator.

To cook

THE SAUCE: Heat the olive oil in a saucepan, add the shallots or onions, fennel trimmings, thyme and basil, and cook until the vegetables turn a light, golden-brown colour. Add the fish stock and Pernod (or Ricard), and reduce to a syrupy consistency. Then add the double cream, bring to the boil and reduce again to a sauce consistency. Pass through a fine sieve into a clean saucepan. Whisk the butter into the sauce and season with salt and freshly ground black pepper to taste. Keep hot.

THE SALMON: Season the strips of salmon and briefly fry in a little olive oil – around 45 seconds on each side. The salmon strips should still be pink in the middle.

To serve

Sprinkle an equal quantity of crisp, sliced fennel on 4 warmed plates. Place 3 pieces of salmon on each plate and pour the sauce around them. Scatter the thin strips of cucumber on top and garnish with the reserved green fennel leaves. Serve immediately.

•

ESCALOPES OF SALMON WITH TURNED VEGETABLES

(Escalopes de saumon aux petits légumes)

The laborious part of this dish is trimming and turning all the different vegetables to a uniform size, but, once this is done, the vegetables can be cooked an hour or two in advance of the meal. It then takes no more than 10 minutes to have this very attractive-looking meal on the table.

Serves 4
•

6 oz (175 g) carrots	1½ lb (750 g) piece middle-cut of salmon, skinned and boned
6 oz (175 g) turnips	
9 oz (250 g) celeriac	4 fl oz (100 ml) fish stock (see page 138)
8 oz (225 g) cucumber	8 fl oz (250 ml) dry vermouth
2 oz (50 g) extra fine French beans	15 fl oz (450 ml) double cream
2 oz (50 g) very small mange-tout	Freshly ground white pepper
Salt	½ oz (15 g) chervil or parsley, stalks removed, washed

Preparation

THE VEGETABLES: Trim and peel the carrots, turnips, celeriac and cucumber, cut them up and trim them into elongated olive shapes. Top and tail and wash the French beans and the mange-tout. Cook all the vegetables separately in boiling salted water until they are just tender, but still have some bite. Drain in a sieve, refresh with cold water, dry on absorbent paper and reserve in a bowl.

THE SALMON: Using a very sharp cook's knife, cut the salmon into 8 fairly thin escalopes. Keep in a cool place until ready to serve.

To cook

Pour the fish stock into a large saucepan and add 5 fl oz (150 ml) of the dry vermouth. Boil briskly until reduced to a slightly syrupy consistency. Add the cream, bring back to the boil and reduce again. Pour in the rest of the vermouth. Reduce to a sauce consistency. Taste, and season with salt and freshly ground white pepper. Stir the prepared vegetables into the sauce and bring back to the boil. As soon as the mixture bubbles, pour the contents of the pan into a warmed serving dish; keep warm.

Heat a non-stick frying-pan, without adding any fat. When the pan is very hot, add 4 of the salmon escalopes, and fry them for 30 seconds on each side. Repeat with the remaining 4 escalopes.

To serve

Sprinkle the sauced vegetables liberally with the chervil or parsley, then arrange the salmon escalopes on top. Serve immediately.

MONKFISH COOKED IN RED WINE

(Gigot de lotte)

Larding is the process of introducing ribbons of pork fat or bacon into meat which lacks sufficient fat of its own and so would otherwise tend to be rather dry when cooked. Here, monkfish is larded with bacon strips. You may not have attempted this before but do try it; it is a French technique that we would do well to use more often. This dish was a great favourite in the Rothschild household.

Serves 4
•

24 baby onions, peeled and left whole	*1 × 3 to 3½ lb (1.5 kg) monkfish, skinned and trimmed, but left whole*
24 small mushrooms, washed and drained	
	Salt and freshly ground black pepper
5½ oz (165 g) clarified butter (see page 16)	*10 fl oz (300 ml) good-quality red wine*
2 tablespoons groundnut oil	*A bouquet garni (see page 22)*
16 tiny new potatoes, peeled	*3 oz (75 g) butter*
6 oz (175 g) streaky bacon slices, rinds removed	*Chopped curly parsley, to garnish*

Preparation and cooking

THE GARNISH: Separately fry the onions and mushrooms, each with 1 oz (25 g) of the clarified butter, until they are golden brown and tender. Season and reserve. Using 1 oz (25 g) clarified butter plus 2 tablespoons groundnut oil, fry the potatoes until they are golden. Season and reserve. Cut 4 oz (100 g) of the bacon into ¼ in (5 mm) wide strips, and put the strips in a small saucepan of water. Bring to the boil and blanch for 1 minute. Drain the strips in a sieve and refresh them under cold running water. Dry them well on absorbent paper, then fry them in a further 1 oz (25 g) of the clarified butter until they are lightly crisp and golden. Combine the vegetables and the drained, fried bacon strips; cover and keep warm.

THE FISH: Cut the remaining bacon into strips ¼ in (5 mm) wide and use a larding needle to 'sew' the bacon strips into both sides of the fish at ¾ to 1¼ in (2 to 3 cm) intervals. Season the fish with salt and freshly ground black pepper.

Heat the rest of the clarified butter in a large pan and fry the monkfish over a moderately high heat until it is browned on all sides. Pour in the wine and add the bouquet garni. Reduce the heat to give a gentle simmer, then cover and cook for 12 to 15 minutes.

To serve

Drain the fish and transfer it to a warmed serving dish. Boil the remaining pan juices until they are reduced by two-thirds. Now whisk in the butter, a bit at a time, to make a smooth sauce. Season and strain a little of the sauce over the monkfish and serve the rest in a warmed sauce boat. Arrange the vegetable and bacon garnish around the monkfish and sprinkle with chopped parsley.

•

SEA BASS WITH FENNEL

(Loup de mer au fenouil)

 In this recipe the sea bass is stuffed with mushrooms, onions and fennel, and baked in greaseproof paper – a style of baking which cooks it to perfection.

Serves 4

•

1 × 3 lb (1.5 kg) sea bass, boned from the back and gutted (see page 141)	*12 oz (350 g) fennel bulbs, trimmed and finely chopped*
3½ oz (90 g) butter	*4 fl oz (120 ml) double cream*
4 oz (100 g) button mushrooms, trimmed, wiped, and finely chopped	*Salt and freshly ground black pepper*
	1 tablespoon Pernod
2 teaspoons lemon juice	*1 tablespoon oil*
4 oz (100 g) onions or shallots, finely chopped	*4 tablespoons fresh white breadcrumbs*
	1 quantity Mousseline sauce (see page 33)

Preparation and cooking

Pre-heat the oven to gas mark 7, 425°F (220°C).

THE FISH: Unless your fishmonger has done this for you, remove the scales by scraping the back of a knife from tail to head on each side of the fish. Then, using scissors, cut off the fins and trim the tail. Rinse quickly with cold water and pat dry with absorbent paper. Wrap in cling film and keep in a cool place.

THE FILLING: Melt $\frac{1}{2}$oz (15 g) of the butter in a frying-pan. Stir in the finely chopped mushrooms and the lemon juice and cook over a moderate heat until all the moisture has evaporated. Transfer to a bowl and keep on one side. Clean the pan with absorbent paper and melt a further 1 oz (25 g) of the butter in it. Stir in the finely chopped onions or shallots and cook over a gentle heat for 2 or 3 minutes. Stir in the finely chopped fennel. Cover and cook gently for 15 minutes, stirring from time to time. Add the mushrooms and the cream and bring to the boil. Continue to cook, stirring frequently, until the cream has reduced and been absorbed by the vegetables. The mixture should have the consistency of a workable paste. Taste, and season with salt and freshly ground black pepper. Remove the pan from the heat and stir in the Pernod; leave until completely cold.

TO STUFF AND BAKE THE FISH: Lay the fish on its stomach. Open up the back where the bone was taken out and lightly salt the inside. Fill the fish with the vegetable mixture, spreading it out evenly. Have ready a sheet of greaseproof paper about 4 in (10 cm) longer than the length of the fish, and lightly oiled. Lay the fish on the paper. Close the paper by folding it like a hem over the centre of the fish and twisting round the ends. Tie with string, not too tightly, at the head, middle and tail. Lay on a baking tray with the fold underneath and put in the oven to bake for 10 minutes. Turn the oven down to gas mark 3, 325°F (160°C) and cook for a further 20 minutes.

To serve

Without unwrapping the fish, use a palette knife to lift the fish from the baking tray to a warmed oval plate. Remove the centre string and cut a three-sided flap to create a door, large enough to expose the flesh of the fish. Fold back the door and make sure the fish is cooked by testing it with the point of a sharp knife: the flesh should flake easily. Remove the skin exposed through the door. Fold the door back into position and replace the fish in the switched-off oven to keep warm. Heat the remaining butter in a frying-pan, stir in the breadcrumbs and fry until golden, stirring constantly. Remove the fish from the oven, pull back the flap and pour the buttered breadcrumbs through the hole over the fish. Replace the door flap and take the fish to the table still wrapped in its greaseproof envelope. Serve immediately, with the Mousseline sauce handed separately.

MARGUERITE OF SALMON AND TURBOT WITH CHAMPAGNE SAUCE

(Marguerite de saumon et turbot sauce champagne)

 In this dish the colours of the thinly sliced white turbot and pink salmon fillets are used in alternating concentric circles to create a stunning daisy-like pattern.

Serves 6
•

1 oz (25 g) butter, melted	*1¼ lb (500 g) skinned salmon fillet*
1 large courgette, topped and tailed	*12 oz (350 g) skinned turbot fillet*
1 medium carrot, topped and tailed and peeled	*15 fl oz (450 ml) fish stock (see page 138)*
Salt	*1 quantity Champagne sauce (see page 35)*
1 tomato, skinned and de-seeded	*Sprigs of chervil, to garnish*

Preparation and cooking

Pre-heat the oven to gas mark 9, 475°F (240°C).

You will need 6 × 5 in (13 cm) squares of thin cardboard. Cover these with foil and brush the tops with melted butter.

THE GARNISH : Prepare the garnish using a cannelising knife to cut grooves the length of the courgette and carrot. Slice into rounds about ⅛ in (3 mm) thick. Put the carrot into a small saucepan of cold salted water and bring to the boil. Add the courgette and blanch until both are barely cooked, then drain in a sieve and refresh with cold water. Cover and leave on one side until ready to serve. Cut the tomato into diamond shapes and set aside.

ARRANGING THE FISH : Using a very sharp knife, slice the salmon fillets across into strips ¼ in (5 mm) wide, then the turbot into slices ⅛ in (3 mm) wide. Sprinkle the surfaces of the foil-covered squares with a little salt, then arrange some strips of salmon in a circle up to the sides of each square. Inside this first circle place some strips of turbot, just over-lapping the circle of salmon. Repeat this pattern again with salmon, then turbot, creating decreasing circles. Finally, roll up a small strip of salmon and place this in the centre. When all 6 marguerites are complete place the squares in a roasting tin, pour over the fish stock, season with a little salt and bring to the boil. Cover the dish with buttered greaseproof paper and poach in the oven for 3 to 4 minutes, until just cooked.

To serve

Use a fish slice to drain and remove the foil squares. Very carefully lift each marguerite on to a warmed plate. Quickly arrange the garnish around the edge of each plate, alternating slices of carrot and courgette. Put diamonds of tomato in the centre of each marguerite. Place in the oven to re-heat for 1 minute, then, finally, pour the Champagne sauce around the edge of the fish. Garnish with sprigs of chervil and serve immediately.

•

LOUISIANA CRAB
(Crabe Louisiane)

We tend to spurn the humble crab in favour of the more luxurious lobster, which is a pity. Its texture and flavour are worth more consideration – and in this recipe they receive it. If small crabs (weighing about $1\frac{1}{4}$ lb (500 g) apiece) are not available, then one weighing about $2\frac{1}{2}$ lb (1.25 kg) will do – but a single, larger crab will need 30 minutes to cook.

Serves 4
•

$2 \times 1\frac{1}{4}$ lb (500 g) live crabs	$\frac{1}{4}$ teaspoon snipped fresh thyme leaves or a generous pinch of dried thyme
Salt	
$1\frac{1}{2}$ oz (40 g) butter	10 fl oz (300 ml) white wine (e.g. Riesling)
8 oz (225 g) button mushrooms, trimmed, wiped, and finely chopped	2 thin slices of boiled ham, about 4 oz (100 g), diced
	Salt and freshly ground black pepper
2 oz (50 g) onion or shallots, finely chopped	Snipped flat-leaf parsley, to garnish

Preparation

Boil the crabs in heavily salted water, cool them and extract the crabmeat, following the instructions given in figs. 1 to 7, below and overleaf. Keep all the crabmeat together in one bowl, as there is no need to separate brown meat from white for this recipe; you will have about 12 oz (350 g) in all. Ideally you should not use more than 2 tablespoons of the brown meat, as its flavour will overpower the white meat. A warning – do check carefully that there is no broken shell among the meat!

To cook

In a frying-pan, heat $\frac{1}{2}$ oz (15 g) of the butter until it is foaming. Stir in the finely chopped mushrooms and cook over a high heat for 3 minutes. When all the moisture has evaporated, transfer them to a bowl. Melt the rest of the butter in the same pan and stir in the finely chopped onion or shallots. Cover and cook over a low heat for 3 to 4 minutes, then uncover and stir in the crabmeat and the thyme. Stir and continue cooking for 1 minute before pouring in the wine. Bring to the boil, boil for 1 minute, then stir in the reserved mushrooms and the diced ham. Mix well, taste, and season with salt and freshly ground black pepper, if necessary. Remove the pan from the heat, cover, and keep warm.

To serve

The crabmeat mixture can be served either on a warmed shallow dish, or divided between the crab shells (cleaned and oiled), arranged on a flat plate. Sprinkle with the snipped parsley and serve immediately.

•

PREPARING COOKED CRAB

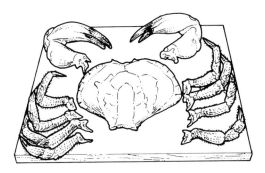

1 Turn the crab on its back, with the pointed tail nearest to you. Twist off the legs and claws.

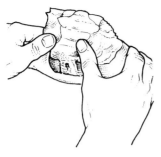

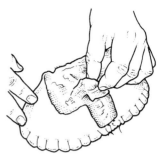

2 Use your thumbs to push the central body section up and out of the main shell.

3 With your thumb, press down and break free the shell section behind the eyes. Remove this and the stomach sac.

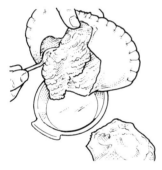

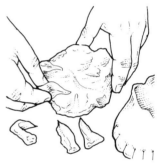

4 Use a teaspoon to scrape all the brown meat from inside the main shell.

5 Remove and discard the feathery gills (or 'dead men's fingers') surrounding the central body section.

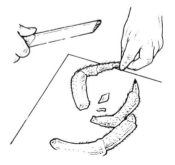

6 Cut the central body section into 4, and use a skewer to pick the white meat out of the crevices in the shell.

7 Crack the legs and claws, and extract the white meat.

SQUID IN SAUCE ARMORICAINE

(Calamars sauce Armoricaine)

The preparation of squid in theory seems lengthy and involved, in practice it is quickly and easily done. This recipe is a marvellous opportunity to use up any form of prawn heads that you have stored in the freezer. If you have none, let it be an object lesson to you to save any bones or trimmings that could usefully go into a stockpot!

Serves 4

•

8 oz (225 g) prawn heads	2 to 2¼ lb (1 kg) squid
4 tablespoons well-flavoured olive oil	3 fl oz (85 ml) brandy
1 carrot, peeled and coarsely chopped	2 large tomatoes, about 7 oz (200 g), peeled, de-seeded, and diced
2 onions, coarsely chopped	
2 cloves of garlic, peeled and chopped	1 to 2 teaspoons lemon juice
1 teaspoon mild paprika	Salt and freshly ground black pepper
5 fl oz (150 ml) dry white wine	Snipped fresh flat-leaf parsley, to garnish
1 teaspoon tomato purée	

Preparation

THE SAUCE: Start by briefly blending the prawn heads in a food processor or liquidiser, or pass them through the coarse plate of a mincer; reserve.

In a medium-sized saucepan, heat 2 tablespoons of olive oil and stir in the chopped carrot, onions and garlic. Cook over a moderate heat, stirring frequently, until the vegetables are lightly coloured. Sprinkle in the paprika, stir, then add the prawn debris. Pour in the white wine, 1 pint (600 ml) water and the tomato purée. Bring to the boil, then adjust the heat to give a gentle simmer and leave to cook, uncovered, for 25 minutes. Have ready a fine sieve set over a clean saucepan; strain the sauce, rubbing through sufficient vegetables to give it body. You should have about 1 pint (600 ml); cover and keep on one side until ready to use.

THE SQUID: Hold the squid sac in one hand and gently pull out the head with the other (see figs. 1 to 6, overleaf). As the head comes away, so too will all the innards. Pull off and discard the membrane covering the sac, so the creamy white skin underneath is revealed. Withdraw the transparent quill from the body sac and

PREPARING SQUID

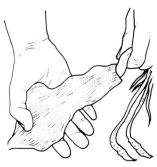

1 Hold the squid firmly with one hand and pull out the head and innards with the other.

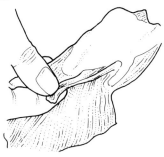

2 Carefully pull the grey membrane off the white sac, but leave the tentacles intact.

3 Feel inside the sac for the transparent quill and pull it out.

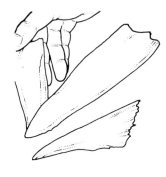

4 Pull the two flaps away from the body.

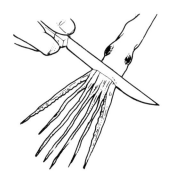

5 Cut off the tentacles just below the eyes and remove the hard beak.

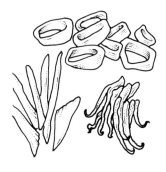

6 Rinse well, drain and cut into rings and pieces about $\frac{1}{2}$ in (1 cm) wide.

throw away. Cut off the tentacles just below the eyes, discard the hard beak from among them, then cut into approximately 1 in (2.5 cm) lengths; rinse, dry and reserve. Rinse out the squid sacs, drain and cut across into pieces about $\frac{1}{2}$ in (1 cm) wide. Dry the squid rings thoroughly on absorbent paper.

To cook

In a large frying-pan, heat the remaining 2 tablespoons olive oil until it starts to smoke. Add the squid gradually, so the temperature is not lowered too much. Fry until lightly coloured. Warm the brandy in a soup ladle or small saucepan, ignite, and pour over the squid, shaking the pan as you do so. When the flames have died away, transfer the contents of the pan to the strained sauce and add the diced tomatoes. Bring to the boil, then simmer gently, uncovered, for 15 to 20 minutes, until the squid is tender.

To serve

Taste, and if you feel the flavour of the sauce needs a little reinforcing, add the lemon juice. Taste again and season with salt and freshly ground black pepper. Serve piping hot, sprinkled thickly with snipped parsley.

MUSSELS WITH NORMANDY CIDER

(Moules au cidre de Normandie)

Mussels make an excellent meal. If you have any doubt about their preparation, please refer to Sole heart's desire (page 139). Here the recipe calls for $4\frac{1}{2}$ lb (2 kg) mussels for 6 people, which allows about 20 mussels each. Exactly how you serve them depends on the occasion. For the family, the mussels can simply be piled into deep bowls and served with a large bowl in the centre of the table for the discarded shells. For a more formal presentation you can remove the half-shells and arrange the mussels on deep plates, but you will have to do this job quickly if the mussels are to go to the table nice and hot.

Serves 6
•

$4\frac{1}{2}$ lb (2 kg) prepared mussels	2 bay leaves
5 oz (150 g) butter	6 fl oz (175 ml) double cream (optional)
4 shallots, finely chopped	Salt and freshly ground white pepper
12 fl oz (350 ml) medium-dry cider	Snipped fresh chives, to garnish
A sprig of thyme	

To cook

Discard any mussels that have remained open throughout the cleaning process. In a large pan, melt 1 oz (25 g) butter and stir in the shallots. Cook over a low heat for 2 or 3 minutes, until softened but not coloured. Turn up the heat and pour in 10 fl oz (300 ml) of the cider. Add the thyme and bay leaves and boil to reduce the cider by one-third. Pour in the cream and add the mussels to the pan; cover with a well-fitting lid and cook over a fairly high heat for 3 to 5 minutes, jumping the mussels in the pan to ensure even cooking. Have ready a colander positioned over a clean saucepan. Pour the mussels and cooking liquor into the colander. Discard any mussels that have remained firmly closed. Return the juices in the saucepan to the heat. Boil until reduced to a syrupy consistency. Add the remaining cider and whisk in the rest of the butter, about a teaspoon at a time. Do not allow the liquid to boil, or it will curdle. Taste, and season with salt and freshly ground white pepper.

To serve

Pour the sauce over the mussels, scatter with the snipped chives, and serve immediately.

MY QUICHE

(Ma quiche)

 Dublin Bay prawns, confusingly, do not come from Dublin Bay. In fact, they are fished from Morocco, through the Mediterranean, and on up to Iceland. However, Dublin Bay recognised them for the delicacy they are, a trade developed and the name stuck. But so too have other names! Just to add to the confusion, they are also known as Norwegian lobsters, and they are also often sold under their French name, *langoustine*.

Sad to say, they are rather expensive, but a few mussels (about one-third) can be substituted for the same number of prawns, if you prefer. To prepare and cook the mussels follow the directions given in the recipe Sole heart's desire (page 139), heating the mussels in some of the stock. Strain the cooking juices and return them to the rest of the stock, then cook the Dublin Bay prawns as instructed in this recipe.

This recipe is for one 8 in (20 cm) quiche, but the same quantities of pastry and filling could alternatively be used to make four individual quiches. For these, use fluted tins with removable bases, base measurement $3\frac{1}{4}$ in (8 cm), depth $1\frac{1}{4}$ in (3 cm). To line the tins, cut out four 5 in (13 cm) rounds, using a pastry cutter or a small saucer or saucepan lid as a guide.

Serves 4 or 6
You will need a fluted metal tart tin, base measurement 8 in (20 cm), preferably with a removable base.

•

20 live Dublin Bay prawns, or raw prawn tails	5 fl oz (150 ml) double cream
1 quantity Aromatic stock (see page 19)	2 eggs
2 tomatoes, chopped	Salt
$\frac{1}{2}$ teaspoon tomato purée	A pinch of cayenne pepper
6 oz (175 g) shortcrust pastry (see page 162)	A few parsley sprigs, to garnish
$\frac{1}{2}$ oz (15 g) Chinese thread egg noodles	

Preparation

THE PRAWNS: Put the prawns in a colander and rinse thoroughly with cold running water.

When the stock has cooked for 20 minutes, throw in the prawns, bring back to the boil, and boil for 1 minute. Immediately remove the pan from the heat and strain its contents through a large sieve into a bowl; reserve the cooking liquor. When the prawns are cool enough to handle, pick them out and shell them. If using Dublin Bay prawns, first twist off the two large claws, then bend and detach the body from the tail section. Using a small sharp knife, or nail scissors, cut a slit the length of the tail on the underside, then peel off the shell and remove the black intestine; reserve the meat separately and keep it covered in a bowl; keep the heads but discard the tail shells. Sometimes the claws are too small to contain much meat but if it is worth it, crack them and extract the meat using the point of a knife, and add to the bowl. If using prawn tails the job is straightforward: peel them, reserving the meat and shells in separate bowls.

To crush the reserved head and body shells, put them through the coarse plate of a mincer, or process for 1 minute in a food processor or blender. Then return the strained stock to the saucepan with the shells, chopped tomatoes and tomato purée. Bring to the boil, then simmer, uncovered, for 20 minutes. Strain the stock, then return it to the saucepan and boil to reduce to 5 fl oz (150 ml); reserve in a measuring jug.

THE PASTRY CASE: Roll the pastry out to a round about 12 in (30 cm) in diameter and line the tart tin. Push the pastry gently into the flutes with a floured finger, then trim off the excess pastry around the rim. Prick the base well with a fork and chill for 20 minutes.

Meanwhile, pre-heat the oven to gas mark 5, 375°F (190°C), and put a baking tray in the oven to heat. Line the pastry case with a circle of silicone paper and fill it with an even layer of baking beans. Transfer the tin to the baking tray in the oven, and bake the pastry case for 10 minutes.

Remove the tart tin from the oven and take out the paper and beans; leave the baking tray in the oven. Reduce the temperature to gas mark 4, 350°F (180°C).

To assemble the tart

Soak the Chinese noodles in boiling water for 4 minutes (or follow the cooking instructions on the packet). Drain, then dry on absorbent paper; spread the noodles in the pastry case.

Halve the prawn tails lengthways; arrange the tails in a rosette on top of the noodles, with the claw meat, if you have it, in the centre.

Add the cream and the eggs to the reduced stock; whisk lightly to mix, then taste, and season with salt, if necessary, and a pinch of cayenne pepper.

To bake

Put the tart back on the baking tray in the oven and carefully pour in the cream and egg mix. Bake it for 35 to 40 minutes, until it is slightly puffed and set in the centre.

To serve

Remove from the oven and serve warm, garnished with sprigs of parsley.

Opposite: My quiche

Overleaf: Escalopes of salmon with turned vegetables (see page 146)

DESSERTS

The dessert has often been described as the crowning glory of a meal. Here, we show you how to make a whole selection of desserts, ranging from the simple to the elaborate, but all worthy of being the culmination of a marvellous meal. In this chapter, which covers hot and cold desserts and baking, we have included some classic French favourites as well as some new recipes which we created specially for the television series and this book.

Originally, we both trained as *pâtissiers* and that is still Michel's first love, perhaps because he has a sweet tooth. Although in France it is considered derogatory to call a *pâtissier* a baker, we both admit that there is something electrifying about working with flour. It is a commodity that is taken for granted, yet it is so precious. Without it there would be no bread, no pastry, no brioches or mille-feuilles, no gougère or blinis.

This chapter also contains some recipes that remind us of our childhood in France. Our mother believed that if you were happy with your food you were happy with life, however humble your home. Certainly her pancakes and waffles kept us very happy with life! It was our mother who first made us realise what cooking was all about. Cooking is international; it requires no passports. There are no language barriers when it comes to eating and appreciating good food: it is to do with love.

Please do not be intimidated by the number of ingredients or the length of the instructions in the recipes; just follow them through and we promise you will be delighted by the results. So will your guests!

•

Opposite: Iced strawberry soufflé (see page 188)

Previous page, top: Tarte Tatin (see page 206); below left: Soft cheese hearts with red fruit (see page 175); below right: Raspberry and orange shortbread (see page 179)

BASIC DESSERT PREPARATIONS

This section includes those recipes which are absolutely fundamental to our dessert-making: several pastries, two different types of meringue, a basic sorbet syrup, and some sauces which will make any dessert really special.

•

SHORTCRUST PASTRY
(Pâte brisée)

The most fundamental pastry of all; if you succeed with this pastry and no other, you will be able to get by: it is the pastry most commonly used as container for all manner of fillings.

Makes 1 lb (450 g)

•

9 oz (250 g) plain white flour	*A pinch of sugar*
5½ oz (165 g) butter, slightly softened, cut into small pieces	*¾ teaspoon salt*
	1 tablespoon cold milk
1 egg	

Preparation

Sieve the flour on to a work surface and make a well in the centre. Put the butter pieces in the well with the egg, the sugar and the salt. Using the fingertips of your right hand, rub together the egg, sugar and salt, then use the left hand to sweep in a little flour at a time. Use the right hand to rub the flour into the fat mixture. When the ingredients have almost come together, add the milk and lightly press the mix together to form a dough. Using the palm of your hand, knead the dough for 2 or 3 turns to combine smoothly. Form into a ball, put into a plastic bag, and refrigerate for several hours before using.

The dough will keep successfully in a plastic bag in the refrigerator for a few days, or in the freezer for several weeks.

SHORTBREAD DOUGH
(Pâte sablée)

 A dough that gives a buttery, rather crunchy texture when baked. It is ideal for small biscuits (*petits fours*), to serve with ice-creams, sorbets, cream and fruit desserts, and coffee. To make biscuits, roll the dough out to $\frac{1}{8}$ to $\frac{1}{4}$ in (3 to 5 mm) thick, cut into different shapes and bake at gas mark 2, 300°F (150°C) until pale golden.

Makes about $1\frac{1}{2}$ lb (750 g)

•

9 oz (250 g) plain white flour	*A pinch of salt*
7 oz (200 g) butter, at room temperature, cut into small pieces	*2 egg yolks*
	1 drop of vanilla or lemon essence (optional)
$3\frac{1}{2}$ oz (90 g) icing sugar, sifted	

Preparation

Sieve the flour on to a work surface and make a well in the centre. Put the butter pieces in the well, then work with your fingertips until it is very soft and creamy. Add the sifted icing sugar and the salt and work this into the butter. Add the egg yolks to the butter mixture and when they are thoroughly mixed in, begin to incorporate the flour. Work the mix as little as possible and stop as soon as you have a smooth dough. If you are using vanilla or lemon essence, add this at the final stage of mixing, rubbing it into the dough with the palm of your hand.

Put the dough in a plastic bag, and chill it for 2 hours before use. When you roll out the dough, work quickly – at room temperature it soon becomes soft and difficult to handle.

To store

The dough will keep in a plastic bag in the refrigerator for a few days, and also freezes successfully for several weeks.

FLAN PASTRY

(Pâte à foncer)

This is a classic lining for tarts and flans. A little less crumbly than traditional shortcrust pastry, it will add an extra touch of elegance to your baking.

Makes about 14 oz (400 g)

•

9 oz (250 g) plain white flour	*1½ teaspoons caster sugar*
4 oz (100 g) butter, softened	*¾ teaspoon salt*
1 egg	

Preparation

Follow the method for making shortcrust pastry (see page 162) to the stage when the egg, sugar and salt have been incorporated with the flour but the mixture is still rather crumbly. Now add 2 fl oz (50 ml) water and gradually mix together to form a dough. Using the palm of your hand, knead the dough for 2 or 3 turns to combine smoothly. Form into a ball, put into a plastic bag and refrigerate for several hours before using.

To store

The pastry will keep for several days if stored in a plastic bag in the refrigerator, or for several weeks if frozen.

•

CLASSIC PUFF PASTRY

(Feuilletage classique)

Your efforts to make your own puff pastry will find their reward in its irresistibly rich, buttery flavour; no shop-bought product is half as good. If you plan to make the pastry some time before using it, give it only 4 turns before chilling or freezing, then the final 2 turns just before you use it.

Makes about 2 lb (1 kg)

•

1¼ lb (500 g) plain white flour	*1¾ teaspoons salt*
1 fl oz (25 ml) white wine vinegar	*Additional flour for rolling out*
2 oz (50 g) butter, melted	*14 oz (400 g) block of butter, thoroughly chilled*

Preparation

Sift the flour on to a work surface and make a well in the centre. Pour in 7 fl oz (200 ml) cold water, the white wine vinegar, the melted butter and the salt. Use the fingertips of your right hand to work the ingredients together, while using the left to sweep in the flour little by little. When the ingredients are thoroughly combined, use the palm of your hand to knead the mixture to a smooth dough. Form it into a ball and cut a cross in the top (this breaks the elasticity in the dough). Put into a plastic bag and chill in the refrigerator for 2 to 3 hours.

Lightly dust the work surface with a little flour. Shape the dough to a rectangle and using a rolling pin roll out each corner, leaving a raised central area of dough. Use the rolling pin to lightly beat the chilled butter into a slightly flattened rectangle and place it on top of the raised dough. The butter should cover this area with no overhang. Now fold the 4 rolled-out portions inwards so that the butter is wrapped in an envelope of dough. Put the butter parcel into a plastic bag and chill for 30 minutes before going on to the next stage.

Lightly dust the work surface with flour again. Then roll the dough out to a 27 × 16 in (70 × 40 cm) rectangle. Use a pastry brush to flick off the excess flour and fold the rectangle 3 times – the bottom third folded over the central third, and the top third brought down to cover the bottom third. This is the first turn. Give the dough a quarter turn to the right, so the pastry fold is on your left. Then roll out the dough to the same size rectangle and, again, fold into 3. This is the second turn. The pastry now needs to be put into the plastic bag and chilled for a further 30 minutes. Make 2 more turns, as before, and chill again for 1 hour. Finally, give the pastry 2 more turns, making a total of 6. It is now ready to use.

Note: having cut the pastry into the required shape, e.g. palmiers, vol-au-vents, fleurons etc., put on a dampened baking tray and chill for a minimum of 30 minutes before baking; this will help minimise any shrinkage or distortion. Bake puff pastry in a hot oven, gas mark 7 to 9, 425° to 475°F (220° to 240°C).

To store

Stored in a plastic bag in the refrigerator the dough will keep for up to 3 days, or it can be frozen for several weeks.

SWEET SHORTCRUST PASTRY
(Pâte sucrée)

This is a well-behaved pastry – easier to prepare than the richer shortbread dough. Its more robust qualities make it good for tarts and sweet pies in general, and ideal for anything which has to be transported.

Makes about 1¼ lb (500 g)

•

9 oz (250 g) plain white flour	*4 oz (100 g) icing sugar, sifted*
4 oz (100 g) butter, at room temperature, cut into small pieces	*A pinch of salt*
	2 eggs

Preparation

Sieve the flour on to a work surface and make a well in the centre. Put the butter pieces into the well and work them with your fingertips until they form a soft mass. Pour the sifted icing sugar on top and add the salt; work thoroughly into the butter. Break the eggs on to the butter and work them in also. Now gradually incorporate the flour into the butter mixture, still using the fingertips, until the ingredients come together to form a dough. Knead the dough for 2 or 3 turns to combine smoothly. Form into a ball, put into a plastic bag and refrigerate for several hours before using.

To store

The dough keeps happily in a plastic bag in the refrigerator for several days, or in the freezer for several weeks.

QUICK PUFF PASTRY
(Feuilletage minute)

 This is a very simple and quickly made version of puff pastry. The rise will be some 30 per cent less than with the classic type, and it will not keep as long. Nonetheless, it is a very useful pastry, as you will find if you try it for dishes such as Potato pie (see page 71), Le Poulbot pasties (see page 66) or *Tarte Tatin* (see page 206). It is worth noting that, as always with pastry, the temperature of the butter is important. Here, it needs to be firm but not hard, so remember to remove some butter from the refrigerator about 2 hours before making the pastry.

Makes about $2\frac{3}{4}$ lb (1.25 kg)

•

$1\frac{1}{4}$ lb (500 g) plain white flour	1 teaspoon salt
$1\frac{1}{4}$ lb (500 g) butter, cut into small cubes	9 fl oz (275 ml) ice-cold water
	Additional flour for rolling out

Preparation

Sift the flour on to a work surface and make a well in the centre. Put the butter cubes in the well and sprinkle in the salt. Use the fingertips of your right hand to work the ingredients, combining them, while you gradually sweep in the flour with your left hand. When the butter is mostly in flakes and the rest of the mixture is looking grainy, pour in the water. Work the water into the pastry, but stop as soon as the mixture comes together to form a dough – do not knead it. The dough should still retain flakes of butter here and there.

Lightly dust the work surface with a little flour and roll the dough away from you into a 16 ×8 in (40 ×20 cm) rectangle. Fold into 3 and proceed as for Classic puff pastry (page 164) to the point where you have given the pastry 2 turns. Put into a plastic bag and transfer to the refrigerator for 20 minutes. Give the pastry a further 2 turns, then use as required.

To bake

Roll the dough out into the required shapes, put it on a dampened baking tray and chill it for 20 minutes before baking. Bake in a hot oven, gas mark 7 to 9, 425° to 475°F (220° to 240°C).

To store

This dough will keep for 2 days in a plastic bag in the refrigerator, or 3 weeks in the freezer.

FRENCH MERINGUE

(Meringue française)

A very delicate, melting meringue, excellent as an accompaniment to fresh fruit salads, sorbets or ice-creams. If you prefer a very pale golden meringue with a slight flavour of caramelised sugar bake at gas mark 3, 325°F (160°C) for about $1\frac{1}{4}$ hours only. However, even when using the very lowest temperature, keep an eye on them. Domestic ovens are often inaccurate at low temperatures, and it may be that the meringues are better baked with the oven door slightly open.

4 egg whites	*4 oz (100 g) icing sugar, sifted*
4 oz (100 g) caster sugar	

Preparation

Pre-heat the oven to gas mark $\frac{1}{2}$, 250°F (120°C). Line 2 large baking trays with silicone or greaseproof paper. If you use greaseproof paper, brush it with melted butter, then dust it with flour.

In a clean bowl, whisk the egg whites until they form soft peaks. Gradually whisk in the caster sugar, about a tablespoon at a time, whisking well between additions. When all the caster sugar has been incorporated, continue whisking steadily for 10 minutes. By this time the meringue will be very firm, dense and glossy, and the mixture will be stiff enough to hold needle-sharp points. With a large metal spoon, fold in the sifted icing sugar a little at a time, using the minimum number of strokes needed to incorporate the sugar, in order to keep the meringue as stiff as possible. Use immediately as required in a large piping bag fitted with the appropriate piping tube; or use 2 tablespoons to shape the meringues into ovals and place on the prepared baking trays.

To cook

Put into the oven and lower the temperature to gas mark $\frac{1}{4}$, 225°F (110°C). Bake for about $1\frac{3}{4}$ hours, until the meringues are crisp and dry – check on the underside, in the centre. Cool on a wire rack.

To store

Store in an airtight container. They will keep for up to 2 weeks.

ITALIAN MERINGUE
(Meringue italienne)

Italian meringue is made by pouring sugar syrup *of the correct temperature* on to beaten egg whites. It is foolproof – provided the sugar syrup is at the right temperature; so a sugar thermometer is an essential. The meringue is never cooked on its own but it is used as an ingredient in other dishes. It can be used to lighten iced soufflés, as in Iced strawberry soufflé (see page 188), and is useful for folding into *crème pâtissière* (see page 171) and whipped cream, because it gives a lighter, smoother texture than plain sugar. The liquid glucose in the recipe is optional, but a very useful addition: it stops crystals forming in the sugar syrup and around the edge of the bowl. It is readily available from chemist's shops.

This type of meringue cannot be made successfully in smaller quantities than those given here.

6 egg whites	*1 fl oz (25 ml) liquid glucose (optional)*
12 oz (350 g) caster sugar	

Preparation

Have the egg whites ready in a large grease-free mixer bowl. In a small thick-based saucepan combine 3 fl oz (85 ml) water with the sugar and the glucose (if used). Start to heat the sugar gently so the crystals dissolve before the syrup boils. Once the sugar has dissolved, skim off any foam on the surface. Using a pastry brush dipped in cold water, brush down the sides of the pan to remove any sugar crystals. Insert a warmed sugar thermometer, and bring to the boil. Boil rapidly, continuing to wash down the sides of the pan.

When the temperature of the syrup reaches 230°F (110°C), beat the egg whites in an electric mixer until stiff. As soon as the sugar syrup reaches 250°F (121°C) remove the saucepan from the heat. Set the mixer at low speed. Pour the sugar syrup on to the egg whites in a thin stream, away from the beater. Continue to beat for about 15 minutes, until the meringue is cold. The meringue is now ready to use.

To store

The raw meringue can be stored in an airtight container in the refrigerator for several days.

SORBET SYRUP

This syrup provides a basis for sorbets, or it can be used to poach fruits, e.g. the pears in Pear clafoutis (see page 213). Stored, covered, in the refrigerator, the syrup keeps for up to 2 weeks. Liquid glucose is readily available at any chemist's shop.

Makes 2½ pints (1.5 litres)

•

1½ lb (750 g) sugar	*3½ fl oz (100 ml) liquid glucose*

Preparation

Put the sugar and glucose in a saucepan with 22 fl oz (650 ml) water. Cook gently, stirring often, until all the sugar has dissolved. Then stop stirring, bring the syrup to the boil, and boil for 3 minutes. Pour through a fine metal sieve into a bowl and leave until cold before using.

•

FRUIT SAUCE
(Coulis de fruit)

This kind of sauce can be served with a wide variety of tarts, ices, mousses and cakes, and also with other fruits. The choice of fruit can either complement or contrast with the dessert, but we recommend you use only one type of fruit at a time. Allow a minimum of 4 fl oz (120 ml) sauce per person.

Makes 1¾ pints (1 litre)

•

1½ lb (750 g) fresh fruit (e.g. apricots, peaches, pineapple, redcurrants, raspberries or strawberries)	*8 fl oz (250 ml) sorbet syrup (see above)*
	Juice of 1 lemon

Preparation

Prepare the fruit, washing and draining it if necessary, then peeling, coring, or hulling as required.

In a food processor or blender, purée the fruit with the syrup and the lemon juice. Rub the purée through a sieve, then chill it in the refrigerator until you are ready to serve it.

To store

Fruit purées freeze well, but you do need to beat them well once they have thawed, to regain a smooth consistency.

•

CRÈME PÂTISSIÈRE

Without *crème pâtissière* there would be little or no *pâtisserie*. So it is well worth learning to make it properly. It is not difficult, but it is important to get it just right. One common mistake is failing to cook it thoroughly, for the full 2 minutes; and then a taste of raw flour remains. Don't assume that, because a sauce has thickened, the flour is cooked. Curiously, the sauce will thicken, then thin very slightly, and it is this thinning that indicates that the flour is completely cooked.

Makes about 1½ lb (750 g)

•

6 egg yolks	*18 fl oz (500 ml) milk*
4½ oz (120 g) caster sugar	*1 vanilla pod, split*
1½ oz (40 g) plain white flour, sifted	*A little butter or icing sugar*

Preparation

In a bowl, whisk the egg yolks with about 1 oz (25 g) of the sugar, until the mixture is thick and mousse-like. Add the sifted flour and mix it in smoothly.

In a saucepan, bring the milk, the remaining sugar and the vanilla pod to the boil. Remove the vanilla pod and pour about a third of the boiling milk on to the egg yolk mixture, whisking as you do so. Return this to the rest of the milk in the pan and, stirring all the time, bring to the boil over a gentle heat. Simmer for 2 minutes, then remove the pan from the heat. To prevent a skin forming on the cooling custard, dot the surface with butter or dust it with icing sugar. Use immediately, or store, covered, in the refrigerator for up to 24 hours.

Alternative flavourings

COFFEE: Omit the vanilla pod and add 2 tablespoons of instant coffee (or a little more or less, according to how strong you want it), to the milk and sugar mixture, before you bring it to the boil.

CHOCOLATE: Mix 2 tablespoons of sifted cocoa powder into the eggs with the flour. Omit the vanilla pod, and add a little extra sugar – up to 1 oz (25 g) – to the milk.

•

CRÈME CHANTILLY

A sweetened cream that can be served as it is with desserts, or folded into sauces such as *crème pâtissière* (see page 171) to lighten and enrich them. Notice that the lighter whipping cream is used, rather than double cream. If you only have double cream, thin it by adding 3 fl oz (85 ml) very cold milk. The cream will then be very light, but still firm enough to hold its shape.

Makes about 1¼ lb (500 g)

•

18 fl oz (500 ml) whipping cream, thoroughly chilled	*Vanilla essence*
2 fl oz (50 ml) sorbet syrup (see page 170), chilled, or 2 oz (50 g) icing sugar, sifted	*(optional)*

Preparation

Have ready a well-chilled mixing bowl and whisk. If you intend to use a free-standing electric mixer, chill the bowl.

Pour the chilled cream into the bowl and add the sorbet syrup or the sifted icing sugar. Add the vanilla, if used. Whisk until the cream begins to thicken. If you are using an electric mixer, beat at a moderate speed for 1 or 2 minutes, then increase the speed and beat for a further 3 or 4 minutes, until the cream is beginning to thicken. Do not over-beat, or the cream will become too dense, or might even become buttery. Use immediately, or store in the refrigerator for up to 24 hours.

Alternative flavourings

COFFEE: Dissolve 2 tablespoons instant coffee in 1 tablespoon hot milk. Leave to become cold before beating into the *crème chantilly*.

CHOCOLATE: Gently melt 5 oz (150 g) plain dark chocolate in a heatproof bowl set over a pan of hot water. When the chocolate has melted, remove it from the heat and leave it to cool for a few minutes; then beat in a third of the *crème chantilly*. Being as light-handed as possible, fold in the remaining cream. Alternatively, you can fold in 2 tablespoons of sifted cocoa powder just as the cream starts to thicken.

·

CRÈME ANGLAISE

 A remarkably useful and adaptable sauce, both in its own right and as a basis for many desserts, sweets and ice-creams. As little as eight egg yolks can be used if a less rich sauce is preferred, but don't use less than this.

Note: vanilla pods are becoming very expensive so make sure you get the maximum use out of them. Keep several pods buried in your storage containers of caster sugar, then the aroma and flavour taken on by the sugar can be carried through to your baking. When a vanilla pod is used to infuse milk, retrieve it, rinse well, dry and restore to the sugar jar once more. In this way a pod can be used several times over.

Makes 2½ pints (1.5 litres)

·

12 egg yolks	1¾ pints (1 litre) milk
9 oz (250 g) caster sugar	1 vanilla pod, split

Preparation and cooking

In a bowl, combine the egg yolks with 3 oz (75 g) of the caster sugar. Whisk until the mixture is thick and mousse-like.

In a saucepan combine the milk with the remaining sugar and the vanilla pod; bring to the boil. Pour the boiling milk on to the egg mixture, whisking constantly. Pour the mixture back into the pan and return to a low heat to cook, stirring continuously with a wooden spoon until the custard is thick enough to coat the back of the spoon. Do not allow the mixture to boil, or the egg yolks will cook and the texture will be ruined. But if you do let the custard get too hot, immediately remove the pan from the heat and transfer it to sit in cold water; beat vigorously and you may manage to save the sauce.

If you would rather take a slower, safer course, cook the custard in the top of a double saucepan or in a heatproof bowl set over a pan of simmering water. Using this method, the sauce will take about 20 minutes to thicken.

To serve

Strain the custard and serve hot or chilled. The custard will keep well in the refrigerator for 2 to 3 days. Strain again before serving.

•

CHOCOLATE SAUCE
(Sauce chocolat)

 Serve hot or cold with Banana ice-cream (see page 193), Warm pear soufflés (see page 208) or slices of toasted brioche (see page 215).

Makes about 10 fl oz (300 ml)

•

7 oz (200 g) plain dark bitter chocolate	*1 oz (25 g) sugar*
5 fl oz (150 ml) milk	*1 oz (25 g) butter*
2 tablespoons double cream	

Preparation

Gently melt the chocolate in a bowl set over a pan of hot water.

In a separate pan, combine the milk, the cream and the sugar, and bring to the boil, stirring constantly with a wire whisk. Whisking all the time, pour this mixture on to the melted chocolate. Return the sauce to the pan, set it over direct heat and boil for 15 seconds. Remove the pan from the heat and whisk in the butter bit by bit, until the sauce has a uniform consistency throughout. Pour through a sieve into a warmed bowl. Serve hot or cold.

To store

The sauce will keep, covered, in the refrigerator for up to 3 days.

COLD DESSERTS

The advantages of a cold dessert are obvious. You can give the dessert your undivided attention at a time that suits you. The preparation can be done earlier in the day, or on the day before, when you are calm, not under pressure, instead of at the last moment, when everything is happening at once. You can taste as you go along, and if something turns out to be a disaster you will have time to adapt or replace it. You have time, too, to give special care to the presentation. Then, on the night, with one thing less to worry about, you can relax and enjoy the company of your guests, secure in the knowledge that a wonderful dessert is ready for the end of the meal.

·

SOFT CHEESE HEARTS WITH RED FRUIT

(Cœurs de fromage blanc aux fruits rouges)

It is easy to make your own *fromage blanc*, using a blender or food processor. Combine equal quantities of cottage cheese and plain yoghurt, add a little lemon juice, and blend until very smooth.

Serves 4
You will need 4 heart-shaped pierced cœurs à la crème *moulds.*

·

12 oz (350 g) fromage blanc or *curd cheese, drained (choose whichever fat content you prefer)*	*16 dessert gooseberries, topped and tailed*
	4 stalks of redcurrants
4 fl oz (120 ml) double cream (optional)	*4 stalks of white currants (if obtainable)*
12 cultivated strawberries, hulled	*1 egg white (optional)*
12 wild strawberries, hulled	*Caster sugar (optional)*

Preparation

Beat the *fromage blanc* or curd cheese in a bowl until it is smooth. If you want to make the consistency a little richer, add a little fresh cream.

Line the insides of the moulds with slightly dampened muslin, leaving enough cloth to fold over the top of the cheese. Spoon the cheese into the moulds. Get rid of any air by tapping the moulds gently to settle the cheese well into the moulds. Chill in the refrigerator for not less than 2 hours, or up to 24 hours.

To serve

Unwrap the muslin; put a plate on top of each mould and invert it. Lift off the mould and carefully take off the muslin. If you like, spoon some cream on to the surfaces of the little hearts. Arrange the fruit around each heart. If you suspect any of the fruits might be a little sharp, then lightly beat an egg white and dip the fruit briefly, first in the egg white then in caster sugar. Do this just before serving. Serve very cold.

•

RICE TART
(Tarte au riz)

A good family dessert, best served at room temperature, accompanied by an ice-cold mint-flavoured *crème anglaise* (see page 173) made with fresh mint infused in the milk. Do not on any account throw away the syrup you use for poaching the fruit; make it up to its original volume with cold water, and use it to make a sorbet – pear syrup makes a wonderful basis for Cider sorbet (see page 201), and raspberry syrup is of course excellent for a Raspberry sorbet (see page 198).

Serves 8
You will need a flan tin 8½ in (22 cm) in diameter and 1 in (2.5 cm) deep, preferably with a removable base.

•

½ oz (15 g) softened butter	*Vanilla pod, split*
8 oz (225 g) sweet shortcrust pastry (see page 166)	*6 tablespoons double cream*
1 egg yolk, beaten with ½ teaspoon milk	*1¼ to 1½ lb (500 to 750 g) pears or fresh raspberries*
4 oz (100 g) pudding rice	*1 quantity sorbet syrup (see page 170)*
1 pint (600 ml) milk	*2 oz (50 g) caster sugar, for topping*
2 oz (50 g) sugar	

Preparation and cooking

Pre-heat the oven to gas mark 6, 400°F (200°C). Brush the flan tin with softened butter.

THE PASTRY: On a lightly floured surface, roll out the shortcrust pastry to a thickness of about $\frac{1}{8}$ in (3 mm) and use it to line the tart tin. Ease the pastry into the flutes, then trim off the excess level with the tin. Use your thumb and forefinger to crimp the edges attractively, then prick the base well with a fork and refrigerate for 30 minutes. Line the pastry with a circle of greaseproof paper and fill with baking beans. Put on a baking tray and bake in the centre of the oven for 10 minutes. Remove from the oven and carefully take out the baking beans and paper. Return to the oven to bake for a further 5 minutes. Remove again, brush the inside base of the pastry with the beaten egg yolk, and replace in the oven to bake for a final 5 minutes. Remove and leave to cool.

THE FILLING: Put the rice, milk, sugar and vanilla pod together in a saucepan. Cover, and cook gently for about 45 minutes, stirring from time to time, especially towards the end of cooking. The best way to cook this rice is over a heat diffuser mat – then it will cook without any danger of catching on the base of the pan. When cooked the rice should have absorbed all the milk, and should be soft. Remove the vanilla pod and stir in the cream. Cover and leave in a warm place.

Pre-heat the grill.

If you are using pears, peel, halve and core them. Heat the syrup to simmering point, add the pears and poach them for about 10 minutes, until tender; the time they take to cook depends on the degree of ripeness. Drain, dry thoroughly and slice thinly. Arrange in the base of the tart shell.

If you are using raspberries, hull them. Bring the syrup to the boil. Put a small batch of raspberries at a time into a large sieve, plunge them into the syrup for 30 seconds and remove. Drain thoroughly and gently arrange them in the base of the pastry-lined tin. Carefully spoon in the still-warm rice, bringing it right up to the level of the pastry edge. Smooth over with a palette knife.

THE TOPPING: Sprinkle evenly with the sugar, then cover the pastry edge of the tart with foil to protect it. Cook under the grill until the sugar is browned to a deep caramel (but be careful not to let it get too dark, or the flavour will be bitter). Remove from the grill and leave to cool to room temperature.

CHERRY TART

(Tarte aux cerises)

 This wonderful tart is well worth the time spent on stoning the cherries. Serve it as a colourful summer dessert after a family meal or a dinner with friends.

Serves 6
You will need a loose-bottomed flan tin, top measurement $8\frac{1}{2}$ in (22 cm) in diameter.

•

10 oz (275 g) made flan pastry (see page 164)	5 oz (150 g) crème pâtissière (see page 171)
$1\frac{1}{2}$ lb (750 g) fresh red cherries	2 oz (50 g) redcurrant jelly
1 oz (25 g) sugar	

Preparation

Pre-heat the oven to gas mark 7, 425°F (220°C). Grease the flan tin.

THE PASTRY: Roll the pastry out to about $\frac{1}{8}$ in (3 mm) thick and line the tin with it. You will have a small amount of pastry left over. Trim the pastry level with the edge of the tin, then crimp the edge with your thumb and forefinger; leave to rest in the refrigerator for about 20 minutes.

THE CHERRIES: Meanwhile, prepare the cherries. Remove any stalks, and stone the cherries. There is no need to buy a special gadget for this job, just use a small piece of wire bent back at one end to form a loop; this will enable you to take the stones out without cutting the fruit entirely open. Place the stoned cherries in a heatproof dish and sprinkle with sugar.

To cook

Cook the cherries in the oven for about 5 minutes, until the juices flow. Take them from the oven, and drain them in a colander set over a bowl to catch the juices; reserve the juices.

Put a baking sheet in the oven to heat.

Fill the pastry base with the *crème pâtissière*, and arrange the cherries on top in a neat pattern, so that the cream is closely covered. Transfer the tart to the baking sheet in the oven and bake for 40 minutes. When the tart is baked, remove it from the oven and leave it in the tin for 10 minutes, then push the loose base up to remove the flan from the tin, and slide it, still on the base, on to a wire rack.

To glaze

To glaze the tart, heat the redcurrant jelly in a saucepan until it begins to boil. Add the reserved cherry juice, and brush the cherries with the glaze.

To serve

The tart should be served at room temperature, never chilled.

•

RASPBERRY & ORANGE SHORTBREAD

(Sablé aux framboises au confit d'oranges)

 A perfect combination of sweet, crumbly shortbread and soft, sharp fruit. Have each part prepared, then, *just* before serving, assemble. Any delay will mean the shortbread will be softened by the sauce, and the marvellous balance will be upset.

Serves 6

•

1 orange	*1 pint (600 ml) fruit sauce (see page 170), chilled*
1 oz (25 g) caster sugar	*1½ lb (750 g) prepared fresh raspberries*
1½ lb (750 g) shortbread dough (see page 163)	*1 oz (25 g) icing sugar*
A little flour for rolling out	

Preparation

Pre-heat the oven to gas mark 7, 425°F (220°C).

Wash the orange and, using a potato peeler, peel off the zest, taking care to leave behind any bitter white pith. Slice the zest into fine hair-like strips. Pour about 10 fl oz (300 ml) water into a small saucepan and add the strips of orange zest. Bring to a full boil, remove the pan from the heat and drain the strips into a sieve. Refresh under cold running water, then return the strips to the pan together with the sugar and 5 fl oz (150 ml) water. Bring to the boil, then simmer gently for 8 to 10 minutes. Remove the pan from the heat and pour the contents into a sieve set over a small bowl. Tease out the candied strips of peel with a fork, so they do not stick together. Reserve the candied peel strips; in this recipe you will not need any of the syrup drained from the zest, or any of the rest of the orange.

To prepare the pastry, start by dividing the dough in half; the pastry will be easier to manage in these smaller quantities. Lightly dust the work surface with a little flour and roll out one piece of pastry to $\frac{1}{10}$ in (2 mm) thick. Using a fluted pastry cutter, cut out 9×4 in (10 cm) rounds and arrange them carefully on a baking tray. Repeat this procedure with the remaining piece of pastry, so you have a total of 18×4 in (10 cm) rounds. Bake for 8 minutes, until pale golden. Use a palette knife to transfer them to a wire rack; leave to cool.

Before serving, pour two-thirds of the chilled fruit sauce into a bowl. Reserve 6 perfect raspberries for decoration, then add the remainder to the sauce. Gently rotate the bowl to coat them in the sauce; chill briefly.

To serve

Put a pastry base on each of 6 plates. Using 2 forks, lift the raspberries from the sauce, drain them briefly, and arrange some on each pastry base. Put another circle of pastry on top, then more raspberries on top of that. Sieve a generous layer of icing sugar over the remaining biscuits and put one on top of each dessert. Place one of the reserved raspberries in the centre of each of the top biscuits and delicately arrange some candied orange peel around it. You can either serve the remaining sauce separately, in a sauce boat, or spoon a little around each pastry.

ORANGE CHARLOTTE FLAVOURED WITH GRAND MARNIER

(Charlotte à l'orange au Grand Marnier)

 A recipe that may introduce you to making your own sponge biscuit, which, of course, will be much better than any you can buy! Do not be disconcerted by the rather unusual ingredient, potato flour. If this is not available, cornflour is an acceptable substitute. The recipe also suggests an orange jelly topping, but if you prefer, you can make a simple glaze by sieving orange jam and warming it with a little water to thin it down. Allow it to cool, then brush it over the top of the charlotte.

Makes 8 portions
You will need a 9 × 13 in (23 × 33 cm) Swiss roll tin; and a metal pastry ring 9½ in (24 cm) in diameter.

•

For the sponge biscuit:	For the charlotte:
Melted butter	*13 fl oz (375 ml) milk*
A little flour	*5 egg yolks*
4 eggs, separated	*4 oz (100 g) sugar*
1½ oz (40 g) plus 1 teaspoon caster sugar	*1 tablespoon gelatine granules*
2 egg whites	*3 fl oz (85 ml) Grand Marnier*
¾ oz (20 g) plain white flour, sifted	*10 fl oz (300 ml) double cream*
¾ oz (20 g) potato flour	To decorate:
3 oz (75 g) sieved raspberry jam	*4 large oranges*
For the orange syrup:	*2 oz (50 g) sugar*
1 tablespoon Grand Marnier	*2 fl oz (50 ml) Grand Marnier*
2 tablespoons sorbet syrup (see page 170)	*2 teaspoons gelatine granules*

Preparation and cooking

Pre-heat the oven to gas mark 7, 425°F (220°C). Line the Swiss roll tin with greaseproof paper, brush the paper with melted butter and dust with flour. Position the pastry ring on a thin cake board or flat serving plate.

THE SPONGE BISCUIT: Put the egg yolks and 1 oz (25 g) plus 1
teaspoon caster sugar in a bowl and whisk until you can trail a ribbon of the mix
across the surface. In a separate bowl, using a clean whisk, beat the 6 egg whites until
they form soft peaks. Whisk in the remaining caster sugar and whisk until the egg
whites form firm peaks. Using a slotted spoon, fold one-third of the egg whites into
the whisked egg yolks, then use a plastic spatula to fold in the remaining whites, the
sifted plain white flour and the potato flour. To retain air and lightness, mix only as
much as is absolutely necessary. Use a palette knife to spread the sponge mix evenly
in the prepared Swiss roll tin. Transfer to the oven and bake for about 5 minutes,
until the sponge biscuit is pale golden. Turn it out on to a wire rack and carefully
strip off the greaseproof paper before you leave it to cool.

When the sponge biscuit has cooled, put it on a work surface and cut it lengthways
into $6 \times 1\frac{1}{2}$ in (4 cm) wide strips. Gently warm the raspberry jam and spread a little
on one side of each strip of sponge. Then stack the sponge strips on top of one another
in a single pile. Press them together lightly to make sure they stick together, then cut
across into strips $\frac{1}{4}$ in (5 mm) wide. With the aid of the palette knife, transfer them to
the pastry ring, gently pressing each slice on to the side of the ring so the matchsticks
of sponge form an upright band around the edge. The jam will be sufficient to hold
the slices to the pastry ring.

THE ORANGE SYRUP: In a small bowl, combine the Grand Marnier
and the sorbet syrup. Use a pastry brush to dab this mixture on to the sponge biscuit
lining around the edge of the ring.

THE CHARLOTTE: Use the milk, egg yolks and sugar to make a *crème
anglaise* (see page 173). Leave to cool to room temperature. In a small heatproof bowl
combine the gelatine granules and the Grand Marnier and leave for 2 or 3 minutes,
to allow the gelatine to soften. Set the bowl over a small saucepan of simmering water
to warm gently until the mixture has become liquid and clear; cool for a few minutes,
then pour it into the *crème anglaise*.

In a separate bowl, whisk the cream until it will only just hold a shape, and fold
this into the *crème anglaise* also. Pour half this mixture into the sponge-lined pastry
ring and carefully transfer to the refrigerator to set; leave the rest of the mixture at
room temperature until the next stage.

TO DECORATE: Wash and dry all the oranges; set 2 of them aside. Use a
potato peeler to remove strips of zest from the other 2 oranges. Cut the zest into very
fine strips and put them into a small saucepan. Cover them with cold water, bring to
the boil, drain into a sieve, and refresh with cold water. Return the orange strips to
the pan, add the sugar, and cover with cold water. Cook gently until the sugar has
dissolved, then bring to the boil again. Continue to cook until most of the water has
evaporated and only about 1 tablespoon of syrup remains. Pour the contents of the
pan into a small sieve and leave the orange strips to drain.

Segment the 2 oranges as described on page 97, then cut each segment into 3 pieces. Transfer the pieces to absorbent paper to drain.

When the charlotte mixture in the pastry ring is firm, remove it from the refrigerator and lay the pieces of drained orange segment over the surface. Cover with the remaining charlotte mixture, and return to the refrigerator to finish setting.

Squeeze the juice from the remaining 2 oranges and place it in a small saucepan. Cook until reduced by two-thirds, then strain through a muslin-lined sieve into a small heatproof bowl. Add the Grand Marnier and the gelatine and mix. Leave to soften for a few minutes. Put the bowl over a small saucepan of simmering water for the mixture to warm until it becomes liquid and clear. Remove it and leave until cool. When the jelly is just on the point of setting, pour it over the surface of the charlotte mixture. Return to the refrigerator until the jelly has completely set.

To serve

As a final decorative touch, sprinkle the charlotte mixture with the candied orange peel. Carefully run a thin-bladed knife around the inside of the pastry ring to free the sponge, then remove the ring and serve.

∙

WALNUT CAKE
(Gâteau aux noix)

This cake makes a delicious winter dessert. Hazelnut cake made using exactly the same recipe, but substituting hazelnuts for the walnuts, is equally good. To prepare the hazelnuts, toast them in an oven pre-heated to gas mark 3, 325°F (160°C) for about 10 minutes, until the papery skins start to split and flake off. Transfer them to a slightly damp cloth and rub well to remove the majority of the skins. Then chop the nuts finely.

Serves 6 to 8

You will need a sponge tin or flan ring, $8\frac{1}{2}$ in (22 cm) in diameter and $1\frac{1}{2}$ in (4 cm) deep.

∙

2 oz (50 g) butter, for greasing	*$\frac{1}{2}$ teaspoon vanilla essence*
2 oz (50 g) very fine breadcrumbs	*Juice of 1 lemon, strained*
8 eggs, separated	*9 oz (250 g) walnuts, very finely chopped*
9 oz (250 g) icing sugar	

Preparation and cooking

Pre-heat the oven to gas mark 6, 400°F (200°C). Butter the tin or ring, and dust it lightly with half of the breadcrumbs.

Beat the egg yolks with 7 oz (200 g) of the icing sugar in a bowl until the mixture will hold a trail. Using a spatula, fold in the remaining breadcrumbs. Then add the vanilla essence, the lemon juice and the finely chopped nuts. In a separate bowl, beat the egg whites until they reach the soft peak stage. Add the rest of the icing sugar, and whisk until the meringue is dense and glossy. Fold a third of the beaten egg whites into the yolk mixture. Once it is totally incorporated, add the remaining egg white, using the minimum number of strokes so that the air in the mixture is retained. Pour the mixture into the tin or ring and bake in the oven for 55 minutes.

Take the cake from the oven and unmould it on to a wire rack. You will need to give it a 45° turn every 10 minutes or so until it has cooled, to prevent it sticking to the rack.

To serve

Bring the cake to the table whole, dusted lightly with icing sugar and accompanied by ice-cold *crème anglaise* (see page 173).

·

ORANGE CHEESECAKE
(Cheesecake à l'orange)

A simple, well-behaved cheesecake. How it is decorated is a matter of choice, but the sugar-reduced marmalade now on sale in many supermarkets has a piquant, slightly bitter orange flavour that goes very well with the creaminess of the cheesecake. If you do not have a lemon zester, it's worth investing in this most useful piece of kitchen equipment: use it to cut thin strips of zest from the skin of the oranges before segmenting them.

Serves 8
You will need a deep cake tin, 8½ to 9 in (22 to 23 cm) in diameter, with a removable base; or use a spring-form tin of the same dimensions.

·

	To decorate:
8 oz (225 g) shortbread dough (see page 163)	
12 oz (350 g) cream cheese	*6 tablespoons thin-cut orange marmalade, preferably sugar-reduced*
12 oz (350 g) curd cheese	
6 oz (175 g) caster sugar	*Hair-like strips of orange zest, cut as described above*
5 fl oz (150 ml) soured cream	*2 oranges, segmented (see page 97)*
4 eggs	
Grated rind and strained juice of 3 oranges	

Preparation and cooking

Pre-heat the oven to gas mark 2, 300°F (150°C). Butter the cake tin.

On a lightly floured surface, roll out the shortbread dough to a diameter slightly less than that of the tin. Carefully fit the dough into the base of the tin and prick well with a fork. Bake the shortbread for 30 to 35 minutes until it is pale golden and just beginning to firm. Remove from the oven and leave to cool.

Reduce the oven temperature to gas mark 1, 275°F (140°C).

In a large mixing bowl, combine the cream cheese, the curd cheese, the sugar and the soured cream. In a separate bowl, whisk together the eggs until foamy. Pour the eggs through a sieve into the cheese mixture. Stir this in, then add the strained orange juice and the grated rind.

Put the tin containing the shortbread on a baking tray. Pour the cheese mixture into the tin and transfer the tin, on the baking tray, to the centre of the oven. Bake for about $1\frac{1}{2}$ hours, until a thin skewer inserted in the centre comes out clean. Switch off the oven and leave the cheesecake there to cool.

Run a knife carefully around the edge of the cooled cheesecake to free it from the tin, then gently ease the base from the tin. Chill until ready to serve.

To serve

Spread the marmalade evenly over the surface of the cheesecake and decorate with thin strips of orange zest and segments of fresh orange. Chill again lightly before serving.

•

ALMOND MERINGUES WITH PEACHES AND RASPBERRY PURÉE

(Dacquoises aux pêches)

All the components of this dessert can be prepared ahead and quickly assembled just before serving. The dacquoises require a rather unusual size of metal flan ring. You probably will not have this, but don't let that stop you trying the recipe. Simply make a ring of the appropriate diameter and height from a strip of cardboard, seal the ends together with sticky tape and cover the ring with foil. You will find that this home-made substitute will work perfectly well.

Serves 8
You will need a metal ring 2½in (6 cm) in diameter by ½in (1 cm) high, or a cardboard collar of this size,
made as described above.

•

½ oz (15 g) butter, for greasing	Up to 4 oz (100 g) caster sugar
2 lb (1 kg) fresh raspberries, hulled	8 perfectly ripe peaches
1 oz (25 g) plain flour, sifted	Juice of 1 lemon
2½ oz (65 g) icing sugar, sifted	10 fl oz (300 ml) double cream, whipped
2½ oz (65 g) ground almonds	2 oz (50 g) flaked almonds, lightly toasted
4 egg whites	

Preparation and cooking

Pre-heat the oven to gas mark 2, 300°F (150°C), and butter a large baking sheet.

Reserve about 50 whole raspberries for decoration. Purée the rest in a food processor or blender, then pass through a fine sieve into a bowl. Cover and keep on one side.

Sift the flour and the icing sugar into a bowl. Stir in the ground almonds and mix thoroughly so that all the ingredients are evenly combined and no lumps remain.

In a large mixing bowl, start to whisk the egg whites. Once they are foamy, add a pinch of caster sugar. Continue to whisk until they reach the stiff peak stage. Using a large metal spoon, fold in the almond mixture lightly, with a minimum number of strokes, then fold in 2 tablespoons of the raspberry purée (refrigerate the remainder). Dip the flan ring in cold water and place it, wet, on the buttered baking sheet. Immediately fill the ring with some of the egg white mixture, then smooth the top level with a palette knife. Remove the ring by giving a ¼ turn and lifting it straight up. Wash the ring and repeat the process, forming 8 rounds in all.

If you have a matching baking sheet, slip this underneath the one containing the dacquoises (the additional baking sheet will guard against over-browning). Transfer to the oven and bake for 45 minutes. At this stage the dacquoises will be tinged a pinkish pale brown but will still be soft. Remove from the baking sheet with a palette knife and cool on a wire rack.

Meanwhile, peel the peaches. Plunge the peaches first into boiling water for 1 minute, then into cold. Slip off the skins and transfer the peaches to a bowl. Sprinkle them with half the lemon juice, cover and refrigerate.

To serve

When ready to serve, taste the raspberry purée, and add the rest of the lemon juice and sugar to taste. Then add sufficient water to give the sauce a coating consistency; it should not need more than 4 tablespoons. Lightly whip the cream. Arrange a dacquoise base in the centre of each of 8 serving plates and top with a peach. Spoon a little raspbery sauce over each and sprinkle with the flaked almonds. Surround the base of each peach with 6 fresh raspberries and serve with the whipped cream.

PYRAMID OF SNOW EGGS WITH BLACKCURRANT SAUCE

(Pyramide d'œufs, coulis de cassis)

 A variation on Oeufs à la Neige, a great favourite, but made and served in a slightly different way. The meringues are not prepared in milk but piped in ball shapes into $2\frac{1}{2}$ in (6 cm) tartlet tins, and briefly baked. This enables them to keep a better, bolder shape. And instead of caramel, fresh blackcurrant sauce is spooned over the meringues.

Serves 6
•

$\frac{1}{2}$ *quantity* crème anglaise *(see page 173)*	*Juice of 1 lemon*
1 lb (450 g) fresh blackcurrants, stalks removed, well rinsed and drained, or frozen blackcurrants, thawed	*Sugar to taste*
	6 egg whites
5 fl oz (150 ml) sorbet syrup (see page 170)	*6 oz (175 g) caster sugar*

Preparation and cooking

Pre-heat the oven to gas mark 1, 275°F (140°C). Lightly butter 12 tartlet tins. Make the *crème anglaise* and put it in a covered bowl in the refrigerator to chill.

THE SAUCE: Next make the blackcurrant sauce, so this too has time to chill. Put the blackcurrants in a blender or food processor with the syrup and the lemon juice and process until smooth. Strain through a nylon sieve (metal will discolour and taint blackcurrants), into a bowl. Taste the mixture, add additional sugar if you wish, then cover and chill in the refrigerator.

THE MERINGUE: Place the egg whites in a large, very clean bowl. Beat until soft peaks form, then, still beating, gradually add the sugar; continue to beat until the mixture forms stiff peaks.

Using a piping bag on its own, without any nozzle, pipe the meringue into the buttered tartlet tins. Smooth the surface with a palette knife so each ball is nicely rounded, smooth, and even. Cook in the oven for 10 minutes. Have ready a sheet of greased foil or a baking tray; carefully turn out the balls.

To serve

Pour half the chilled *crème anglaise* into a large bowl. Build up a pyramid of the meringue balls in the bowl, then carefully pour in sufficient of the remaining *crème anglaise* to float the balls. Drizzle a little of the blackcurrant sauce over the meringue, and serve, with the remaining blackcurrant sauce in a jug for people to help themselves.

·

ICED STRAWBERRY SOUFFLÉ

(Soufflé glacé aux fraises)

 This dessert can also be prepared in individual ramekins. Follow the method, taking the mixture 1 in (2.5 cm) above the rim of the dish. Freezing time will be about 45 minutes.

Serves 8 to 12
You will need a deep soufflé dish, 7 in (18 cm) in diameter and 4 in (10 cm) deep.

·

$2\frac{1}{2}$ lb (1.3 kg) ripe strawberries	$\frac{2}{3}$ quantity Italian meringue (see page 169)
$12\frac{1}{2}$ oz (360 g) caster sugar	$1\frac{1}{4}$ pints (750 ml) fruit sauce (see page 170), chilled
Juice of 1 lemon	8 extra perfect whole strawberries, for decoration
1 pint (600 ml) double cream, chilled	

Preparation

Encircle the soufflé dish with a triple-thick band of greaseproof paper to stand 3 in (7.5 cm) above the rim; secure in place with string.

Wash, hull and dry the strawberries on absorbent paper. Reserve 7 oz (200 g) of the berries and purée the remainder in a food processor or blender. Strain the purée through a fine sieve, stir in the sugar and lemon juice and chill in the refrigerator for 1 hour.

In a separate bowl, whisk the cream to a soft, floppy consistency, then chill it in the refrigerator also.

Make the Italian meringue according to the recipe on page 169, and whisk it until it is cold.

Using a whisk, fold the chilled cream into the strawberry purée, then fold in a heaped spoonful taken from the measured meringue. Incorporate this with a whisk, then use a rubber spatula to fold in the rest of the meringue. Pour into the prepared soufflé dish so the mixture comes about $1\frac{1}{2}$ in (4 cm) above the rim of the dish. Freeze the soufflé for about 5 hours at a temperature of 5°F (-15°C) at least, until the soufflé is half-frozen.

To serve

Quarter the reserved 7 oz (200 g) of strawberries and fold into half the chilled fruit sauce.

Carefully remove the collar from the half-frozen soufflé and, working as neatly as you can, remove the centre from the chilled soufflé. Fill with the fruit mixture. Replace a little of the soufflé mixture on top and smooth over the surface. Return to the freezer for 15 minutes. Put the soufflé dish on a serving plate and decorate with the extra whole strawberries. Serve immediately with the remaining fruit sauce served separately in a sauce boat.

BEAUMES DE VENISE MOUSSE WITH GREEN GRAPES

(Mousse au vin Beaumes de Venise)

 A very light wine-flavoured mousse. To use a dessert wine like Muscat de Beaumes de Venise may seem a little extravagant, but it gives a wonderful flavour to the mousse.

Serves 6 to 8
•

18 fl oz (500 ml) Muscat de Beaumes de Venise	*1½ oz (40 g) custard powder*
2 teaspoons gelatine granules	*Juice of 1 large lemon*
1 vanilla pod, split	*7 oz (200 g) sugar*
5 eggs	*8 oz (225 g) green grapes, peeled and pipped*
1 egg white	*6 or 8 small fresh mint leaves*

Preparation and cooking

Measure the wine, then take out 2 tablespoons and put in a small heatproof bowl. Stir in the gelatine. Leave to soften for a few minutes, then place over a small saucepan of simmering water and leave to dissolve and become a clear liquid. Pour the rest of the wine into a separate pan, add the vanilla pod and bring to the boil.

Meanwhile, separate the eggs, placing the yolks in one bowl and the 6 egg whites in a large mixer bowl. Beat the custard powder and the lemon juice into the egg yolks. When the wine is boiling, remove the vanilla pod and pour the wine on to the egg yolk mixture, whisking as you do so. Return the mixture to the saucepan and bring to the boil, stirring quickly. Boil gently for 2 minutes, then remove the pan from the heat. Pour into a bowl, stir in the clear gelatine liquid, then place a piece of greaseproof paper directly on top of the custard to prevent a skin forming. Cover and leave aside for a few minutes.

Put the sugar and 5 tablespoons of water into a small saucepan, and heat gently until the sugar has dissolved. Use a pastry brush dipped in cold water to wash down any sugar crystals that may adhere to the side of the pan. Turn up the heat, insert a warmed sugar thermometer and boil rapidly to bring the syrup up to 230°F (110°C). Let the sugar syrup continue to boil while you whisk the egg whites until they are stiff. Keep an eye on the sugar and take the pan from the heat when the temperature reaches 250°F (121°C). Immediately pour the syrup into the egg whites, whisking all the time. Continue to beat until the meringue forms stiff peaks. Using a wire whisk, fold one-third of the meringue into the custard, then use a large metal spoon to fold in the remainder. Finally fold in the grapes, keeping back 6 or 8 for decoration.

To serve

Spoon the mixture into glasses and decorate each portion with a peeled grape and a mint leaf. Chill lightly until ready to serve.

·

ICE-CREAMS AND SORBETS

Ices have a universal appeal for young and old. Commercial products vary greatly, but when you are making ices at home – be they popsicles or champagne sorbets, ice-cream cornets or *petits vacherins glacés aux pistils de safran* (see page 203) – you should never compromise on quality. The fruits, creams, eggs and liqueurs that are used should be the freshest and the best. And the ices need to be eaten when they are freshly made as well, if they are to be enjoyed at their most delicious.

When making a custard-based ice-cream using an infusion such as cinnamon or mint, you should always, if you possibly can, make the custard a day ahead, so that it has 24 hours in the refrigerator to allow the flavour to develop and mature.

All the ices in this section have been tested in a middle-of-the-range ice-cream maker, with a 15 fl oz to $1\frac{3}{4}$ pint (450 ml to 1 litre) capacity of unfrozen mixture. The reason for the difference is that mixtures containing cream or egg whites will increase in volume during the churning/freezing process, so allow for that when filling your machine with the unfrozen mixture. (Study the instruction leaflet that comes with the machine, and make sure you understand exactly how to operate it before you start.)

For those people who are wondering if the recipes can be attempted without a machine, they can, but making ices in a machine is so much less effort – and ice-creams and sorbets are better for being made in a machine. Air is beaten into the liquid as it freezes, giving the finished ice a fine, silky texture.

Once an ice is made it should be packed into a container, right up to the top. If it is not possible to fill a container, put a sheet of greaseproof paper directly on top of the mixture, and this will prevent crystals of ice forming on the surface and spoiling the texture. Without all the stabilisers and preservatives of commercial ice-creams, home-made ices will not keep as long as commercial ones, and we recommend that they should be eaten within 3 days.

After storing in the freezer, some ices need time to mellow in the refrigerator, or they will be too hard and cold to taste. But it is difficult to give any hard and fast rules about this, because the running temperature of a refrigerator will vary according to the amount it is in use. So the times we suggest can only be general guidelines.

Note: ices can provide an environment in which harmful organisms could thrive. This danger can be avoided if the mixture is heated to 176°F (80°C) for 15 seconds. It can then be cooled and churned. All equipment which comes into contact with ice-cream should be scrupulously clean.

·

VANILLA ICE-CREAM
(Glace à la vanille)

 The simplest and most versatile of home-made ice-creams. Serve it with fresh fruit, as an accompaniment to a hot dessert, or on its own.

Makes about 2½ pints (1.5 litres)
·

1 quantity crème anglaise *(see page 173),* *using 8 egg yolks only*	*5 fl oz (150 ml) double cream*

Preparation

Return the vanilla pod to the made custard. When it is completely cold, cover, and chill in the refrigerator for 24 hours.

Remove the vanilla pod and churn the custard in two batches for about 20 minutes, adding half the cream to each batch after 5 minutes.

To store and serve

Pack the ice-cream into storage containers as soon as it is ready; store it in the freezer until you are ready to use it. Allow 15 to 20 minutes in the refrigerator before serving.

Opposite: Meringue nests with saffron ice-cream (see page 203)

BANANA ICE-CREAM

(Glace à la banane)

Make sure that you use very ripe bananas to produce the correct flavour when making this ice-cream. It is particularly delicious served with chocolate sauce (see page 174).

Makes 3½ pints (2 litres)

•

1 quantity crème anglaise *(see page 173), using 8 egg yolks only*	*About 2¼ lb (1 kg) very ripe bananas*
	4 tablespoons white rum
5 fl oz (150 ml) double cream	

Preparation

When the *crème anglaise* is completely cold, stir in the double cream. Peel and weigh the bananas; you need 1½ lb (750 g). Put them in a food processor or blender with the rum and blend until smooth. Stir into the custard and put half the mixture at a time into the machine. Churn for about 25 minutes, until almost firm. Repeat with the remaining mixture.

To store and serve

Pack the ice-cream into storage containers as soon as it is ready; then store it in the freezer until you are ready to use it. Allow about 30 minutes in the refrigerator before serving.

Opposite: Pear clafoutis (see page 213)

CINNAMON
ICE‑CREAM
(Glace à la cannelle)

The flavour of cinnamon combines wonderfully well with the apples of *Tarte Tatin* (see page 206), and there is the contrast of hot and cold as well.

Makes about 1¾ pints (1 litre)

•

½ quantity crème anglaise *(see page 173), made without the vanilla*	*8 cinnamon sticks, about 1½ oz (40 g)*
	4 fl oz (120 ml) double cream

Preparation

Make the *crème anglaise* as instructed on page 173, but replace the vanilla with the cinnamon sticks. Cover the custard, cool it, and chill in the refrigerator for 24 hours. The sticks should remain in the custard until it is churned.

Strain the custard into the ice-cream maker, and process for approximately 10 minutes. While the mixture is still fluid, pour in the cream; continue churning until lightly firm. This will take approximately 20 minutes.

To serve

If possible, this ice-cream should be served at once. It can be kept in the freezer until needed, but only for a limited time.

MINT CHOCOLATE ICE-CREAM

(Glace chocolat menthe)

Because of the chocolate in this recipe the *crème anglaise* will seem to have reached the right texture after being poured on to the egg yolks but it will still be necessary to poach the mixture to ensure it is cooked.

Makes 2¾ pints (1.6 litres)

•

1¼ pints (1 litre) milk	2½ oz (65 g) cocoa powder, sifted
2 oz (50 g) bunch of mint, rinsed and dried	8 egg yolks
9 oz (250 g) caster sugar	4 tablespoons mint liqueur (optional)
5 oz (150 g) plain dark bitter chocolate	5 fl oz (150 ml) double cream

Preparation

To prepare the custard, first bring the milk, the mint and 3 oz (75 g) of the sugar to the boil. Meanwhile, have ready in a bowl the plain chocolate, broken into sections, and the sifted cocoa powder. In a separate bowl, whisk together the egg yolks and the rest of the sugar. When the milk boils, pour it on to the chocolate and cocoa powder, stirring quickly. When the chocolate has melted pour it on to the egg yolks and sugar, again stirring continuously. Pour the liquid back into the pan and set it over a low heat, still stirring, until the custard is thick enough to coat the back of the spoon. On no account let the custard boil. Chill in the refrigerator for 24 hours to allow the flavours to develop.

Strain and stir in the liqueur, if used, and the cream and put half the mixture in the ice-cream machine to churn for about 25 minutes, until the mix is fairly firm. Repeat with the remaining mix.

To store and serve

As soon as the ice-cream is ready, pack it into storage containers, then store it in the freezer. About 30 minutes before serving, remove to the refrigerator.

COUPE ANDRÉ

 This is an unusual method of making ice-cream, and an unusual way of serving it. The delicious combination of caramel-flavoured ice-cream, cream and hot coffee will have your guests demanding more, much more!

Makes 3 pints (1.75 litres)
You will need 10 × 5 fl oz (150 ml) ramekins or heatproof dishes and a roasting tin to contain them (it may be easier to bake the ramekins in 2 batches).

•

10 oz (275 g) caster sugar	*4 fl oz (120 ml) double cream*
1¾ pints (1 litre) milk	To serve:
1 vanilla pod	*5 fl oz (150 ml) double cream, whipped*
4 eggs	*8 coffee beans*
2 egg yolks	*Piping hot black coffee*
Freshly grated nutmeg	

Preparation

Pre-heat the oven to gas mark 2, 300°F (150°C). Line the roasting tin with about 4 thicknesses of kitchen paper.

THE CARAMEL: Put 5 oz (150 g) of the caster sugar into a medium-sized thick-based saucepan. Measure 7 fl oz (200 ml) water into a jug and add half to the sugar. Cook gently, stirring often, until all the sugar has dissolved. Wash down the side of the pan with a pastry brush dipped in water to make sure no sugar crystals are left there.

Once the sugar has completely dissolved, stop stirring, bring the syrup to the boil and boil until it is the colour of light caramel. Immediately remove the pan from the heat. *Please take great care with the next stage.* Standing well back, add the remaining half of the measured water to the caramel. Initially it will spit and bubble furiously, but this will subside very quickly. Stir, and re-heat gently until the caramel becomes a smooth sauce. Pour a little into each ramekin in turn, tilting and turning the dish so the caramel coats the base and sides. Transfer the dishes to sit on the paper in the roasting tin; keep on one side until ready to use.

THE CUSTARD: In a saucepan, bring the milk to the boil with the vanilla pod and 3 oz (75 g) of the sugar. In a separate bowl, whisk the eggs, the egg yolks and the rest of the sugar. As soon as the milk comes to the boil, remove the vanilla pod and pour the milk on to the egg mixture, whisking constantly. Pour an equal quantity of the custard into each dish, grate some nutmeg sparingly over the surface and transfer to the oven. Pour very hot water into the roasting tin to come half-way up the sides of the dishes.

After 25 to 30 minutes, when the sides have begun to set, but the centre is still soft, carefully remove the tin from the oven. Take the ramekins from the tin and leave to cool.

TO CHURN: When cool, pour the contents of the dishes into a food processor or blender and blend until smooth. Add the double cream, blend briefly, and pour half the mixture into the ice-cream maker. Churn for about 25 minutes, until it forms a solid mass. Repeat with the second batch. If possible, churn and serve. If you can't do this, pack the ice-cream into storage containers and store in the freezer until required but preferably for no longer than 2 hours.

To serve

If you have stored the ice-cream in a freezer, transfer it to the refrigerator about 30 minutes before serving. At serving time, have the whipped cream ready in a piping bag fitted with a rosette nozzle. Quickly place a scoop of the ice-cream in the bottom of a tea cup or coffee cup, pipe a rosette of cream on top and decorate with a coffee bean. At the table, pour over piping hot black coffee, and serve.

.

STRAWBERRY SORBET
(Sorbet aux fraises)

 Frozen strawberries can be used to make this sorbet, but the flavour will not be quite as good, nor the colour of the made sorbet so intense as when using fresh strawberries. Defrost 1 lb (450 g) strawberries and proceed as below.

Makes about $1\frac{3}{4}$ pints (1 litre)

.

1 lb (450 g) strawberries, hulled, rinsed briefly, and thoroughly dried	*Juice of $\frac{1}{2}$ lemon*
	8 fl oz (250 ml) sorbet syrup (see page 170)

Preparation

Put the strawberries in a food processor or blender and blend until smooth. Have ready a nylon sieve set over a bowl. Rub the purée through the sieve, then strain in the lemon juice. Add the syrup, stir, cover, and transfer to the refrigerator to chill.

Transfer the mix to the ice-cream machine and churn for about 8 minutes, until it is firm.

To store and serve

Pack into storage containers and store in the freezer until ready to serve. Take the sorbet out of the freezer and place in the refrigerator 20 minutes before serving.

•

RASPBERRY SORBET
(Sorbet aux framboises)

 With their delicious flavour and texture, raspberries make a perfect sorbet. You can use thawed frozen raspberries instead of fresh ones – it will make little difference.

Makes about 1¾ pints (1 litre)

•

1 lb (450 g) raspberries, hulled, rinsed briefly, and thoroughly dried	*Juice of ½ lemon*
	8 fl oz (250 ml) sorbet syrup (see page 170)

Preparation

Put the raspberries in a food processor or blender and blend until smooth. Rub the purée through a nylon sieve set over a bowl, then strain in the lemon juice. Stir in the syrup, cover, and chill in the refrigerator.

When the mixture is thoroughly chilled, transfer it to the ice-cream machine and churn for about 8 minutes, until it is firm.

To store and serve

Pack into storage containers and store in the freezer until ready to serve. Take the sorbet out of the freezer and place in the refrigerator 20 minutes before serving.

BLACKBERRY SORBET

(Sorbet aux mûres sauvages)

Blackberry sorbet is sharper than strawberry and raspberry but just as delicious. You can add an egg white to the mixture, to lighten the texture of the sorbet, if you like.

Makes about $1\frac{3}{4}$ pints (1 litre)

•

1 lb (450 g) blackberries, hulled, rinsed briefly, and thoroughly dried

14 fl oz (400 ml) sorbet syrup (see page 170)

Juice of $\frac{1}{2}$ lemon

1 egg white (optional)

Preparation

Put the blackberries in a food processor or blender with the syrup and blend until smooth. Have ready a nylon sieve set over a bowl. Rub the purée through the sieve and strain in the lemon juice. Cover and chill in the refrigerator.

Lightly beat the egg white with a fork to loosen it, then add it to the blackberry mixture. Churn for 10 to 12 minutes, until it is firm.

To store and serve

Pack into storage containers and store in the freezer until ready to serve. Take the sorbet out of the freezer and place in the refrigerator 20 minutes before serving.

BLACKCURRANT SORBET

(Sorbet au cassis)

 Blackcurrant sorbet makes a very refreshing summer dessert. You may wish to add an egg white to make the sorbet even lighter.

Makes about 1½ pints (900 ml)

•

1 lb (450 g) blackcurrants, stalks removed, rinsed and drained	*Juice of ½ lemon*
	1 egg white (optional)
18 fl oz (500 ml) sorbet syrup (see page 170)	

Preparation

Put the blackcurrants in a pan with half the sorbet syrup. Bring to the boil, and boil for 1 minute. Pull the pan aside from the heat; leave to cool for 10 minutes. Transfer the contents of the pan to a food processor or blender and blend until smooth. Have ready a nylon sieve set over a bowl. Rub the purée through the sieve and strain in the lemon juice. Add the remaining syrup; cover and chill in the refrigerator. Lightly beat the egg white with a fork to loosen it before adding to the mixture; churn for 10 minutes.

To store and serve

Pack into storage containers and store in the freezer until ready to serve. Take the sorbet out of the freezer and place in the refrigerator 20 minutes before serving.

CIDER SORBET

(Sorbet au cidre)

This sorbet includes lemon zest which gives it an unusual tang. It is simple and straightforward to make and utterly delicious at the end of a meal.

Makes about 3½ pints (2 litres)

•

15 fl oz (450 ml) sorbet syrup (see page 170)	*1¾ pints (1 litre) dry cider, chilled*
Zest of 1 lemon	*1 egg white*
Juice of 2 lemons	

Preparation

Make up the sorbet syrup according to the recipe on page 170, but as soon as the syrup has been passed through a sieve into a bowl, add the pared zest of 1 lemon to the measured amount. Leave to cool. Strain the syrup into a bowl, and add the lemon juice. Pour in the cider.

In a separate bowl, lightly beat the egg white with a fork to loosen it. Stir this into the sorbet liquid. Put the mixture in the ice-cream maker. (You will probably need to do this in 2 batches.) Churn for about 18 minutes, until the mix is lightly firm. Repeat with the remaining mix.

To store and serve

Pack the sorbet into storage containers as soon as it is ready; store in the freezer until ready to use. It can be served straight from the freezer.

TEA, MINT AND PRUNE SORBET

(Sorbet aux thé, menthe et pruneaux)

 This combination of Darjeeling tea, fresh mint and prunes may sound unusual but it is simple to make and produces a very successful sorbet.

Makes 2¼ pints (1.25 litres)

•

6 oz (175 g) sugar	*1 oz (25 g) bunch of fresh mint, rinsed and dried*
¾ oz (20 g) Darjeeling tea leaves	*5 oz (150 g) pitted prunes (about 17)*

Preparation

Combine the sugar with 1¾ pints (1 litre) water in a saucepan and bring to the boil. Have the tea leaves and mint ready in 1 bowl, the prunes in another. Pour the boiling syrup over the tea and mint, cover, and leave to infuse for 3 minutes. Strain immediately into the bowl containing the prunes. Cool, cover, and leave overnight in the refrigerator.

The following day, pour the liquid into the ice-cream machine (you will probably need to do 2 batches), reserving the prunes. Churn for 18 to 20 minutes.

Meanwhile, slice the prunes lengthways into 6. Add these in the last minute of churning, when the sorbet is formed.

To serve

Serve at once. You can store this sorbet in the freezer for a brief time, but it is not advisable to leave it there for more than 2 hours. It will need about 30 minutes in the refrigerator before serving. In the freezer, the little bits of prune become frozen hard, and time is needed in the refrigerator to ensure an even texture throughout the sorbet before it is eaten. Otherwise your guests might break their teeth on frozen prunes!

MERINGUE NESTS WITH SAFFRON ICE-CREAM

(Petits vacherins glacés aux pistils de safran)

 This is an impressive dessert that Michel often offers at The Waterside Inn. Each serving is composed of a scoop of ice-cream sitting in a little nest of meringue, topped with a lacy meringue cap decorated with crystallised violets, and surrounded by slices of fruit in a fruit syrup. As a dessert to be served at home, it has the advantage that all its components can be prepared beforehand, and then it can be assembled very quickly just before serving. In fact, making the ice-cream up to a day in advance will accentuate and improve its flavour.

Note: any meringue left over can be piped into other shapes, such as a large case, a base for a Pavlova, or extra nest shapes. They will keep for several days in an airtight container.

Serves 8
You will need 12 small tartlet tins, or similar moulds, $1\frac{1}{2}$in (4 cm) in diameter.

•

4 nectarines or small peaches	*1 oz (25 g) crystallised violets, finely chopped (optional)*
$\frac{1}{2}$ bottle red wine (preferably Burgundy)	
4 oz (100 g) sugar	*12 fl oz (350 ml) crème anglaise (see page 173) made without vanilla*
1 oz (25 g) clarified butter (see page 16), for greasing the moulds	
	A pinch of saffron threads
1 quantity French meringue (see page 168)	*2 fl oz (50 ml) double cream*

Preparation

THE FRUIT: The best way to peel nectarines or peaches is to use a method similar to that for skinning tomatoes. Have boiling water and very cold water ready in two separate bowls. First, cut a tiny nick in the skin of each fruit, then plunge them into the hot water for 1 minute, remove them, and immediately immerse them in the cold water. Remove them after 1 minute and peel them, starting with the little cut you made in the skin. Put them at once in a saucepan with the red wine and sugar and cover with a circle of greaseproof paper directly on top of the liquid. Poach the fruit. The time taken will depend on how ripe they are; 5 minutes should be sufficient, but it must be a very gentle process, so that the fruit does not either overcook or bruise. Remove from the heat; put the fruit and liquid into a bowl, cover with cling film and allow to cool.

THE MERINGUE NESTS AND CAPS: Pre-heat the oven to gas

mark $\frac{1}{4}$, 225°F (110°C). Wash and dry the moulds, then invert them – you will be using their outsides. Grease the outside surfaces with clarified butter, and then put the moulds in the refrigerator for 5 minutes, to harden the butter (this will make the eventual unmoulding easier). Have ready a sheet of silicone paper or buttered greaseproof paper. Make up 1 quantity of French meringue, according to the recipe on page 168.

To make the nests, fit a piping bag with a decorative $\frac{1}{2}$ in (1 cm) nozzle, spoon some of the meringue mixture into the bag and pipe on to the paper rounds 2 in (5 cm) across, with an additional coil on top of the outer edge. Pipe 5 small feet around each nest.

To make the caps, fit another piping bag with a plain $\frac{1}{8}$ in (3 mm) nozzle and spoon in some more of the meringue. Pipe the meringue in a lattice pattern over the outsides of the tartlet tins. Reinforce any points where lines of meringues cross with an additional dot of the meringue mixture. Sprinkle the tops of the caps with the finely chopped crystallised violets, if using.

Put the nests and caps into the oven, and cook for 45 minutes. Take the caps out and leave them at room temperature, in a dry place. Because they are so much bigger and thicker, the nests will need an additional hour in the oven. Then remove them, set them aside with the caps, and allow them to cool. This will take approximately 45 minutes. Transfer the nests to a wire rack by inserting a palette knife very carefully between the paper and the meringue (keep the blade of the knife absolutely flat while you do this). Then slide the nests on to the rack. Next, unmould the caps. They are extremely delicate, so take great care when moving them from the moulds to the rack. But however careful you are it is virtually inevitable that there will be breakages, so we have made allowances for that in the number we have suggested you make.

THE ICE-CREAM: Make the *crème anglaise*. Strain the mixture, add the

saffron threads, and set it aside to cool; stir it occasionally as it cools. Pour the cooled custard into an ice-cream maker and churn for 10 to 20 minutes, adding the cream some 5 to 8 minutes before the end of the process. To make sure all the saffron threads are in the mixture before it freezes, scrape off any that have stuck to the paddle and mix them into the ice-cream.

THE SYRUP: Drain off the red wine and sugar liquid that the fruit was poached

in. Leave the cold fruit in the bowl, and keep it covered with cling film until you are ready to assemble the desserts. In a saucepan, boil the liquid for about 30 minutes, to reduce it to a syrupy consistency. Cool the syrup. If you are in a hurry, you can do this very quickly by putting it in a small bowl inside another bowl of crushed ice.

To serve

Assemble the little desserts on individual plates. Place a nest on each plate, and put a scoop of ice-cream inside each nest. Put a meringue cap on each scoop – do this with great care, remembering that the caps are very fragile. Cut each peach or nectarine into 10 slices and arrange 5 slices around each meringue nest. Pour the syrup over the fruit and serve immediately.

•

HOT DESSERTS

 Although there is an element of risk in serving a hot dessert, some are so delicious that they are well worth a little extra strain. There is the bonus, too, that your guests will appreciate that you have gone to special trouble for them.

However, you don't want to spend the entire meal worrying about your dessert. The aim of this section is not only to teach you how to make splendid hot desserts, but also to enable you to be impressively calm and poised as you do it.

Remember, too, that although hot desserts have to be finished at the last minute, for nearly all of them a good deal of the preparation can be done in advance. Even a soufflé can be fully prepared an hour or an hour and a half before you put it in the oven. That is the sort of thing we do in the restaurants all the time. Just prepare your soufflé, transfer it to its dish, then place the dish in a roasting tin and pour in hot water to come half-way up the sides. Keep the water at simmering point until you are ready to put the soufflé in the oven. Your soufflé will rise like magic.

And magic is what cooking is all about.

TARTE TATIN

This is a classic French winter tart that is very easy to make. It should be served as hot as your family or guests can eat it without the caramel burning their lips. It is especially delicious with Cinnamon ice-cream (see page 194).

In the restaurants we sometimes serve a more exotic version of this dish, making up small individual tarts and substituting mangoes for apples. If you try this, use only half the quantity of butter. We serve the little tarts accompanied by a fruit sauce (see page 170) made with mangoes and passion fruit.

Serves 6

You will need a frying-pan or round fireproof dish approximately 10 in (25 cm) in diameter and 2¼in (5.5 cm) deep. It must be a container that is able to stand direct heat and any handles must also be heatproof, as this dessert is cooked both over direct heat and in the oven.

•

6 medium dessert apples,
preferably Cox's Orange Pippins

Juice of ½ lemon

4 oz (100 g) butter

7 oz (200 g) sugar

9 oz (250 g) Classic or Quick puff pastry
(pages 164, 167)

Preparation and cooking

Peel, halve and core the apples, brush them with lemon juice and put them in the refrigerator. Grease the base of the frying-pan or dish with the butter, and add a generous layer of sugar. Arrange the apples, rounded side down, on the sugar.

Roll out the puff pastry to ⅛in (3 mm) thick. Fit the pastry directly on top of the apples, allowing an overlap of about ¾in (2 cm) all round. Neaten the edge of the pastry with a sharp knife, and leave to rest in the refrigerator for at least 20 minutes.

Pre-heat the oven to gas mark 7, 425°F (220°C).

Put the pan or dish over fierce direct heat, to caramelise the sugar and butter to a light amber colour. This will take about 15 minutes.

Once that stage is reached, place the pan or dish in the oven and cook for 20 minutes, until the pastry is cooked to a golden colour and has risen nicely.

To serve

Take the tart from the oven and put a plate on top of it. Protect your hand and arm with a cloth and, taking great care, turn the whole thing over so that the tart turns out from the pan or dish. The pastry will now form the base of the tart, with the apples in their delicious golden caramel coating on top. You may need to put the fruit back in place, using a small knife.

FRESH FRUITS WITH CARAMEL SABAYON

(Gratin de fruits frais au sabayon de caramel)

 Simple and delicious – the sort of dish that can be put together when you have unexpected guests. The fruits can be almost any you choose, but obviously those that brown once they are cut (apples, pears, bananas) do not look quite so attractive after macerating in rum for 2 or more hours.

Serves 4

•

1¼ lb (500 g) mixed fresh fruits of your choice	*4 egg yolks*
4 tablespoons white rum	*Juice of 1 lemon*
4 oz (100 g) caster sugar	*4 tiny sprigs of fresh mint, to decorate*
4 fl oz (120 ml) double cream	

Preparation

THE FRUITS: Prepare the fruits, washing, peeling, removing stalks, cores, pips, etc., as necessary. Cut into neat sections or slices and put into a bowl. Spoon in the rum, cover, and chill, turning the fruits occasionally, for a minimum of 2 hours.

THE CARAMEL: In a medium-sized thick-based pan, heat the sugar until it begins to liquefy and darken. Stir with a wooden spoon until the caramel is clear and the colour of liquid honey. Immediately remove the pan from the heat. *Please take great care at the next stage.* Standing well back, add the cream to the caramel. Initially it will spit and bubble vigorously, but this will subside very quickly. Stir and re-heat gently until the caramel has completely dissolved and the cream is smooth; cool. Pre-heat the grill.

THE SAUCE: In a separate pan, combine the egg yolks and the cooled caramel cream. Add the lemon juice and whisk together over a low heat. Use a sugar thermometer or dip your finger into the mix to test the temperature. As soon as the sauce reaches 140°F (60°C), remove it from the heat. (At this temperature it will be too hot for your finger to bear any more than a very brief dip.)

To serve

Put the rum-soaked fruit in 4 gratin dishes and spoon an equal quantity of sauce over each portion. Grill very briefly, for a matter of seconds, so that the sauce is just tinged with colour. Decorate with a sprig of mint each and serve immediately.

•

WARM PEAR SOUFFLÉS WITH CHOCOLATE SAUCE

(Soufflés tièdes aux poires, sauce chocolat)

 These little soufflés are very delicate, and must be served as soon as possible after they come out of the oven. They look most attractive garnished with a sprig of mint and a pear fan.

Serves 6
You will need 6 individual ramekins, top measurement $2\frac{3}{4}$ in (7 cm), base 2 in (5 cm), depth $2\frac{1}{4}$ in (6 cm).

•

3 oz (75 g) butter, melted	*2 tablespoons pear eau de vie*
7 oz (200 g) caster sugar	*Oil*
1 oz (25 g) hazelnuts	*6 egg whites*
1 lb (450 g) tinned pears (drained weight)	*1 quantity chocolate sauce (see page 174)*
4 teaspoons cornflour	*6 small sprigs fresh mint*

Preparation

Pre-heat the oven to gas mark 3, 325°F (160°C). Brush the ramekins generously with the melted butter, and dust the base and sides with $1\frac{1}{2}$ oz (40 g) of the caster sugar.

Spread the hazelnuts on a baking tray and toast them in the oven for about 10 minutes, until their skins begin to flake off. Then transfer them to a damp cloth and rub to remove the majority of the skins. Set aside until needed. Increase the oven heat to gas mark 7, 425°F (220°C).

Weigh 12 oz (350 g) of the pears, reserving the remainder. Put the weighed pears in a food processor or blender and blend until smooth. Pour into a small saucepan and heat very gently for 20 minutes, stirring frequently, until the purée is reduced to a thickish paste. Remove from the heat and keep warm.

In a small, thick-based saucepan, combine a further $3\frac{1}{2}$ oz (90 g) of the sugar with 2 fl oz (50 ml) water and heat gently until the sugar crystals have dissolved. Using a warmed sugar thermometer, boil rapidly until the syrup reaches 320°F (160°C). Immediately remove the syrup from the heat and stir it into the pear purée; leave aside.

In a small bowl, combine the cornflour and the *eau de vie* and stir until smooth. Pour into the pear purée and bring to the boil, stirring constantly. Simmer for 2 minutes, then remove the pan from the heat and leave covered at room temperature.

Lightly oil a small baking tray. In a separate, small, thick-based pan, heat the remaining sugar. Heat, stirring with a wooden spoon, until the sugar becomes liquid and darkens to a golden caramel. Quickly remove the pan from the heat and stir in the prepared hazelnuts. Pour the mixture on to the oiled baking tray and leave to become cold and brittle. Tap the caramel with a rolling pin to break into small pieces, then, to reduce the caramel to small pieces, either crush in a bowl with the end of a rolling pin or briefly process in a food blender. Reserve in a non-humid atmosphere until you are ready to assemble the soufflés.

Take the reserved pears and trim them into 6 ovals $\frac{3}{4}$ in (2 cm) long and $\frac{1}{4}$ in (5 mm) thick. With a small, sharp knife, slice these lengthways to form fan shapes (see illustration on page 214). Dice the remaining pear pieces and reserve.

To assemble and bake the soufflés

Put a large baking tray in the oven to heat. In a large clean bowl, whisk the egg whites with a pinch of caster sugar until they form soft peaks. Use the whisk to incorporate one-third of the egg whites into the pear purée mixture; then, using a plastic spatula, gently fold in the remainder. Half-fill the prepared ramekins, spoon a little heap of the crushed hazelnut caramel into the centre of each dish, then fill the dishes to the top with the remaining soufflé mix.

Transfer the soufflés to the pre-heated baking tray and bake for 3 to 5 minutes, until they are risen and golden.

To serve

Gently unmould the soufflés on to warmed plates and quickly pour a ribbon of chocolate sauce around each soufflé. Put a sprig of mint and a pear fan on top of each soufflé and sprinkle a little diced pear into the sauce on each plate. Serve instantly.

CRÊPES WITH LIME SOUFFLÉ

(Crêpes soufflées au citron vert)

 A delicious light dessert of pancakes filled with a lime-flavoured soufflé mixture. It needs last-minute attention and must then be served very quickly, so have the ingredients well organised.

Makes 10 pancakes

•

2 lemons	*Juice of 4 limes*
3½ oz (90 g) caster sugar	*10 × 6 in (15 cm) pancakes (see page 27)*
5 fl oz (150 ml) sorbet syrup (see page 170)	*6 limes, segmented (see page 97)*
8 fl oz (250 ml) crème pâtissière (see page 171)	*1 oz (25 g) icing sugar*
5 egg whites	

Preparation and cooking

Pre-heat the oven to gas mark 7, 425°F (220°C).

Wash the lemons and use a potato peeler to peel off the zest, leaving behind the white pith. (You will not need the rest of the lemons in this recipe.) Slice the zest into fine strips. Put them into a saucepan with about 10 fl oz (300 ml) water, bring to the boil, then immediately remove the pan from the heat. Drain the strips into a sieve. Refresh them under cold running water, then return them to the pan with 1 oz (25 g) of the caster sugar and 5 fl oz (150 ml) water. Bring to the boil, simmer for 8 to 10 minutes, then take the pan from the heat and pour the contents into a sieve set over a small bowl. Use a fork to tease out the candied strips of peel, so they do not stick together. Reserve. Combine the drained syrup with the sorbet syrup and reserve.

Put the *crème pâtissière* in a heatproof bowl and heat gently over a pan of simmering water. Pre-heat the grill.

In a large bowl, whisk the egg whites until they are stiff but not dry. Gradually whisk in the rest of the caster sugar, a little at a time; continue to beat until the meringue forms stiff peaks. Remove the custard from the heat: it should by now be just warm. Whisk in the lime juice, use the whisk to incorporate one-third of the egg whites, then fold in the remainder with a large metal spoon.

Have the pancakes ready, lying flat on a baking tray. Put a large spoonful of the soufflé mixture in the middle of each one, press 2 segments of lime into the filling, then gently fold the pancake in half. Lightly press the edges of the pancakes together, then transfer them to the oven to bake for 2½ minutes. Meanwhile quickly prepare the warmed serving plates. To one side of each plate arrange 2 lime segments with a little heap of lemon zest between. Pour a little of the lime juice remaining from the segments into the syrup, then put about a tablespoon of the syrup on each plate. As soon as the pancakes come out of the oven sift icing sugar over them and put them under the hot grill for about 45 seconds, so that the sugar melts and becomes partly caramelised.

To serve

Use a palette knife to transfer each pancake to the prepared warmed serving plate. Serve instantly.

·

MANDARIN AND COINTREAU SOUFFLÉS

(Soufflés mandarines et Cointreau)

A delightfully easy soufflé that has a nicely developed orange flavour. With this, and all the other recipes using orange or citrus fruits in general, make sure you give the skin a good vigorous wipe or a gentle scrub before using them. With most fruits nowadays, it is quite likely that they have been sprayed with protective wax sealant, citrus fruits in particular. So make sure that this is removed before using the grated or peeled skin in a recipe.

There is another important point to watch when orange or lemon zest is used. Should you not own that very useful gadget, a lemon zester (we have mentioned it before), then the alternative is to simply pare the skin with a potato peeler or small knife. However, with this method, there is a danger that the white pith is peeled as well as the coloured zest. Try to make sure that only the zest is removed, as the pith will implant a bitter flavour, to the detriment of the finished dish.

Serves 4
You will need 4 soufflé dishes, 4 in (10 cm) in diameter and $2\frac{1}{2}$ in (6 cm) high.
Brush with melted butter, then dust base and sides with caster sugar.

·

1 oz (25 g) butter, melted	*1 tablespoon granulated sugar*
A little caster sugar	*3 fl oz (85 ml) Cointreau*
$\frac{1}{2}$ quantity crème pâtissière *(see page 171)*	*6 egg whites*
3 mandarins, washed	*$2\frac{1}{2}$ oz (65 g) caster sugar*
1 orange, washed	

Preparation

Pre-heat the oven to gas mark 7, 425°F (220°C) and put a baking tray in the oven to heat. Put the *crème pâtissière* in a heatproof bowl and heat gently over a pan of simmering water. Grate the zest from the mandarins and reserve. Peel and segment them (according to the instructions for segmenting oranges on page 97), then put on one side until ready to use. Remove the orange zest with a zester, or use a potato peeler to remove only the coloured peel and cut this into very thin, hairlike strips.

Bring a small saucepan of water to the boil, add the orange strips and boil for 2 minutes. Drain in a sieve and refresh under cold running water. Return the strips to the rinsed-out pan with 1 tablespoon granulated sugar and 1 tablespoon water. Boil gently until the liquid has almost evaporated, and reserve the candied peel to decorate the soufflés.

Squeeze the juice from the orange. Pour into a small saucepan and boil gently until reduced to about 1 teaspoon. Combine the *crème pâtissière* with the reduced orange juice, grated mandarin zest and Cointreau.

In a separate, large bowl whisk the egg whites until they form soft peaks; gradually whisk in the caster sugar and continue whisking until the meringue will hold firm peaks. Now use the whisk to incorporate one-third of the egg whites into the flavoured custard, folding in the remainder with a large metal spoon.

Divide half the mixture between the 4 soufflé dishes, then use two-thirds of the mandarin segments to form a layer on top of the mixture in each dish. Cover with the rest of the soufflé mix.

To cook

Immediately place the soufflé dishes on the hot baking tray and bake in the oven for 10 to 12 minutes. The soufflés should be well risen but still a little creamy and soft in the centre.

To serve

Quickly arrange the remaining mandarin segments on top and surround with the reserved candied orange strips. Serve instantly.

PEAR CLAFOUTIS
(Clafoutis aux poires)

Clafoutis is usually associated with cherries, but in fact it can be made with many other fruits. Pear clafoutis is particularly good. Don't waste the syrup you use for poaching the pears. Add cold water to make it up to its original volume, and use it as the basis for a sorbet: it makes a particularly good Cider sorbet (see page 201).

Serves 8

You will need a 9 in (23 cm) diameter flan tin, $\frac{3}{4}$ in (2 cm) high, preferably with a removable base.

•

$\frac{1}{2}$ oz (15 g) butter, at room temperature	4 fl oz (120 ml) milk
10 oz (275 g) shortbread dough (see page 163)	4 fl oz (120 ml) double cream
A little flour	$\frac{1}{2}$ vanilla pod, split
Juice of 1 lemon	4 eggs
4 large pears	6 oz (175 g) caster sugar
1 quantity sorbet syrup (see page 170)	1 oz (25 g) granulated sugar

Preparation and cooking

Pre-heat the oven to gas mark 7, 425°F (220°C). Brush the inside of the tin with the butter.

Roll out the pastry on a lightly floured work surface and use it to line the flan tin, easing the pastry into the flutes, then trimming off the excess level with the tin. Using your thumb and forefinger, crimp the edge attractively. Prick the base of the pastry all over with a fork, and refrigerate for 20 minutes. Line the pastry with a circle of greaseproof paper and fill it with baking beans. Put the tin on a baking tray, transfer it to the centre of the oven, and bake the pastry case for 15 minutes. Remove it from the oven, carefully take out the beans and paper, and leave it on one side until you are ready to use it. Reduce the oven temperature to gas mark 6, 400°F (200°C).

Have ready a bowl of cold water with the lemon juice added. Peel and halve the pears. Use a teaspoon or a melon baller to scoop out the core neatly. Now use a small knife to cut a small 'v'-shaped channel to remove the stalk from the top of the pear down to the core. Have the syrup ready in a medium-sized saucepan and bring to the boil. Cook the pears in the simmering liquid until they are tender; this will probably take about 20 minutes, but it depends very much on how ripe they are. Drain, then dry on absorbent paper; leave to cool.

Pour the milk and the cream into a saucepan and add the vanilla pod. Bring to the boil.

In a bowl, beat the eggs with the caster sugar until they are light and frothy. Whisk in a pinch of flour. Remove the vanilla pod and, whisking constantly, pour the boiling liquid on to the eggs. Leave the mixture to cool, stirring occasionally.

Use a small sharp knife to slice the pear halves thinly from the floweret end, towards the stalks, leaving the slices attached at the stalk end (see illustration). Arrange the pieces in a fanned-out shape on the pastry base. Pour the custard around the pears and transfer the tart to the oven. Bake for about 25 minutes, until it is golden-brown and set.

To serve

Take the clafoutis from the oven and leave it until it is just warm before you remove the flan ring, dust with the granulated sugar, and serve.

•

PREPARING PEARS FOR PEAR CLAFOUTIS

Thinly slice the rounded portion of the pear
halves to within about $1\frac{1}{2}$ in (4 cm) of the
stalk end, so the slices remain attached.
Arrange in a fanned-out shape.

BRIOCHE

 It is a mystery why the British have taken to the croissant in such a big way, and almost totally ignored the brioche. It is supreme among French breads, its unique, feathery, buttery lightness putting it in a class of its own. The characteristic fluted tins, large and small, in which brioches are usually baked are fairly widely available. However, if you don't have any of these tins, then brioches can be baked in saucepans (as long as they have heatproof handles) or deep muffin tins (the kind sometimes used for individual Yorkshire puddings). Brioche is, of course, delicious for breakfast, served either by itself or with butter and jam.

Makes 1 large brioche or 20 small brioches
You will need either 1 large brioche mould, $9\frac{1}{2}$ in (24 cm) top measurement, $4\frac{1}{2}$ in (12 cm) at the base; or 1 × 7 in (18 cm) diameter saucepan (with a heatproof handle); or 20 small brioche moulds, $3\frac{1}{4}$ in (8 cm) top measurement.

•

3 fl oz (85 ml) milk, warmed to blood heat	*12 oz (350 g) butter, at room temperature*
$\frac{1}{2}$ oz (15 g) fresh yeast	*1 oz (25 g) sugar*
2 teaspoons salt	*1 egg yolk beaten with 1 tablespoon milk, to glaze*
$1\frac{1}{4}$ lb (500 g) plain white flour	*Icing sugar (optional)*
6 eggs	

Preparation

If you are using a saucepan, line it with buttered greaseproof paper to twice the height of the pan.

Pour the milk (at blood heat) into a large (mixer) bowl. Crumble in the yeast and stir until dissolved. Add the salt, then the flour and the eggs and knead, using a wooden spoon or the dough hook of an electric mixer, until the mix is smooth and elastic. If you are using a mixer, have it at a very low speed to start with. Once the ingredients are incorporated, increase the speed to medium. Increase again to high for the final 1 or 2 minutes.

In a separate bowl, beat together the butter and sugar until the butter is very soft. Add this mixture to the dough a little at a time, making sure each addition is thoroughly mixed in before adding the next. When all has been added continue to beat for a further 15 minutes by hand or 5 minutes in the mixer, until the dough has become smooth, shiny, and fairly elastic. Cover the bowl with a damp cloth and leave in a warm place (about 75°F/24°C) for about 2 hours, until the dough has risen and doubled in bulk.

Knock back the dough, turning it over quickly by hand not more than 3 times. Cover again and refrigerate for several hours, but not more than 24 hours.

MAKING BRIOCHE IN A MOULD

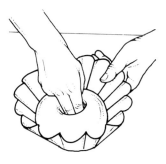

1 Place two-thirds of the dough in the mould and make a circular hollow in the centre.

2 Insert the remainder of the dough in the hollow. Glaze with egg yolk and milk.

3 Leave to rise. Then glaze again, and snip edges, if making a large brioche.

4 When baked, turn brioche out on to a cloth and cool on a wire rack.

•

On a lightly floured work surface, shape the dough into a large ball. If using a saucepan, place the dough in the lined pan. If you are making brioche in a mould, follow the step-by-step instructions in figs. 1 to 4.

Glaze the top of the brioche with the egg yolk and milk glaze, brushing from the outside towards the centre, and being careful not to let the glaze fill any crevices in the dough, or splash on to the edges of the mould, as this will restrict the way the dough rises.

Leave to rise in a warm draught-free place until the dough has almost doubled in bulk. This will take about 20 minutes for small brioches and $1\frac{1}{2}$ hours for a large one.

To cook

Pre-heat the oven to gas mark 7, 425°F (220°C). Glaze the top of the brioche again, then if you are making a large brioche, snip all round the edges with scissors, or a razor-blade, dipped in cold water. Do not snip small brioches. Bake the small brioches for 8 minutes, the large one for 40 to 45 minutes. Protect your hand with a cloth, and turn out the brioche on to it. Immediately turn the brioche on to a wire rack to cool.

To serve

Serve the brioche by itself for breakfast, or with butter and jam, or sift a little icing sugar over some slices of brioche and place under a very hot grill to glaze.

•

WAFFLES
(Les gaufres)

Waffles make a wonderful impromptu dessert. How you serve them is up to you. They are absolutely delicious with fresh strawberries and *crème chantilly* (see page 172); and children love them with Vanilla ice-cream (see page 192). They are also good served for tea on a cold winter's afternoon, accompanied by home-made preserves, or American-style with maple syrup and butter. Just make sure that your supply can cope with the demand!

Makes 12 single waffles or 6 doubles, to serve 6

•

9 oz (250 g) plain white flour	*14 fl oz (400 ml) milk*
1 oz (25 g) sugar	Flavourings:
A pinch of salt	*e.g. orange or lemon zest, Grand Marnier, rum, orange flower water*
3 eggs, separated	
3 oz (75 g) butter, melted and cooled	*Clarified butter (see page 16), to brush waffle iron*

Preparation

In a large bowl, combine the flour, sugar and salt. Make a well in the centre and put in the egg yolks and the cooled melted butter. Whisking all the time, gradually add the milk, incorporating the flour, little by little into the liquid, to give a smooth batter. Cover and leave at room temperature for 15 to 30 minutes.

Pre-heat the waffle iron. If you have an electric iron, just turn it on; if you are using a non-electric iron, put it to heat on the stove.

Have the egg whites ready in a large bowl. Add a pinch of sugar and beat until almost stiff. With a large metal spoon and using the minimum number of strokes, fold the egg whites and whatever flavouring you choose into the batter.

To cook

Lightly brush the waffle iron with clarified butter. Pour in just sufficient batter to cover the waffle area. Close and leave to cook. If you are using the non-electric variety, after 2 minutes turn over and cook the other side. Whichever type of iron you are using, the waffles will take 3 or 4 minutes to cook, according to taste. Turn out on to warmed plates and serve at once.

•

KOUGLOF

A sweet yeast bread that many nations have adapted and taken on as their own. With each slightly differing recipe there is a variation on the name; the Austrians have *Gugelhupf* (or *hopf*) and the Alsatians have *Kougelhopf* – with many permutations on this throughout Austria, Germany and Alsace; the Russians have something very similar and call it *Kulich*; the Poles claim it as their *Babka*; Italians insist that *panettone* is the original and the best, and so on. The rich yeast dough means that the bread has a moist texture and keeps fresher longer. It is baked in a traditional mould that has fluted, sloping sides and a central funnel through which the heat of the oven is able to penetrate the centre of the cake. It is said that the best moulds are earthenware. These, being porous, get a little more seasoned each time they are used so each yeast cake is reputedly better than the last. But these moulds are very hard to come by. It is a little easier to find the tins, but even these are only available in specialist cookery equipment shops.

If the unthinkable happens and you have some *Kouglof* left over, toast it and serve it for breakfast or tea with butter and home-made preserves.

Makes 1 large Kouglof (about 25 slices) or 2 medium (about 16 slices each)
You will need either 1 × 6 pint (3.5 litre) or 2 × 3 pint (1.75 litre) Kouglof moulds.

•

$\frac{1}{2}$ oz (15 g) butter, for greasing mould(s)	12 oz (350 g) unsalted butter, at room temperature
4 fl oz (120 ml) milk, warmed to blood heat	3 oz (75 g) caster sugar
1 oz (25 g) fresh yeast	9 oz (250 g) raisins
2 teaspoons salt	2 tablespoons rum
1¼ lb (500 g) plain white flour	4 oz (100 g) whole almonds, skinned
6 eggs	Icing sugar

Preparation

Butter the mould, or moulds, generously.

Using the ingredients listed above, follow the instructions given for making brioche (see page 215), to the stage where the dough has been knocked back and refrigerated for up to 24 hours.

Put the raisins in a bowl, spoon the rum over them, and leave them to soak for at least 2 hours. Lightly brown the almonds under the grill. When the almonds have cooled place one in the base of each flute at the bottom of the mould (about 17 in the large mould, 10 in each small mould). Chop the remainder.

Take the dough from the refrigerator and, working the mixture as little as possible, incorporate the raisins and rum and the chopped almonds. Turn the dough out on to a lightly floured surface and form into a rounded sausage shape; drop this very gently into the base of the mould or moulds, so the almonds remain in place. Cover with a damp cloth and leave in a warm place to rise to within about $\frac{1}{2}$ in (1 cm) of the top of the mould. This will take $1\frac{1}{2}$ to 2 hours.

To cook

Pre-heat the oven to gas mark 4, 350°F (180°C).

Bake the *Kouglof* in the centre of the oven. The large version will take 45 to 50 minutes to cook, the smaller ones 30 to 35 minutes. Free the top edges with a knife and gently turn it out of the tin. The *Kouglof* will be very fragile at this stage, so return it to the oven for a further 5 minutes to crisp and lightly colour it. Leave to cool on a wire rack. Dust with icing sugar and serve.

To store

To freeze the *Kouglof*, wrap it in foil while it is still warm, or seal it in a strong plastic bag after it has cooled. It will keep in the freezer for 6 weeks. Thaw at room temperature for 2 hours.

INDEX